The Powerholders

David Kipnis

The Powerholders

The University of Chicago Press
Chicago and London

DAVID KIPNIS is professor of psychology
at Temple University. He is the author of
Character Structure and Impulsiveness
and numerous journal articles.

The University of Chicago Press,
    Chicago 60637
The University of Chicago Press,
    Ltd., London

80 79 78 77 76   987654321

Library of Congress Cataloging in Publication Data

Kipnis, David.
    The powerholders.

    Includes bibliographical references and index.
    1. Control (Psychology)   I. Title.
BF632.5.K56   301.15′5′019   75-43230
ISBN 0-226-43731-0

To Andrew and Elliot

Contents

Preface

Modern technology, modern communication systems, and the accumulation by individuals, corporations, and states of enormous amounts of "slack" capital provide a surprisingly large number of people with occupations in which they make decisions that affect the lives of still larger numbers of other people. Moreover, people can make these decisions without once having seen or known personally those whose lives are being influenced.

Thus persons can be hired, fired, placed under surveillance, drafted into the military, moved to new cities, required to learn new skills, or have their tastes and values subtly altered without once meeting those whose interests are served by such changes. Each party then is cushioned from the other by time, space, and technology. For many persons, power appears to be exercised without human feelings being at all important.

It is only when forces of resistance are mobilized in response to some particularly gross act of influence that we obtain firsthand knowledge of the actors who are in positions of power. For instance, the recent articles in the public media reporting the Vietnam War and the political scandals of the second Nixon administration revealed the very human motives underlying the seemingly impersonal decisions that were made.

We can conclude from these brief insights that, despite the fact that modern-day exercises of power appear to be devoid of human content, there is much that psychologists can learn from examining this process. The observations on the use of power that are given in this book are based on the assumption that the exercise of power is an important concern for many people.

There are two themes here; broadly speaking, the first examines how power is used, and the second examines what happens to powerholders as a result of using power. The book is intended to provide a conceptual framework for viewing these events. Wherever possible I have based my conclusions on my own research or on research done by others who deal with these topics. Since empirical research by psychologists is sparse, I have frequently made educated guesses concerning the psychological processes that are involved. In addition I have included materials from other social science disciplines. These sources help show that power is a central concern of all people. Scores of scholars from Thomas Hobbes in the seventeenth century to Harold Lasswell in our times have viewed the question of power as one of the central issues of society. Basically the major question is, Can individuals who have access to resources needed by others be trusted to use these resources without destructive consequences either for themselves or for others? A related concern examined in this book considers what if any alterations take place in the values of powerholders so that their original humanitarian impulses are replaced by selfish and egoistic ones.

In writing this book, I have foraged among the writings of many social scientists. I hope that I have given credit where it is due. Of particular value in forming my thoughts was an integrative review by Dorwin Cartwright (1965) of what is known about the use of social power.

Many of my colleagues and friends have given generously of their time and knowledge in preparing this book. My good friend Richard Petrow instructed me in the art of writing. Both Louise Kidder and Ralph L. Rosnow provided many comments and criticisms which have been incorporated into the book's content. Much of my early laboratory research was done in collaboration with Barry Goodstadt, whose contributions I am happy to acknowledge. Parts of chapter 1 were taken from an unpublished article prepared by Goodstadt and myself. Appreciation is expressed to Carolyn Hegeler, who provided editorial assistance in preparing the manuscript, and to Sondra Candeub, who patiently deciphered my writing while typing the final draft of this book. Last, Temple University provided me with small grants of money to conduct research and, more important, the time to write. My thanks, indeed.

as representing our finest moments. When we speak about exploiting natural forces, most persons can agree with the conclusions of the political scientist Adolph Berle that the use of power is a refuge from chaos. Without the striving to exercise control over forces impinging on our lives, we would not be able to live in society. Intuitively, people know that to deny the existence and importance of power is to invite personal disaster. Yet still, when we seek to increase the comforts of our lives by directly attempting to cause behaviors in our fellow human beings, we feel uneasy. Hence the substitution of more acceptable words such as "social influence," "leadership," or "persuasion" as a means of signaling that we have caused other persons to do what we want.

In this book I propose to examine the use of power from the perspective of the powerholder. My focus on the powerholder is based on the conviction that he plays a critical dual role in social and behavioral change processes. First, as a result of the power he controls he can shape outcomes for others. Even the most ordinary people can change the course of society if they have access to resources that are needed by others. The politician controls patronage, the banker money, the military officer weapons, the college professor the baccalaureate degree. In all instances, access to these resources increases the individual's potential for controlling the behavior of others, and so for shaping society.

A second reason for studying the psychology of the powerholder is that he himself may change because of the resources at his disposal and his use of these resources to change others. As Sigmund Freud pointed out in his description of "countertransference," therapists are often very much influenced by the role they play in therapy sessions and, as a function of such therapy, come to change their feelings toward patients. A somewhat analogous process may be operative among powerholders, who are themselves affected by the act of influencing others.

In order to understand the role of the powerholder in the process of social and self change, it is essential that some systematic and rational meaning be given in the language of psychology to the problems outlined above. In particular there are two major issues involving the use of power that are of concern to psychologists and that shall be examined in this book. The first issue is: What determines how power is used once it has been obtained? That is, what social-psychological forces can be isolated that determine the powerholder's decisions to change another's behavior? For example, what are the circumstances surrounding a father's decision in one instance to threaten his child as a means of obtaining compliance, and in a second instance to spend long hours teaching his child in order to obtain compliance?

The second major issue deals with the question of how the control and use of power can change the powerholder's view of himself and his view of others who are subject to his influence. That such changes occur have been well documented in literature and in history. Furthermore the kinds of forces that seem to bring about such changes are social-psychological forces. They include the fact that the control of power tends to make people more likely to have the "last word," provides them with greater life-satisfactions, and tends to encourage others to flatter them. Needless to say, these events, if repeated often enough, cannot help but cause profound changes in the powerholder's conscious representation of himself and his world.

Despite the importance of these issues, psychology has had surprisingly little to say about the use of power. Almost several decades ago, Dorwin Cartwright (1959) wrote that psychology was "soft on power." By this he meant that psychology was willing to examine such issues as persuasion, leadership, education, and others that involved changing the lives of people but was unwilling to admit that it was in fact studying some of the many faces of power. As a result, to this day, we find comparatively few mentions of the topic *social power* in reference periodicals that list topics studied in psychology.

Moreover, the mainstream of social-psychological thought and research on power has focused on the target of power. That is, it has been concerned with how individuals and groups respond to social forces designed to change beliefs, cognitions, and behavior. With but few exceptions, social psychologists have tended to ignore the person trying to change these beliefs, cognitions, and behavior. In this regard Harvard psychologist Herbert Kelman has observed that psychologists prefer to study the powerless rather than the powerful. That is, psychologists will study the problems of the black minority but, as many critics have noted, do not study the problems of the white majority that produced the minority's problems in the first place. Considerable time and scientific effort have been expended by social scientists deter-

mining the conditions under which individual attitudes can be
changed and private compliance obtained. Far less time has been
spent studying the person doing the persuading. As a result of
this emphasis on the target of power, there are large gaps in our
knowledge which pertain to some very practical social questions.
Let us examine instances where psychologists must remain silent
for lack of information.

Organizational use of power. Within work organizations there are
known to be wide variations in how managers use their authority
to conduct business. In dealing with subordinates, for example,
some managers seem to rely heavily on the use of threats and
punishments as a means of exacting conformity, while others rely
much less on punishments. Why the differences in use of coercive
power? Further, the same manager may use threats with one
worker but say nothing to a second worker doing equally poor
work. Again, why the selectivity in the use cf coercive power by
managers? Perhaps we may obtain some insights by asking the
managers to justify their actions. If we do this we are likely to
hear managers tell us that the worker he threatened was a born
troublemaker, while the second worker had a "good deal of promise." If we pursue the matter further, we might find that the second worker spends a lot of time talking to the manager—that is,
apple-polishing, a tactic frequently noted in the literature as a
way to gain the esteem of a superior (Kipnis 1960; Kipnis and
Vanderveer 1971). Then again, we might find that the manager
was emotionally upset because of a fight with his boss the day before he threatened the first worker. Obviously, there are many
possible factors that could have determined this particular use of
power beyond the stated reason that the worker was a "born
troublemaker." Unfortunately, social sciences have few generalizations to offer in this area.

Political office. Another arena of power usage about which psychologists have little to say concerns the use and abuse of power
in public office. For instance, a recent presentation to the Philadelphia Court of Common Pleas documented an instance in
which the president of a local corporation that provided services
to city-controlled transportation facilities paid a city official a
large amount of money in exchange for certain guarantees from
the city. How do we explain this bribery? Psychologists would
tend to first ask questions about the president's moral and ethical

development, as these might serve to guide his behavior. However, we would probably find that the president had a strong
superego and completely accepted the norms and values of our
culture as they related to ethical practices. Perhaps a further examination might find that the president had conducted his business in a climate in which "payoffs" were the norm and were not
considered unethical behavior. Thus the president's role demanded that he violate the law, since if he refused to participate
in the bribery racket his company would not have survived. In
this instance we would have to turn our attention from the individual to the cultural context in which the decision to exercise
power was carried out.

Furthermore, in both of the above instances we have very
little idea of what was happening to the beliefs and values of the
manager and the company president as they pursued their day-
to-day exercise of power. Did they enjoy seeing others "dance to
their tune"? What did they think of themselves as they threatened
and bribed? What did they think of the target persons who had
complied with their influence attempts? Will they get along with
others better or worse as a result of causing them to carry out
their wishes? These and similar questions have not received systematic attention in psychology.

Reasons for Not Studying the Powerholder

Some years ago Marwell and Schmitt (1967) defined social behavior as the manipulation of other people to achieve one's own
goals and the study of interactions between people as really, the
study of how people control each other. This definition suggests
that the use of power and influence should be the central focus
of study by social psychologists. The fact that it is not deserves
comment.

There are several overlapping explanations, I believe, for psychology's lack of concern with the powerholder.

First of all, persons in positions of power resist being studied.
It is far easier to carry out research among the labor force than
among top business executives. Since people in positions of
power tend to control the funding of research, it is most likely
that they will encourage research on topics that are of concern
to themselves. These might include, for example, building tests
to select persons for social roles, or finding the best means of

socializing our children. Rarely will they encourage study of themselves. Historians and political scientists are fully aware of the difficulty of obtaining documents that describe the forces shaping the decisions of political leaders. Most of the time these documents are locked away with the proviso that they cannot be made public for thirty to one hundred years after the actor's death. Thus one block to research in this area is the power-holder's penchant for secrecy. Power, then, tends to preserve itself from scrutiny by directing the efforts of potential examiners elsewhere. In fact, one can make fairly shrewd estimates of a person's or group's status and power from the frequency with which he is placed under systematic surveillance. The more he is studied, the less his power.

A second and related reason for the absence of studies of the powerholder has to do with the cultural context in which research originates. Despite the many wars, scandals, and outrages that periodically erupt, one can still argue that most persons in Western society lead comfortable lives. As a result, the goal of persons in society, including behavioral scientists, is to maintain and improve this state of affairs. We want to know how to eliminate delinquency and criminal behavior. We want to improve methods of education and training so that our children as adults can contribute to society and prosper. The goal of psychotherapy is to increase a person's ability to cope with the world rather than to change the patient's world. In this regard Caplan and Nelson (1973) have pointed out that social science usually attempts to change the deviant's behavior rather than the social conditions producing this behavior. The natural assumption is that whatever is causing the patient's defects are his fault rather than society's. In short, when society provides benefits for most of its citizens, an accepted goal of science becomes the devising of means that will bind the individual to his society. This collective goal tends to exclude examining persons who represent society.

A last reason why psychology has not systematically studied the powerholder is that most persons, at most times, hold normative values that stress the importance of accepting legitimate authority. As a result, the act of studying the powerholder has the unpleasant implication that one is challenging authority. Such emotional feelings are less likely to be experienced by the researcher when investigating the *target* of power. Only when society enters a period of crisis and disorganization are social scientists likely to become interested in the person making the decision. To live in an age where the major collective question is, "What went wrong?" leads inevitably to an examination of authority. To live in an age where most persons feel all is right with the world leads to the study of the target of power.

Definition of Power

Social-psychological descriptions of human behavior are plagued by the fact that there may be no single correct perspective from which to view events. If we consider the act of love, for instance, we find that some social scientists choose an "X-rated" description of what is going on behaviorally or physiologically at the moment (e.g., Masters and Johnson 1966). That is, they are concerned with the process of interaction between the parties making love. Still others are concerned with the outcomes of love and analyze the subsequent quality of married life as a function of the initial attractions between the lovers. Others are concerned with the resources of the lovers, such as beauty, wealth, and status, that may have initially attracted each to the other (Walster et al. 1966); and, finally, still others are concerned with a description of the cultural context which produced the particular interaction in the first place.

While the eventual expectation of all researchers is that their particular perspective will dovetail with other views of the same problem, this hardly ever occurs. Lacking both a common vocabulary and a common conceptual frame of reference, each researcher experiences bafflement when attempting to integrate his findings with those of others.

The problems of perspective and boundaries are particularly troublesome when we consider the power act. Like love, we know that power exists, but we cannot agree on a description of it. Pollard and Mitchell (1973) point out that most theories of power offer explanations that cannot be precisely translated into each other's terms. Yet it is difficult to find direct contradictions between them. In commenting on this state of affairs, Cartwright (1965) has suggested that the literature on social power requires the construction of a theory-map to plot the linkages between the various approaches to social influence and power. The theory-map, as sketched by Cartwright, includes identifying the person who exercises power, the methods used by the powerholder to gain compliance, information about the target of power, the target's motives, and the conditions under which the target will oppose or comply with the powerholder's influence attempts.

Since this book covers only part of the range of thinking about social power, it is necessary to first describe on Cartwright's map the major approaches to viewing power, so that the reader can understand which areas have been left out of this book.

The Target's Response to Power

Perhaps the most widely accepted treatment of social power is in terms of the outcome of power acts. From this perspective, the focus is on the interaction between two parties, the powerholder and the target person, in which the target person's behavior is given new direction by the powerholder. That is, power is said to be exercised when changes occur in the target person's behavior that can be attributed to the powerholder's influence and that serve the powerholder's interests or intentions (Dahl 1957). Furthermore, these changes would ordinarily not have been carried out by the target person. Thus the elements of a power act include the facts that person A caused person B to do something that B would not do ordinarily. Research stemming from this view tends to focus on when B will comply and when he will resist influence.

Within this focus on the process and outcomes of influence there is considerable variation as to what kinds of acts can properly be labeled as power acts. Some argue that power acts should be limited to the target person's response to force (Bierstedt, 1950). Bachrach and Baratz (1963) have proposed a stringent view of power in which a distinction is made between exacting compliance from a target person through using appeals based upon (a) one's legitimate role, (b) force, (c) influence that involves simple persuasion, and finally (d) threats. The power act in Bachrach and Baratz's view is reserved for the last instance, in which the powerholder causes compliance by threatening to deprive the target person of things he values.

Perhaps the most influential view of power in social psychology was provided by French and Raven (1959) almost two decades ago. The goal of these investigators was to describe the various ways in which "person A could cause person B to do something

which was contrary to B's desire." Furthermore, the authors were
concerned with the consequences of using various power tactics
on: (a) the target person's subsequent liking for the powerholder
and (b) the target person's willingness to obey. A critical distinction offered in this regard by French and Raven was whether the
power tactic caused public compliance but not private acceptance by the target person, or private acceptance as well. Private
acceptance implies that a relatively permanent change in the target's behavior has taken place that will continue independently
of the powerholder's influence. Thus, for instance, teachers hope
that they can develop a permanent love for scholarship among
students, so that their students will continue to study even when
teachers no longer assign books to read. The distinction between
public and private compliance is perhaps critical in any analysis
of the long-range effects of using power. A failure to cause private compliance requires that the powerholder continually monitor the behavior of the target person, producing a situation of
mutual distrust and antipathy (Raven and Kruglanski 1970).

The important elements of French and Raven's conception of
power include the resources held by the powerholder and the
needs, or "motive bases," of the target person. The use of different resources, or power bases in French and Raven's terms, will
result in differing amounts of private acceptance and liking for
the powerholder. The following classifications of power stem
from use of various resources in the French and Raven taxonomy.
The reader may note the wide divergence from Bachrach and
Baratz's definition, especially with regard to the use of persuasion,
legitimacy, and referent power. These bases of power do not rely
upon threats and yet are labeled as power acts.

Reward power. The powerholder may influence behavior because he controls rewards that are wanted by the target person.
Over a short range, the use of rewards will engender public, but
not private, compliance, and the target may regard favorably the
powerholder.

Coercive power. The powerholder may influence behavior because he can control the punishments experienced by the target
person. Threats engender public, but not private, compliance.
However, the use of threats leads to the target person disliking
the powerholder.

Legitimate power. The legitimate power of the powerholder stems from internalized values of the target person which dictate that the powerholder, by virtue of his role, has the right to prescribe behavior. The use of legitimate power tends to produce both public and private compliance. The target person tends to view the powerholder with indifference.

Expert power. Expert power is based upon the target person's belief that the powerholder possesses superior knowledge or ability. In terms of compliance and liking, the outcomes are similar to those believed to occur for legitimate power.

Referent power. The powerholder has power because the target person admires him and identifies with him. Thus power can be exercised because the target person wishes to please the powerholder. Use of this power base leads to the most favorable outcomes for the powerholder, according to French and Raven. The target person readily complies with the powerholder, accepts privately his suggestions, and admires him even more for exerting power.

We see that in this view the powerholder can cause changes in the target's behavior through reliance on a variety of means of influence. Successful influence stems from the fact that the power base used is coordinated with some motive of the target. Person A controls some resource to which person B will respond, be it expert knowledge, rewards, or threats. Thus person A can use these resources in exchange for compliance.

French and Raven's approach has the advantage for psychologists of subsuming a wide variety of social-influence acts under the general rubric of power. Furthermore, it focuses the investigator's attention upon the kinds of resources that are available to the powerholder when attempting to influence others. In addition, it provides very specific predictions about the immediate and long-range effects of invoking various bases of power. For example, the use of coercive power will produce public compliance, but not private compliance, in a target person. Reliance on expert power, however, is likely to produce both public and private compliance. A large variety of ingenious laboratory experiments and field studies have been carried out over the last fifteen years to test these predictions. Basically, this research has examined the target person's response to influence acts, as the power base used by the powerholder has varied.

Power as an Exchange of Influence

The previous approach to power focuses mainly on the responses of the target person. The concern is with the reasons for the target's compliance and how the target feels about himself as a result of this compliance. A second major approach to power examines the interactions between two contending parties who vary in the benefits and costs they may provide each other. This approach has been affiliated with a more general conception of human interactions called "exchange theory." Here interpersonal relations are considered social exchanges in which each party's behavior toward the other yields benefits, although often at some costs. Power is seen in this approach as the ability of one person to affect the balance of rewards and costs of the other party. The more one party can adversely affect this ratio without costs to self, the greater the first party's power over the second (Thibaut and Kelley 1959).

This conception of power leads to study of it in terms of bargaining and negotiations (Swingle 1970), or in terms of how the contending parties evolve norms to regulate the use of power (Thibaut and Faucheux 1965), or in terms of how systems of justice and equity serve to guide the distribution of rewards and costs in a power relationship (Emerson 1962). Whatever the particular focus, the core idea is retained of two or more parties attempting to influence each other in order to get the most for the least cost. Furthermore, the emphasis is on rationality. Both parties, it is assumed, are guided in their negotiations by logically working out how to maximize gains and minimize costs. The literature in this area does not examine in any depth the emotional feelings of the persons contending for control, except as these emotional feelings distort a person's ability to reach logical conclusions (Brown 1970; Tedeschi, Schlenker, and Bonoma 1973). The darker forces that may be generated by the exercise of power (Zimbardo 1970) tend to be left unexamined, or considered simply unnecessary "noise" in the process of conflict negotiation.

An "End-Run" Approach to Power

In terms of Cartwright's theory-map of the terrain of power, we have so far charted the region that deals with the interaction between the powerholder and the target person, or with two parties struggling for control of some desired outcome. Many people think of these kinds of situations when they are asked to define power.

There are several problems, however, in defining power in terms of its outcomes for one or both persons. One basic problem is that it is very difficult, outside of the laboratory, to decide when a target person's behavior was "caused" by the powerholder and when in fact the target person was acting independently of the powerholder but on a parallel course (Dahl 1957; Gamson 1968). For instance, Dahl (1957) provides us with an instance of a Senator X, whose vote on any congressional bill is perfectly correlated with whether or not the bill passes. On the surface it would appear that Senator X exerts considerable influence with his colleagues. However, Dahl points out that Senator X may first informally poll the sentiments of his colleagues and then vote the way he predicts the majority would. Thus rather than exerting influence, he is in fact being influenced by others.

In psychology, a good example of this problem of deciding whether the actions of the powerholder changed the behavior of the target person can be found in attempts to evaluate the outcomes of psychotherapy. The difficulty here is in deciding when the therapist's advice and counsel in fact caused the client to change his behavior and when the observed changes were due to the effects of other influences simultaneously acting on the client.

A second problem with focusing on the process and outcomes of power is that the image of the powerholder is blurred. We don't know what motivated him in the first place, nor do we have a psychological profile of what he is like. All we know is that by using various strategies of influence he was successful in getting the target to do what was wanted.

Because of these two difficulties—the inability to measure satisfactorily the effects of power and the need to bring the powerholder into sharper focus—several investigators (e.g., Cartwright 1965; Mott 1970) have attempted what Gamson (1968) calls an "end run" approach to the study of power. Instead of examining the outcomes of influence, Gamson suggests, examine the behavior of the powerholder in terms of how he attempts to influence others and the kinds of resources he possesses. This shift in emphasis moves the center of study from the behavior of the target to the behavior of the powerholder.

As Gamson points out, it is far easier objectively to determine the capabilities or the resources of the powerholder and the frequency with which he attempts to exert influence, than it is to determine whether or not influence has caused changes in the target's behavior.

It is precisely these sets of questions that are examined in this book. Thus the reader should recognize that when mention is made of the exercise of power, I am referring to the powerholder's attempts to influence others. Whether or not the target person complies is an issue which will not be examined. Discussions pertaining to the circumstances under which target persons comply to power acts may be found in books edited by Dorwin Cartwright (1959) and by James Tedeschi et al. (1973). In terms of Cartwright's map of power, this book will describe the region concerned with the people and the events that set the stage for the moment when the target of power must decide what he is going to do.

2

The Power Act: A Descriptive Model

There is no one theory of power usage but a multitude of overlapping descriptions. Even when we seem to fully understand the forces shaping the decisions of the powerholders, a slight shift in perspective can reveal new and at times even contradictory information about their actions. For example, the political scientist Harold Lasswell has continually pointed out the importance of early childhood experiences of political figures in shaping their adult actions. In his view, powerholders' actions are determined to a fair extent by the kinds of deprivations they experienced as children. Yet C. Wright Mills (1956) in his analysis of powerholders offers equally compelling arguments that we can gain better understanding of the use of power by examining the resources controlled by individual powerholders; still other social scientists (A. Berle 1967; P. Zimbardo 1969) suggest that the use of power cannot be understood without considering the restraints elaborated by society to govern its use.

Cartwright (1965) has provided what may be the most useful clarification of the many views of power. This chapter will present a descriptive model of the power act from the point of view of the powerholder that is a partial adaptation of Cartwright's system, with additions by the present author. The model does not attempt to integrate the various views of power that have been described in the first chapter. It does provide the reader with (in Cartwright's term) a theory-map of the terrain of power, as this terrain is seen by powerholders. The model is summarized in figure 1. It is basically an attempt to describe the chain of events that culminates in the decision of the powerholder to invoke his resources as a means of exercising power.

Power Motivation

We start at Step 1, with the initial motivations of the powerholder to influence others. We can begin by asking why power is exercised. That is, why does a powerholder want to make a target do something he ordinarily would not do? Why does he want to change the behavior of others? The answer originates, of course, in people's dependence on others to mediate important outcomes for themselves. When this dependence on others is combined with the belief that others are unwilling to provide what is wanted, then the powerholder experiences an inclination to influence others, and so gain satisfaction. We designate these inclinations to influence others as power motivations. *Power motivations arise when an individual experiences an aroused need state that can only be satisfied by inducing appropriate behaviors in others.* Power motivations are reduced when the target performs the desired behavior.

This definition of power motivation is an extension of Lewin's definition of power as the "possibility of inducing forces in another person." However, the idea of satisfying personal wants is stressed here, in that the individual is inducing forces in another person in order to achieve some personal goal. Stress is also placed on the term "induction." The definition assumes that the target will not respond appropriately without some urging by the powerholder. As a trivial example, if A's back itches and he is willing to scratch it himself, or others willingly do so, no power motivations are involved. If, however, the itching can only be relieved by having to convince someone else to do the scratching, then power motivation would be involved. (Minton [1972] has also defined power motivation as the need to obtain social compliance and thus achieve intended effects.) Power motives, then, are least likely to arise when the relations are between persons who freely give to each other, without hesitation, and out of

1. Power Motivation
    Aroused need state satisfied by
    appropriate behaviors in others.
2. Request for Compliance
3. Resources
4. Region of Inhibition
    Physiological
    Values
    Costs
    Self-confidence
    Institutional norms
    Culture
5. Means of Influence
    Persuasion
    Threats
    Promises
    Rewards
    Force
    Ecological change

Target's Motivations and Resources ► **6. Response of Target**
    Compliance
    Private acceptance
    Self-esteem
    Esteem for powerholder
7. Consequences for the Powerholder
    Changes in need state
    Self-perceptions
    Perception of target
    Changes in values

Fig. 1. A Descriptive Model
of the Power Act

mutual affection. (Schermerhorn 1961). They are most likely to arise in the absence of such mutual feelings.

Power motives are also less likely to arise when the individual has reached a point in life when his psychological needs can be satisfied by his own actions rather than by the actions of other people. Maslow (1955) makes this point in his discussions of differences between persons seeking to satisfy higher-order needs and lower-order needs. Maslow points out that the "needs for safety, belongingness, love relations, and respect can only be satisfied by other people, i.e., from outside the person. . . . In contrast, the self-actualizing individual, by definition gratified in his basic needs, is far less dependent, far less beholden, far more autonomous and self-directed. Far from needing other people, growth-motivated people may actually be hampered by them" (p 127).

Maslow goes on to point out that since self-actualizing people depend less on other people, they are less ambivalent about them, less hostile, and less anxious. In short, to the extent persons have extensive needs which require the service of others, stresses and strains occur in interpersonal relations. In our own research, support has been obtained for Maslow's views in that we have found that the process of inducing behaviors in others appears to cause distortions of the powerholder's perceptions of others (Kipnis 1972).

Origins of Power Motives

Power motives can be classified in many ways depending upon the particular personal wants that the individual is seeking to satisfy through influencing other people.

Let us briefly examine some of the more important reasons why power motivations may be aroused. By so doing we can distinguish between different conceptions of power motivation as these are currently emphasized in the literature.

Power motivation as irrational impulse. Power motivation is frequently defined in psychology as gaining satisfaction from manipulating and influencing others. When defined in this way, the act of manipulation is seen as both the means and the end in itself. In essence, the powerholder derives satisfaction from perceiving that he has shaped outcomes for others, either because he derives enjoyment from these activities (Christie and Geis 1970; McClelland 1969) or because such activities allow him to avoid feelings of weakness and loss of control (Adler 1956; Fromm 1959; Veroff and Veroff 1972). Dynamically oriented psychologists have variously ascribed the origins of the need to influence others to either the developing individuals way of responding to an absence of love (Fromm 1959), or to his feeling of inferiority (Adler 1958), or to continual anxiety (Horney 1950). It should come as no surprise that when we talk of power motivations in terms of gaining satisfactions from influencing others many people see power needs as representing the irrational, neurotic, and perverted aspects of man's nature.

Power motivation as role behavior. A second and more pervasive reason why people attempt to influence others' behavior derives from their involvement in their institutional roles. Here, the needs to be satisfied originate in the individual's desire to do his work well. When the powerholder perceives that other persons in his "role set" (Kahn et al. 1964) are behaving in ways that interfere with the goals of the organization, feelings of distress are aroused within the powerholder which subsequently lead to attempts by him to correct this deviant behavior. It is important to note that, under these circumstances, the powerholder may not experience any personal satisfaction from influencing others and indeed may find the act of influencing distasteful (Milgram 1963). In a sense the individual is trapped by his own loyalties to legitimate authority; he discovers that it is almost impossible to ignore the demands of authority.

When power motivations arise as a result of institutional involvement, the individual frequently finds himself forced to deliver noxious stimuli to a target in order to influence his behavior. On the surface, the individual should experience shame and guilt over his own action, and over time he should refuse to continue this kind of influence. Yet, this rarely happens.

What mechanisms allow individuals in their institutional roles to carry out behaviors that they would personally condemn if done outside the institution? The answer appears to be that the individual believes that the institution has granted him absolution for his acts. Since the individual perceives that he has no choice but to obey, he also sees himself as not being responsible for the suffering he causes. He views himself as a "pawn" rather than as an "origin of behavior," to borrow DeCharms' (1968) phraseology. Blame, if placed, is directed toward the institution, the rationalization being that "If I don't do it, someone else will." Thus, the banker who forecloses, the instructor who flunks a student, the supervisor who makes a worker redo his work, the mother who spanks, may all believe themselves absolved from blame because they are "doing their duty".

Power motivation as instrumental behavior. A third and equally important explanation of why people are motivated to use power arises from the fact that the induction of behavior in others can be instrumental in obtaining rewards for oneself. This source of power motives is frequently associated with the view that power motivation is a universal attribute of human beings (e.g., Hobbes and, more recently, Mulder, 1963). When this attribute is viewed as a universal drive, the emphasis is on the pursuit of resources which in turn enhance each individual's ability to influence others and to enjoy the "good life." In contrast, there is a deemphasis on the enjoyment of seeing others "dance to your tune."

Cartwright (1965) describes this version of power motivation as follows: "All men seek to influence others and to strive for positions of influence, because they seek certain objectives whose attainments require the exercise of influence" (p. 7). Both the criminal's need for money and the lonely man's need for affection can only be satisfied by convincing someone else to take appropriate actions, that is, to part with money in the first instance and return affection in the second.

In summary, power motivations arise when people have needs that can be satisfied only by inducing appropriate behavior in others. Three reasons why these motivations arise have been described. It is proper to assume that the three reasons mentioned here can overlap. In addition to his need for money, the criminal may come to enjoy frightening his victims and seeing them grovel. The police officer may use the authority of his office to "finagle" a bribe from a motorist. There are obviously many other reasons for the motivations to arise. Frequently, the mere possession of these resources can instigate new needs, setting up an endless procession of reasons for influencing others. We stress, however, that what is common to all these reasons is the fact that they can be satisfied only by inducing appropriate behaviors in others.

Request for Compliance

Given an aroused need, the next step, as shown in figure 1, is for the individual to induce appropriate behavior in a target that will satisfy this need. In theory, this induction begins with a simple request, for example: "I love you. Will you marry me?" Frequently, of course, this step is omitted since the individual anticipates refusal. The consumer knows that, without money, his request for a new car from the automobile dealer will be refused, and the criminal knows that a polite request for money from passersby will often be ignored. When the target ignores such requests, the individual is tempted to invoke whatever resources are available to him in order to convince the target to comply.

Resources

We cannot understand the action of a powerholder after a target person has refused some request unless we have information about the powerholder's resources. Gamson (1968) whimsically calls resources "influence in repose." This is because resources represent the powerholder's *potential* for successful influence. Stress is placed on the term "potential" because there are many reasons why persons who control resources hesitate to invoke them in order to gain compliance. We shall touch on these reasons in a later section of the chapter which discusses factors inhibiting the use of power.

Let us begin with a definition. Resources are commodities, tangible or intangible, (a) that are possessed by powerholders, (b) that if given to target persons will provide them with positive outcomes, or if withheld will prevent the occurrence of negative outcomes, and (c) that target persons believe cannot be obtained outside of their relation with the powerholder. The powerholder possesses something that target persons want and cannot get elsewhere. The scarcer the commodity and the more it is valued, the greater the powerholder's potential for exercising influence. The dependence of the target person is, fundamentally, the reason why the powerholder has the potential for exercising influence.

Of course, if a target person gives up wanting the resource possessed by the powerholder, then the powerholder no longer has the potential to influence the target person. To illustrate, an acquaintance of mine was bitterly complaining to me that the next week of his life had to be spent in entertaining an elderly couple from out-of-town, whom he detested. When I asked why he bothered, his answer was quite simple: "I have to, I'm in their will." Thus the elderly couple had power over my friend so long as he wanted their money.

Classification of Resources

Figure 1 lists some of the common resources available to individuals in our society. We have found it useful to distinguish between resources that reside within the individual (*personal resources*) and resources available to the individual by reason of his *institutional* role.

Personal resources are fashioned out of each individual's unique endowments and include superior intelligence that can be used to convince the target to comply, superior physical strength to intimidate the target, personal beauty to seduce the target, and the ability to grant or withhold affection and services. The reader may think of many other personal resources that a target person will give weight to and that can, accordingly, be used as a base of influence. What all personal resources have in common is that they go where the person goes, that is, they are part of the person's makeup.

The second grouping of resources available to the individual is derived from his participation in institutional life. These resources detach themselves from the individual at the time when he decides to leave the institution. It can be a shock to a person who has spent years in a position of power to leave his office. The trauma arises from the fact that he can no longer issue orders and that he ceases to receive deference and compliments from his associates. Stripped of his institutional resources, he finds that life has become far less pleasant.

There are several ways of distinguishing between personal and institutional resources. Of central interest is the fact that the control of institutional resources increases the individual's potential for controlling the behavior of others. For example, in my personal relations I have the potential for influencing a few people because they admire or in some way depend on me. Yet, my personal resources are limited and so, too, are the sheer number of people I am liable to influence. In my role as college instructor, however, I exercise my influence over several hundred people a week. I say, "Speak," and people speak. I say, "Write," and people write. What power! Since this compliance never occurs outside of the classroom, it would seem foolish to attribute my success to my personality or other personal attributes. Quite simply, the fact that I can invoke the college's resources (to flunk, grant degrees, and so on) provides the added weight that produces student compliance. The same is true of countless others who find themselves unable to get even the least of what they want in personal relations, despite the fact that they shout and scream and rage, but in their roles of supervisors, managers, military leaders, political officeholders, teachers, and government representatives can easily cause the behavior of many thousands of others by merely whispering. Thus, access to institutional powers transforms insignificant men and women into giants.

Adolph Berle (1967) has pointed out a second distinction between institutional and personal resources. This is that institutional resources can be preserved for longer periods of time. Personal resources soon disappear, because the individual encounters someone who is stronger, more loquacious, or simply because personal bases of power erode with time—beauty fades. Resources controlled by institutions, however, are less dependent upon the vitality of any single person. If one person resigns from an institution he may only take with him his hat and coat and letters of appreciation that were gathered along the way. What he must leave for his successor is the right to use the institution's resources, be they the command of other people, the command of machinery, or the command of money. Nothing can be taken away; even ideas developed while in the service of the institution must remain. In this way institutions preserve their resources against forces of decay which inevitably must reduce all individual powerholders.

The Relation between Available Resources
and the Satisfaction of Power Needs

Several points need to be made in connection with the control of resources.

First of all, consider what happens when an individual has few or no resources. It follows that he must cease in his attempts to induce the target to comply. His needs must remain unrequited since he lacks the resources needed to convince others to take appropriate action. Thus, small businessmen may desire to control the pricing strategies of their sources of supplies but cannot even attempt to induce such changes due to their limited monetary resources. Large corporations, however, tend to be more successful in this regard (Galbraith 1967).

Another point is that there are functional relations between the nature of the powerholder's demands from the target and the kinds of resources it is proper to invoke.

For example, in a work context it has been found (Goodstadt and Kipnis 1970; Kipnis 1972) that when they had a choice between invoking personal or institutional resources as a means of influencing the behavior of their subordinates, supervisors overwhelmingly preferred the institutional. That is, attempts to change subordinates' behavior were based almost exclusively upon economic resources (offers of pay raises, and the like) rather than simple persuasive attempts that made no mention of institutional resources.

The most general statement of the relation between available resources and wants of the powerholder is provided in the theory of resource exchange (Foa and Foa 1975). These authors present evidence that particular needs may only be satisfied by a reliance upon particular resources. For example, Foa and Foa's theory suggests that, to obtain love and affection from a target, an individual should invoke his persuasive resources rather than, say, economic resources—at least initially.

Furthermore, the Foas pointed out that some resources are rapidly expended, such as the offer of money in exchange for compliance, while the use of other resources, such as the offer of love and affection, leaves the powerholder as well-off as before. Thus, to the extent a powerholder can achieve his goal of exercising influence through the invoking of nonmaterial resources such as his intelligence, persuasive powers, or the ability to grant or withhold love and companionship, he will not have much concern for exhausting his bases of power. Offering material goods, on the other hand, leaves the powerholder in the position of having to exercise "sharp" bargains so that his power base is not weakened.

Region of Inhibition

So far the potential user of power has proceeded part way along the route to his goal of influencing a target person and thus gaining satisfaction. We began with a person who wanted something that could be gained only by convincing a target to take appropriate action. To the annoyance of the powerholder, the target simply ignored, or worse, refused the request. At this point, it was suggested that the powerholder would be tempted to invoke his resources as a means of reinforcing his demands.

In many instances, the foreplay of first asking and then demanding does not occur. Because of previous experience with the target, the powerholder may realize that the target person will resist a gentle request, and therefore the powerholder may be tempted to invoke his resources without first asking. For example, members of President Nixon's staff, prior to the well-publicized Watergate break-in, did not go to the Democratic party and ask for information. Rather, Nixon's staff was immediately tempted to invoke various resources that might provide this information, despite Democratic party objections.

With the powerholder at the point of invoking his resources, what then remains to be considered? There is one major barrier that must be dealt with by the powerholder. That is, before resources can be involved, there is a region of inhibition, as shown in figure 1, that the powerholder must successfully navigate. We next consider the problems presented to the powerholder by this inhibitory region.

The study of factors inhibiting behavior has been a traditional concern of the social sciences. Hence, the reader should not be surprised to find that factors inhibiting the invocation of resources to satisfy power needs have been analyzed at many different levels of abstraction. For some (Delgado 1969; Moyer 1971), the problem has been stated in physiological terms; here the emphasis is on the inhibition of aggressive behaviors that are instigated by such negative emotional states as frustration, fear, humiliation, pain, and anger. Evidence is now available that these aggressive behaviors may be inhibited through direct brain stimulation or extirpation, through alterations in hormonal balance, or through the use of calming drugs.

The possibility of an emerging psychotechnology capable of inhibiting temptations to invoke resources for coercive means was recently noted by Kenneth B. Clark (1971) in his presidential address to the American Psychological Association. While perhaps speculative, and surely controversial, Clark's address urged that biochemical substances should be developed which rulers and important political figures would be required to take during their terms of office. Noting, how easily individuals with access to great power are tempted to use this power for selfish ends, Clark argued that biochemical interventions could stabilize and make dominant the "moral and ethical propensities of man by *inhibiting his primitive aggressive behaviors*" (p. 1055; emphasis added).

Others think of the region of inhibition of power at a cognitive level in terms of the costs of attempting to influence others (Dahl 1957; Harsanyi 1962; Tedeschi, Schlenker & Bonoma 1973; Thibaut and Kelley 1959; Pollard and Mitchell in press). As Cartwright (1965) points out: "When an agent is deciding whether to exercise influence, it must be assumed that he calculates in some sense the net advantage to him of making an influence attempt" (p. 8). If the results of his calculations indicate that he will lose more than he will gain, presumably the individual does not attempt to influence others. Thus, what inhibits the invoking of resources at this level of abstraction is a hedonistic calculus that yields negative results.

Still others view the problem of inhibition in terms of subjective values and attitudes (Berkowitz and Daniels 1963; Levanthal and Lane 1970; Pepitone 1971; Staub 1971; Walster, Berscheid, and Walster 1973). Despite the fact that the individual may gain substantial advantage by invoking his resources, it frequently happens that he inhibits the invoking of resources because he questions the propriety of the act. Hence, the need to act in an ethical manner overrides the temptation to maximize gains.

To use the example of the Watergate incident, it seems clear that the participants erroneously discounted the possible costs involved in invoking the resources of the office of the president. Notions of the ethics of public office that might have also served to inhibit their actions were missing. Further, there was little public surveillance of how presidential aides used resources. Congressional constraints over activities of members of the executive branch have also lessened in the past two decades thereby minimizing control by other government branches. Such anonymity then, as suggested by Zimbardo (1968), produces a state of affairs in which few means are taboo. In the absence of these forms of restraint on presidential aides, decisions were apparently made to use resources of uncertain legitimacy to get the desired information regarding Democratic party campaign strategies.

Returning to the general question of inhibitions, the decision as to whether to invoke resources can also be related to stable individual differences in personality and values (Christie and Geis 1970; Megaree 1971). For example, in several studies that have directly investigated individual differences in relation to choice of resources (Kipnis and Lane 1962; Goodstadt and Kipnis 1970; Goodstadt and Hjelle 1973), it has been found that appointed leaders who either lacked confidence or believed that external forces such as luck and chance controlled their lives were reluctant to invoke personal resources as a means of inducing behaviors in others. Rather than trying to persuade others to comply, less confident or externally controlled individuals either did nothing or else relied exclusively on institutional resources. Thus, tempermental factors inhibited the use of some resources and favored the invoking of others.

Finally, still other investigators discuss factors inhibiting the invoking of resources in terms of restraints that originate in the norms of groups, institutions, and society (Berle 1967). Powerful guidance is given to when and where resources will be used by these norms, laws, traditions, and values. While not absolute, these written and unwritten norms tend to form a moral climate which serves to restrain the use of resources, even though their use would be considered completely appropriate in a different moral climate. Today, managers of modern corporations are restrained by law from using their vast economic resources to openly intimidate potential business competitors, although in the late nineteenth century, use of economic resources for this purpose was not uncommon (cf. Tarbell 1904). Daniel Elazar (1969), in his book *The Politics of American Federalism,* has discussed how variations in political morality in different regions of the United States directly determines the frequency of corrupt practices in government. In the northeast region of the country, where an individualistic political morality exists, few persons see anything wrong in "dipping into the public till." Such behaviors, however, appear to be restrained in states like Minnesota and Wisconsin where a moralistic orientation toward political office tends to guide an officeholder. Beliefs about public service, rather than personal gain, serve to direct the behaviors in this midwest area.

From these remarks it can be seen that the use of power is not simply a function of the motives of the powerholder and the possession of adequate resources. The burden of our argument is that the description of the power act can be understood more precisely by explicitly taking into account the nature of the restraining forces acting on the powerholder. At all levels one may note the operation or the failure of the operation of these restraining forces. To ignore their presence would drastically simplify our understanding of what is happening when "Person A influences B to do something B would ordinarily prefer not to do." Chapter 6 will explore in greater detail the issues raised in this section.

Means of Influence

If the potential powerwielder has not been restrained by the various means of inhibition mentioned in the previous pages, the next step in the power act, as shown in figure 1, is for him to invoke his resources in order to induce compliance from the target. At this step the question is, How shall the resources be presented to the target—as a promise, as a threat, or what? To answer this question it is suggested that the powerholder must carry out an active cognitive search for the best means to influence the target person. These decision-making steps incorporate an evaluation of the powerholder's own needs, his resources, the presumed responsiveness of the target person, as well as existing social constraints on the powerholder's behavior.

To illustrate this point, let us consider the various contingencies that government planners must consider when deciding on how best to influence the policies of other countries. David Baldwin (1974), a political scientist, provides us with insight into this issue in his discussion of the pros and cons that planners must weigh when deciding whether to exert influence through promise of economic aid or through the threat of military intervention. It is clear that such a decision is not a matter of momentary impulse but rather involves an active cognitive evaluation of the immediate and long-range consequences associated with each of these means of influence.

a) Economic techniques tend to have widespread general effects on another nation's future behavior, while military techniques tend to have limited, specific effects on a nation's present behavior.

b) Economic techniques tend to be slow, continuous, and circuitous, whereas military techniques tend to be fast, intermittent, and direct.

c) A nation provided with economic aid will lose social cohesion, and the aid provided is less visible than military intervention.

This concern with consequences can be found at all levels of usage. Sometimes the concern will be a rather primitive calculation that the target person is too strong to risk directly threatening him. At other times, a more elaborate cognitive search for the best means will be employed, as, for instance, when parents confer on the best means of changing the behavior of their child. Later chapters will examine in detail the various factors influencing this decision-making process. It suffices to say here that the decision as to how to use power is not a simple matter of provocation followed by an instinctive response.

Classification of Means of Influence

Attempts to influence suffer from the same basic ambiguities as attempts to precisely define power. These ambiguities arise from the fact that influence attempts are social acts and, hence, subject to various interpretations as to their intent by each actor involved (Tedeschi, Smith, and Brown, 1972). Thus, a wife's threat to divorce her husband may be viewed by the husband as an appeal to be more accommodating, while the wife, in fact, may be deadly serious. Despite these problems, several writers have discussed various classification schemes for analyzing power strategies. These schemes can be briefly reviewed at this point.

In Chapter 1, we reviewed the classification of means of influence proposed by John French and Bert Raven. A somewhat similar classification has been proposed by Cartwright (1965) who suggests that the powerholder may exploit a base of power by exercising control over: (a) the target's physical movements or his environment; (b) over the gains and costs that the target will actually experience; (c) over the information available to the target; or (d) by making use of the target's attitudes about being influenced. A study by Kipnis and Cosentino (1969) of how supervisors exercise influence over their workers readily illustrates Cartwright's classifications. Some supervisors exercised influence by controlling the workers physical environment, that is, by shifting them to a new job or work location; other supervisors attempted to control the money earned by workers by assigning them to work that allowed overtime pay or higher piece rates; some supervisors attempted to influence their workers by discussing the work with them; while

still other supervisors exercised control by means of their legitimate
authority and simply ordered their workers to carry out some behaviors. The effectiveness of this last power tactic hinges on the
worker's beliefs that supervisors have a legitimate right to exert
influence and that he (the worker) is obliged to accept this influence.

The tactical use of power has been approached in yet another
way by Michener and Schwertfeger (1972), who view the powerholder as attempting to increase the value of the resources he controls and so gain for himself in an exchange with a target. Michener and Schwertfeger, drawing on the writings of Emerson (1962)
and Blau (1964), describe four strategies that powerholders may
use to increase their outcomes. *Blocking outcomes* consist of blocking another person's access to valued outcomes. By restricting the
access of the United States to their oil reserves, for example, the
Arab nations increase their bargaining position with this country
on other matters, such as the United States' support of Israel. *Demand creation* is a second power tactic that may be used to influence a target. Here the powerholder attempts to "create a need"
for his resources so that a target will pay more for them. Thus,
merchants may advertise their product to increase its value in the
eyes of the customer. If the demand is increased as a result of the
advertisements, then more money can be asked for the product,
since it is seemingly worth more to the buyer. *Extension of the
power network* is a third strategy that powerholders may use. Here
the powerholder develops alternate sources of supply for his wants
so that he is not solely dependent on the target. Thus, if two persons who are dating disagree on whether to get married, one of
them may threaten to date others if the partner will not comply.
Withdrawal is the last strategy described by Michener and Schwertfeger. Here the powerholder decides that the price demanded by
the target is more than he wishes to pay. Hence, he abandons his
needs that gave rise to the influence act in the first place. This is,
of course, the extreme case and represents a failure of the act of
power.

Still another mode of classifying influence attempts has been
offered by Tedeschi and his co-researchers in their book, *Conflict,
Power, and Games* (1973). This classification scheme considers
the extent to which the powerholder controls adequate resources.
Furthermore, Tedeschi et al. considers whether the powerholder

wishes openly to manipulate the target or prefers to do so "behind the scenes." These two dimensions of influence result in a classification scheme shown in table 2.1. The particular means of influence used under each of these circumstances are shown as cell entries.

Table 2.1 Classification of Influence Tactics

| | | Powerholder Intends to: | |
		Openly Influence Target	Manipulate Target
Powerholder controls resources	Yes	Threats and promises (A)	Reinforcement control (B)
	No	Persuasion, noncontingent promises, or threats (C)	Information control (D)

Adapted from Tedeschi, Schlenker, Bonoma (1973, p. 88)

It can be seen in cell A that, when a powerholder has available sufficient resources, he can openly attempt to obtain compliance by threatening punishment if the target does not comply or by promising specific rewards if the target does comply.

If the target has a more clandestine bent, as shown in cell B, then he may exert influence without the target being quite aware of what is happening. Studies by Bachrach and Baratz (1963), dealing with what they call "nondecisions," illustrate this clandestine method of exerting influence.

Nondecision-making occurs when a powerholder mobilizes his resources to suppress the demands for change by targets before these demands are made public. University instructors may be unhappy over the amount of "say" they have in running their department affairs. The instructors decide that at the next department meeting they will offer a resolution that faculty be given voting rights on teaching loads, tenure committees, review of salary, and other relevant department issues. The chairman may suppress these demands in three ways before they emerge for public debate. First, he may decide not to call any department meetings. Second, if the meetings are called, he may not recognize the dissident instructors when they request permission to speak. Third, if the instructors are recognized, the chairman may simply rule the motion "out of order," thus stopping debate.

Through these various tactics, the department chairman has exercised power in such a manner that the viewing public has not even been aware that authority has been challenged. This is a tactic of power that can be expected to be continually used in situations where the powerholder suspects that his influence is resisted. It is to his benefit to prevent public debate from even arising.

Bachrach and Baratz suggest that nondecision-making can take several forms, from direct physical harassment of persons liable to demand change, such as the killing of several civil-rights leaders in the South during the early 1960s, to such parlimentary tactics as those described above, which prevent issues from being raised.

When a powerholder does not control the appropriate resources, but still wishes openly to influence a target (the tactic indicated in cell c of table 2.1), then his position is weak. Tedeschi et al. indicate that the powerholder must rely on noncontingent promises or threats, such as are frequently used in advertisements, in order to induce target compliance. An audience is told, for instance, that the use of a particular toothpaste will gain one more friends or prevent the loss of one's teeth. "In this way the powerholder can attempt to tie his own interest to those of the target, so that their interests appear to correspond" (p. 90). However, the advertiser in these instances cannot directly cause the target to buy his product, since he has no direct control over the consumer's behavior.

The last means of influence considered by Tedeschi et al. in table 2.1. concerns instances in which the individual does not possess the appropriate resources needed to influence a target and decides to act in an undercover way in order to get what he wants. To satisfy his wants in these instances, the powerholder must first arouse the fears and credulities of the target without the target fully realizing what has happened. Once these fears and credulities have been aroused, the powerholder can openly offer to reduce them in exchange for compliance. The goal is to make the target falsely believe that he has more to lose than gain by not accepting the advice of the powerholder.

Fear arousal, stealth, and Machiavellian tactics serve the wielder of power very well in these instances, since his real aims must not be publicly revealed at the outset. In *King Lear,* for instance, Edmund, the bastard son of the Earl of Gloucester, seizes his father's wealth and title by first arousing his father's suspicions concerning the loyalty of the legitimate son, Edgar. Once these fears have been falsely aroused, it is a simple matter for Edmund to act as the defender of his father's safety. Similarly, Iago destroys the noble Othello by first convincing him that Desdemona could not really love him. What Shakespeare tells us is that the tactics of bluff and deceit, used covertly, must serve in the absence of real resources by arousing new concerns within the target that can be satisfied by the powerholder. Recent studies of ingratiation (Jones 1964; Kipnis and Vandeveer 1971) provide support for this process of covert influence.

Restraints on Choice of Means

While not shown in figure 1, restraints exist which shape the particular means of influence chosen by a powerholder. For instance, discipline in the armed forces can no longer be maintained by arbitrary threats of loss of leave and furlough, although this means of influence was acceptable prior to revisions in the Uniform Code of Military Justice. Or again, union contracts markedly limit the range of influence companies may use with their employees. While coercive means may still be used, government laws forbid such modes of influence as "yellow dog'" contracts, blacklisting of employees, as well as actual physical force against workers.

How Means of Influence Determine Interpersonal Relations

As could be expected by examining figure 1, there is also a relation between the resources invoked and the means of influence that are attempted. Some resources—guns and knives, for example, are particularly suited for threatening and intimidating targets. Others, such as the possession of superior knowledge, mainly favor the use of persuasion. Money provides the powerholder with a broad spectrum of means of influence, with a particular emphasis on rewards and punishments.

The relation between resources and means of influence has far-reaching consequences for the kinds of social relations that evolve between powerholders and target persons. Etzioni (1968) has classified institutions in terms of the means of influence that are used to exact compliance from their members. Those institutions whose representatives can only rely on coercive means produce, according to Etzioni, hostile and destructive forms of interpersonal relations.

Institutions that provide their members with only coercive means include most prisons, correctional institutions, custodial mental hospitals, and coercive unions. Persons working in such institutions in supervisory roles tend to encounter intensive negative involvement from those under their control. This is because supervisory personnel find that the institution has provided them only with the authority to use threats and punishments as means of influencing others.

An experimental study by Berger (1973), dealing with the control of coercive power, found results that were consistent with Etzioni's views. Managers in a simulated organization, who were delegated only coercive means to influence their workers (pay deductions), generally believed that their workers disliked them. Further, Berger found that the managers who possessed only coercive means directed most of their attention toward the marginal workers who were the potential targets of this means of influence. Satisfactory workers were ignored. These results seem consistent with Etzioni's assumption that the kinds of means available structure both the sort of relations powerholders may enter into with others, as well as the powerholder's feelings about these others.

The Target's Response to the Influence Attempt

Consider now the target's response to the powerholder. This step has received considerable attention from psychologists using the brilliant conceptualization of the problem by French and Raven (1959). Here one asks: Does the target comply with the source of influence? And, if so, under what circumstances does this occur? How long does it last? Is this willing compliance or is it given grudgingly? What are the processes within the target that produce yielding? Further, when will a target person ignore or actively resist the powerholder's influence? These questions and many more like them have, since World War II, been the basis for much social-psychological research dealing with power and related areas such as attitude change and leadership.

Here we ask another question. If the target resists, what happens next to the powerholder? We suggest that the powerholder must recycle through earlier stages (a procedure not shown in figure 1). Depending upon the strength of the original need that aroused the motive to influence others, a reexamination of the resources that are available, and the strength of the restraining forces in the field, the powerholder may decide either to abandon his influence attempt, to modify his original needs, or to persist by invoking different means of influence.

If he persists, then the question of tactics becomes important. What new means of influence are liable to convince the target? While in many instances these new means of influence will take harsher forms (Deutsch and Krauss 1960), or will escalate in intensity (Goldstein, Davis, and Herman, 1975), that will not always be the case. Rather, the new means of influence will be selected to increase pressure for change on the target. Not only may they include threats but also promises of additional rewards, or even greater reliance on informational modes of influence.

Basically, the choice of means depends upon the powerholder's ability to diagnose the causes of the target's resistance. A wrong diagnosis may increase rather than decrease resistance. This cycling through various means of influence in order to induce compliance is well illustrated in the government's attempts to achieve racial balance in public schools during the 1960s and into the early 1970s. Among the means used were threats of economic sanctions against state school systems in the form of withdrawal of federal money; new information on the utility of integration—provided through public information programs; court orders to force the bussing of school children; and in Alabama military force.

This continual pressure to bring about compliance could only be brought to bear on the target because of the wide variety of resources available to the government.

Individuals may also cycle through various influence tactics, although each of these tactics will be considerably weaker than those used by the government. A parent, attempting to make his child improve at school, may promise an extra allowance for better grades or threaten to reduce the child's allowance if the grades remain poor. At the same time, he may have a serious talk with the child on the relation between school performance and the child's adult career; he may appeal to the child's love for his parents, or he may even physically threaten him. And, if all else fails, the parent may consult with the teacher for additional means to apply pressure, such as using the schools' counseling services. This continual pressure will stop only if the parent becomes convinced that his son is not destined to achieve in school, or if the child finally complies and raises his grades.

Consequences for the Powerholder

Up to this point we have described the decision processes of the powerholder in his attempts to induce change in the behavior of others. Still to be reckoned with is the notion that the simple possession and use of power may affect the powerholder himself. If the powerholder's influence attempts are resisted and his needs remain unfulfilled, he should experience frustration and self-doubt. Furthermore, his views of the target will fluctuate in relation to the amount of resistance shown by the target. Will the powerholder like the target more or less if he complies? The last step in the descriptive model of the power act is concerned with the reaction of the powerholder to his own use of power. These reactions can be called the *metamorphic* effects of power and refer to how the exercise of power may transform the powerholder's self-concepts, his values, and his views of the less powerful.

Since Chapter 9 is concerned with a full discussion of the metamorphic effects of power, here I will only briefly indicate the basis for my interest, as a psychologist, in this subject.

Basically, this interest was stimulated by writings of political scientists and philosophers in which persons who control economic and political power are viewed, at best, with mixed emotions. On the one hand, there is admiration for their ability to amass great power and, at times, admiration for the way in which their power is used to influence events in society. On the other hand there is profound suspicion that these powerholders, no matter what their original motives, will use their resources to exploit others and further enrich themselves. This suspicion of the corrupting influence of power has been voiced by political scientists for many centuries. There is fear that power, once consolidated, will become used for despotic ends. Indeed, Hobbes in *Leviathan* maintained that men formed societies as a means of limiting the exploitive consequences of the unequal division of power. The system of checks and balances and the separation of powers between the executive, legislative, and judicial departments contained in the American Constitution are based on the same fears of the consequences of excessive power. Underlying these fears is the assumption that human nature is mean and self-serving. Hobbes viewed all men as moved by a never-ending stream of appetites which could only be satisfied by the control of power. Similarly, James Madison, writing in the

Federalist Papers (no. 14), viewed men as "ambitious," "vindictive," and "rapacious" and believed their access to power had to be limited.

The important question, then, for psychologists is to understand the relation between appetitive drives, the control and use of power, and changes in self-image. Why do we continually find references in the literature to the idea that persons with power become "puffed up with importance," devalue the worth of others, and deny that ordinary morality applies to their acts? What processes underlie these changes? To anticipate the arguments that are presented in Chapter 9, I suggest that individuals take cues as to their own worth from the quality of interaction they have with others. To the extent that these interactions are continually supportive, self-esteem may rise. To the extent that they are less so, self-esteem may fall. Simply put, control of resources gives the powerholders an "edge," so that society tends to act "extra nice" when interacting with them. These kinds of positive feedback gradually allow power-holders to believe that they are more worthy than others and, in fact, deserve more as a simple matter of justice.

Summary

From the point of view of the powerholder, the power act is like a game. Each step flows from the previous one with penalties continually arising to block progress. The contingencies are such that, without a need, an attempt to influence others is unlikely. Without resources, influence is unlikely to be attempted. In the presence of strong inhibition, influence is also unlikely to be attempted. Again, without the proper means of exercising it, influence is unlikely to be attempted. Strong resistance from a target will make the powerholder move back several squares and recycle through all the various steps mentioned. A serious consideration of the use of power must in fact consider all of these points to describe adequately what is happening when influence is exerted.

The initial sequences of the power act can be described in terms of an instrumental view of motivation. The perception that others mediate desirable outcomes for the powerholder provides the incentive to take action. Expectation of successful influence, the second major variable in instrumentality theories, is provided by the kind and amount of resources available. The more that resources can be used without cost to the powerholder, the broader the scope of the resources, the more the resources are given weight by the target —then the higher the powerholder's expectations of successful influence.

As the individual proceeds from step to step in the power-act sequence, expectancies of success and the incentive value of influencing the target take on new values. Further, the region of inhibition adds negative values to the instrumentality act.

Several other investigators (Pollard and Mitchell 1973; Tedeschi, Schlenker, and Bonoma 1973) have also stressed the usefulness of some form of instrumentality theory for explaining the power act. An added value of the present analysis is its consideration of how the availability of resources can shape the initial expectations of the powerholder. In addition, this approach requires the analysis of behavior to begin with a classification of the objective environment in terms of the resources possessed by the person, as well as with some hypothesized psychological state of the person. Both units of information are needed to predict behavior of the powerholder, since the combination of an aroused power need and the possession of resources can be expected to lead to action, while the absence of either will lead to inaction.

3　　The Use of Power

Once a person has gained control of resources that are given weight by others he must consider how best to use these resources. Statesmen must decide when to offer to negotiate, and when threats will produce the advantageous outcome. Parents must similarly decide how to convince their children to eat their food, to dress properly, and to study.

And so it goes—for all levels of society the perplexing problem is how to gain compliance without losing the long-term affection of the target person, and yet use one's resources economically. In the face of these uncertainties, it is not surprising that there is a continual demand for books that promise to give advice on these matters. Niccolò Machiavelli in *The Prince* provides extensive advice to rulers on how to extend and consolidate their power. Similarly, books on leadership provide advice to managers on the best way to influence subordinates, and books on child psychology are continual best-sellers among parents groping their way from one "identity crisis" of their children to the next.

In the present chapter, rather than offering advice on how best to exert influence, I shall more prudently limit myself to the question of what influences a powerholder's selection of influence tactics, regardless of whether the consequences of this choice lead to favorable or unfavorable outcomes.

The reader should be aware that I have adopted the perspective of the powerholder in discussing the particular means of influence that are used. That is, if the powerholder believes he is offering to reward the target for compliance, I will accept this belief as valid, even though the target may view the offer as an insult and an outside observor may see the same promise of reward as a threat. This kind of relativity exists in defining power relationships, since they represent social acts rather than processes that are invariant with respect to who is doing the observing (Tedeschi, Smith and Brown, 1972; Bachrach and Baratz 1963). Hence different observors may disagree sharply on the benefit and meaning of any social exchange.

Instincts and Power Usage

One possible answer to the question of what determines the choice of means of influence comes from social philosophers who stress man's inherent enjoyment in exercising power in order to inflict harm on others. Freud, writing in *Civilization and Its Discontent*, described man's destructive impulses this way:

> Men are not gentle, friendly creatures wishing for love, who simply defend themselves if they are attacked . . . a powerful measure of desire for aggression has to be reckoned as part of their intrinsic, instinctual endowment. The result is that their neighbor is to them not only a possible helper or sexual outlet, but also someone who tempts them to satisfy their aggressiveness on him, to exploit his capacity for work without compensation, to use him sexually without his consent, to seize his possessions, to humiliate him, to cause him pain, to torture, and to kill him. Homo homini lupus. Who in the face of all his experience of life and history will have the courage to dispute this assertion?
>
> As a rule this cruel aggressiveness waits for some provocation or puts itself at the service of some other purpose, whose goal might also have been reached by milder methods. In circumstances that are favorable to it, when the mental counterforces which ordinarily inhibit it are out of action, it also manifests itself spontaneously and reveals man as a savage beast to whom consideration to its own kind is something alien. . . . The existence of this inclination to aggression, which we can detect in ourselves and justly presume to be in others, is the factor which disturbs our relations with our neighbors and which makes it necessary for culture to institute its highest demands.

Here we have Freud enumerating various coercive means by which man may harass his neighbor, and for no other reason than to satisfy primitive aggressive instincts that make up his natural endowment. If we are to take Freud seriously on this matter, the decision as to what particular means of influence to use will depend primarily on the presence or absence of societal restraining forces. In their absence, the powerholder will choose the cruellest means available. In this way he may satisfy both the manifest reason for exerting influence and the instinctual reason relating to the gratifications achieved by inflicting harm on others.

Freud's assumptions, however, are not easily verified when we examine the day-to-day behaviors of powerholders in the process of exerting influence. Except under special circumstances of intense anger we find that most powerholders tend to reject the immediate use of coercive means of influence. There is a preference for using less harsh means that will preserve a friendly relationship if possible. And if friendship is impossible, means of influence are sought that will at least allow civil intercourse between the powerholder and the target.

A study by Michener and Schwertfeger (1972) illustrates how the choice of destructive modes of influence are reserved for those persons we dislike to begin with, rather than being used indiscriminately. These investigators reported that, in conflict with a landlord over a rent increase, tenants who liked the landlord either attempted to change his decision through persuasion or by offering to move into a cheaper apartment in the same building complex. Tenants who disliked the landlord, however, appeared to follow the destructive pattern described by Freud, in that their choice of influence tactics were more likely to cause pain to the landlord. That is, tenants who initially disliked the landlord favored either forming a tenant's union to militantly resist the landlord's demands for higher rent or threatened to move elsewhere, thus depriving the landlord of any rent at all. It is mainly when strong antipathy is felt toward a target person that we appear to deliberately make our first choice of influence coercive rather than gentle.

Institutional Settings Guide the Choice of Influence Tactics

Any discussion of decisions concerning how power is used, whether benignly or with malevolent application, properly begins with the setting in which the influence is to be exercised. Each formal grouping in our society possesses some unique repertoire of influence means that are considered proper to use in that setting. This repertoire exists to provide persons directly responsible for goal achievement with the means to coordinate and guide the behavior of other participants, and so to achieve the setting's goals. In business organizations, Pelz (1951) and Godfrey, Fiedler, and Hall (1959) have found that when appointed leaders were deprived of power usually associated with their positions (by superiors not supporting their decisions), the appointed leaders were less able to influence their employees. Few of the employees listened when they realized that their supervisor's opinions about their work no longer counted. Clearly, personal charm may have only limited value for inducing behavior in settings that traditionally rely on institutionally based means of influence.

Table 3.1 shows the kinds of coercive means of influence that were found to be available to powerholders in three different settings—marriage, work, and custodial mental hospitals. These means of influence were gathered by the writer and his colleagues while interviewing marriage partners, first-line supervisors, and psychiatric aides. The targets of influence were the respondent's spouse, the employee, and the mental patient.

One of the first impressions gained from examining these listings is that the coercive power in each of these settings directs itself toward different values and needs within the target person. In marriage the coercive means of influence are based upon the ability of one spouse to withdraw emotional support and services from the other. The threat is to "move away" from the other partner. Further in the marriage setting, one has an impression that the threats used are vague and do not precisely specify exact consequences for noncompliance. In the mental hospitals, however, the threats appear to be quite precise. Also, the coercive means tend to be directed at the physical well-being of the patient. Rather than withdrawing emotional support and "moving away" from the target, psychiatric aides may threaten to "move against" the patient if compliance is not forthcoming. Among first-line supervisors the threats are directed toward withholding economic support or toward reducing the employee's self-esteem.

Another impression that is gained from examining table 3.1 is that the first-line supervisors appear to control a wider range of coercive influence means than do marital partners or psychiatric aides. That is, supervisors appear to control "low keyed" threats for minor forms of resistance and massive threats (firings or suspensions) for strong forms of resistance. Having access to this range of influence means should make the first-line supervisors far more flexible in their attempts to influence employees than either marital partners or psychiatric aides, who may have to choose threats that are inappropriate for the kinds of opposition being encountered from their spouses or patients.

A good deal can be learned about the attempts of powerholders to influence others from simply tabulating the means of influence available to them in each setting. Can rewards be given out freely?

Table 3.1 Coercive Means of Influence Available in Three Settings

Marriage

1. I act cold and say very little to him/her.
2. I make the other person miserable by doing things he or she does not like.
3. I get angry and demand that he/she give in.
4. I threaten to use physical force.
5. I threaten to separate or seek a divorce.

Work

1. I chewed him out.
2. I gave him a verbal warning.
3. I threatened to give him a written warning.
4. I ignored him while being friendly with everyone else.
5. I kept riding him.
6. I scheduled him to work hours he didn't like.
7. I gave him work he didn't like.
8. I put him in a work area he didn't like.
9. I put him in an area of lower premium pay.
10. I gave him a written warning.
11. I took steps to suspend him.
12. I recommended that he be brought before the disciplinary committee.
13. He was suspended from work.
14. He was fired.

Custodial Mental Hospital

1. Warn the patient of loss of privileges (passes, cigarettes).
2. Put the patient in isolation.
3. Scold the patient.
4. Physically control the patient (restraints, etc.).
5. Give medicine to the patient (to sedate).
6. Discipline the patient by removing things or privileges that the patient wants.

What types of punishments may be threatened for noncompliance? Can the target person's environment be altered? If the answer to most of these questions is "no," one can suspect that the influence potential of the individual will be low, regardless of his personality, loquacity, or personal charm.

Suppose we observe two persons attempting to influence target persons. The first adopts a pleasant, democratic style in which mild *requests* for compliance predominate. The second person adopts a brusque, demanding tone with little concern for the feelings of the target person. If asked to explain these differences, we might guess that the first person is rather timid, while the second has an authoritarian personality. However, we would probably alter our interpretation if we were told that the first person was the president of the local Parent-Teacher Association interacting with one of the members, while the second person was a business manager talking with a subordinate. Rather than resulting from personality differences, the two styles of influence can at least in part be attributed to the fact that the PTA president has no formal sanctions available to induce compliance, while the business manager has such sanctions available.

As a general rule, one should look for increased assertiveness in powerholders as the number of ways in which they can influence others increases. Support for this general rule can be found in several studies by psychologists of the relationship between the availability of means of influence and the assertiveness of the powerholder. In one study by Columbia University psychologists Morton Deutsch and Robert Krauss (1960) it was found that persons running a simulated business game who were given the power to threaten their rivals became far more demanding and less willing to compromise with their business rivals. Seemingly, the added power encouraged the development of a belief system: "We're stronger—we deserve more."

Somewhat similar findings were also obtained by the present writer (1972) in an experimental study in which managers ran a simulated business. The job of manager required the supervision of the work of four employees. There were two conditions in the study. In the first, managers were provided with a number of different ways of influencing the employees; that is, the managers were allowed, if they chose to do so, to give pay raises, pay deductions, to shift their employees from one job to another, to train their employees, or to fire them. In a second condition, the managers were not provided with any of these means of influence. Instead they had to rely on their personal ability to persuade their employees, or on their legitimate rights as managers to issue orders.

The results of this study were that managers who controlled a broad range of ways of influencing were far more assertive and demanding in their relations with their employees than were managers who were not provided with this range of influence. Managers with many institutional powers made twice as many demands upon their employees to work harder as did managers with no institutional powers.

It seems clear, then, that as we move individuals into settings that provide additional ways of influencing others, these individuals will respond by making far more demands upon the world.

There is also a hint in the experimental literature that the kinds of demands made upon others will vary with the kinds of means of influence that are available. In a study of how two people make concessions when bargaining with each other, Schlenker, and Tedeschi (1972) provided some participants with the power to reward their opponents if the opponents complied, other participants with the power to punish noncompliance, and still other participants with both the power to reward compliance and to punish noncompliance. The finding of considerable interest was that the type of power available had important effects on the behavior of the powerholders.

Powerholders sent more threats, and actually invoked coercive power more frequently when they possessed *only* coercive power than when they possessed both coercive and reward power. Thus persons acted more aggressively when they could only punish to gain compliance than when they could choose to either punish or reward. Further, powerholders promised fewer rewards when they possessed *only* reward power than when they possessed both reward and coercive power. These findings suggest that users of power will be less benevolent and more coercive in situations where they can only reward, or only punish, as compared to situations where they control the power to both reward and punish. Perhaps the power of prison guards to threaten and coerce should be augmented with the power to provide genuine rewards to prisoners in exchange for compliance. One wonders if by this means we could reduce the number of prison-abuse incidents that occur. For if the only way we have to get our way is to threaten and bully, it seems clear from everyday observation that most of us, sooner or later, will get used to the idea of threatening and bullying.

The Influence of Status on the Choice of Means

So far we have stated that simply tabulating the number and kinds of means of influence available to a powerholder in a given setting will tell us a good deal about how the powerholder is likely to behave. Here we wish to consider the implication of this statement as it relates to a person's status within the setting. To state an obvious fact, persons with high status tend to have available a wide variety of means to influence. There are also few restraints on their use of these means as compared to the restraints on persons of lower status. Children can only beg, ask, plead, or whine in order to influence their parents. Parents can legitimately punish, reward, and train their children—that is, bring strong means of influence to bear on their children.

Within institutional settings individuals with high status and great office may have unlimited access to resources, while those with less status, such as supervisors or teachers, will have only limited access to the institution's resources. A study of role conflict among business managers by Robert Kahn and his associates at the University of Michigan (1964) nicely illustrates how access to influence varies with the person's work status in the organization. In this study managers were asked the extent to which they could use a variety of means to influence various target persons with whom they worked. The respondent was either a superior, peer, or subordinate of the target person.

Table 3.2 shows these responses in terms of average rating by each respondent of his ability to use four means of influence: legitimate power, reward power, coercive power, and expert power. Quite clearly, top supervisors reported that they had greater latitude to use legitimate, reward, and coercive powers than did subordinates. It may also be seen that all persons in the organization, regardless of level, felt that they could use their expert power to influence a target person.

This indicates that powers derived purely from participation in the organization, such as the power to reward and punish, are closely linked with level in the organization. High-status persons have a wider range of influence to choose from than low-status persons. On the other hand, when the means of influence depend upon the individual's own abilities, such as his expert knowledge, we are more likely to find persons at all levels using such means. Thus first-line supervisors can change their superiors' behavior by using professional knowledge. However, first-line supervisors will hardly ever attempt to change this behavior by promising to raise their bosses' pay, that is, by using reward power. This latter power tactic is reserved for those with higher status.

Table 3.2 Ability to Use Various Means of Influence at Differing Organizational Levels

	Top Supervisor	Immediate Supervisor	Peer	Subordinate
Legitimate power	4.6	4.3	2.3	1.6
Reward power	4.0	3.7	2.2	1.5
Coercive power	4.1	3.6	1.3	1.3
Expert power	4.1	4.1	4.1	4.1

NOTE: The higher the score the greater the ability to use the given power.
*Estimated from text's statement that all respondents averaged above 4.0 on a scale of 1 to 5 (Kahn et al. [1964], p. 200).

Calculation and the Choice of Influence

The previous two sections pointed out that powerholders' willingness to assert themselves is closely tied to the kinds and amount of power bases that are available to them. Assume now that a powerholder does possess a suitable position and an array of means of influence that can be freely used. That is, assume the powerholder can choose to do whatever he wants to make the target person comply. In these circumstances, what determines the powerholder's particular choice of influence from this array? Why does he use one particular means of influence in one situation but not in another? Why in one instance does a teacher use flattery to encourage a student to study but flatly order a second student to engage in similar behavior? Why does a supervisor in one instance spend long hours training an incompetent worker to reach acceptable levels of performance but in another instance threaten to fire an equally incompetent worker? Is the answer, as Freud suggests, simply that powerholders select the means liable to do the most harm, so long as they are not punished themselves? Or are more rational processes involved?

All evidence indicates that more rational processes are almost always involved in decisions concerning tactics of influence. As Raven (1974) points out: "On the assumption that man is rational we would expect him to use the base of power which would most likely lead to successful influence" (p. 192). Raven goes on to point out that if the goal of the powerholder was to produce long-lasting changes in the behavior of the target person, then the powerholder would probably avoid coercive means of influence and perhaps attempt to influence through providing the target person with new information. If long-lasting compliance was not an issue, however, then the powerholder might decide to obtain immediate satisfaction by invoking strong sanctions.

Planning and rationality can almost always be found when powerholders are deciding which of several means of influence should be used in a given situation. This does not mean of course that emotions and feelings do not affect the powerholder's decisions. Such emotional feelings, however, appear to act by narrowing or expanding the range of influence means that the powerholder is likely to believe effective in that situation.

Gamson (1968) illustrates how emotions serve to guide the powerholder's choice of influence means. When the powerholder trusts the target person, persuasion is most likely to be used to convince the target person. Because of this trusting relationship, the powerholder is willing to allow the target person the freedom to make up his own mind, confident that the target person will freely do what the powerholder has requested. If the powerholder does not trust the target person, then it is quite likely that he will decide to invoke threats and punishments. The assumption here is that one cannot rely on influence means that allow the target person freedom of choice (such as persuasion), because with freedom the distrusted target person will probably do exactly the opposite of what the powerholder wants him to do. As Gamson notes: "Since the probability of favorable outcomes is already very low . . . , it is hardly necessary to worry about [the target's feelings]. The attitude then that 'the only thing they understand is force' is a perfect manifestation of this trust orientation" (p. 169).

Choice of Influence—A Two-Stage Process

If we assume that powerholders act rationally when choosing
how best to influence a target person, then it follows that there
must be at least two stages involved in the choice of a particular
means of influence. First the powerholder must diagnose the reasons for the target's refusal to comply with his request. Is the
reason for the target's refusal due to the target's dislike of the powerholder, or is it because the target person does not possess the ability to do what the powerholder wants? Perhaps it is because a lack
of trust exists between the two parties so that the target person
will refuse any suggestion made by the poweholder, no matter how
beneficial the suggestion is to both parties. Clearly, there is no end
to the number of possible reasons why the target person has offered resistance.

Yet if the powerholder does not understand the reason for this
resistance, he will be forced to flail about until by chance he discovers the one influence means that will produce compliance.
Given this time-consuming alternative, the rational powerholder,
before taking further action, prefers to spend some time analyzing
why the target person has refused his request.

Frequently this stage in the decision-making process is complicated by the lack of open communication between the powerholder
and the target person. The target person may lie about his reasons
or sullenly refuse to talk, since once the causes of resistance have
been discovered the powerholder may attempt to overcome the
resistance.

Further, the powerholder can make mistakes in his diagnosis.
He is in the position of the sixteenth-century physician who possessed only the crudest of diagnostic tools with which to decide
what was bothering his patient. As mistakes were common then
among physicians, so too are they today among powerholders. The
history of modern international negotiations contains many examples where signals of one nation were misperceived by another
nation, which saw hostility where in fact peace overtures were intended. We have no X-ray devices available to peer into the mind
of the target person and discern there the reasons for his refusal
to comply with our request. Our closest approach to such a device
is perhaps the consumer surveys that seek to discover the cause of
citizen antipathy toward consumer products, or toward politicians,
so that precise campaigns can be planned to overcome these resis-

tances. For most powerholders, however, diagnosing the causes of the target persons' resistance remains a subtle art based upon past encounters with the target person, hunches, and the powerholder's own perceptiveness.

Once the diagnosis is reached, regardless of whether it is correct, we reach the second stage of the decision-making process, which involves the actual choice of means of influence. Assuming that the powerholder is acting rationally, this stage is almost completely dependent upon the powerholder's initial diagnosis of the cause of the target's resistance. As the powerholder's diagnosis of the reasons for the target's lack of cooperation varies, so too will his choice of tactics vary.

This two-stage process has an analogy in the practice of medical diagnosis and treatment. When a patient appears at a physician's office and complains of feeling sick, the physician must first decide what is causing these complaints. It is only after the diagnosis has been made that the physician can select a particular mode of treatment. Furthermore, the treatment that is selected must be the one that holds the highest promise of cure. If the physician ignores this treatment in favor of another, his action tends to be viewed as a breach of medical ethics. The concept of "treatment of choice" in medicine refers to this general rule that the treatment with the highest probability of cure must be used before any other is tried. Once the diagnosis has been made, one can predict with almost complete certainty the kinds of treatments the physician will use.

There is also a "treatment of choice" rule associated with the selection of means of influence. We have found that if powerholders agree on the reason for a target person's resistance to their influence, they will also agree on the proper means of influence to use. This two-stage process can be illustrated by studies done by myself and my colleagues William Lane and Joseph Cosentino (1962; 1969) among Navy and industrial supervisors.

The purpose of these studies was to determine how appointed leaders used their delegated powers to influence the performance of their subordinates. At the beginning of the studies we had no particular preconceived ideas as to how power would be used. Rather it was hoped to catalogue the range of means of influence that were relied upon, and to get some idea of when each means was used.

Our procedure consisted of asking supervisors in both the Navy and in various business organizations to describe a recent incident in which they had to correct the behavior of one of their subordinates. We asked the supervisors to describe the problem they faced and what they or someone else did about it. In telling us what they did, the supervisors were in effect telling us about the kinds of influence they had the authority to use.

In terms of the model of the power act given in Chapter 2, we note that the reason for these influence attempts did not arise from any particularly sinister motives. Rather they arose from the supervisors' involvement in their work. As part of this work there were obligations to make sure that employees performed at acceptable levels and to force changes if this level was not reached.

The nature of the employee problems that disturbed the supervisors in the first place was also tabulated. Basically the problems could be diagnosed as those caused by an inability of the employee to do his work or by a lack of motivation to do the work or by problems of discipline, in which company rules were violated (such as the problem of habitual lateness). Sometimes a supervisor would describe a subordinate whose poor performance was due to a combination of these problems. These employees were described as manifesting "complex" problems.

Next we looked at the ways in which the supervisors said they attempted to correct their employees' performance. Their attempts involved the use of a variety of institutional means of influence, which we classified as follows: (*a*) coercive power—threatening or actually demoting the subordinate or assigning him to less pleasant or lower-paying work, or reducing his responsibilities, or sending him an official letter of warning, or suspending or firing him; (*b*) ecological control, in which the subordinate was shifted to a new job, work shift, or a new job location but not for the purpose of punishment; (*c*) expert power, in which new information or new skills were shown the worker; (*d*) legitimate power expressed in terms of direct requests or orders for change.

In addition to these institutional means of influence, supervisors also relied upon their personal powers of persuasion convincing subordinates to change by praising, reprimanding, and encouraging them to expend additional efforts. Readers who adopt a historic or cultural perspective on these kinds of findings will be quick to see how bound by time and space such attempts at influence are. That is, no supervisors mentioned physically striking their employees, as would have been done prior to the twentieth century, and no supervisors mentioned using appeals based upon family and company loyalty, as is still done in some Japanese industries.

One of the strongest findings that emerged from these studies was the discovery that there was a "treatment of choice" rule associated with the selection of means of influence. That is, the kinds of influence invoked by the supervisors were found to vary systematically with the nature of the subordinate's problem as diagnosed by the supervisor. Without any particular instruction in the use of power, most of the supervisors converged on the selection of a given means of influence for a given type of problem. These findings are summarized in table 3.3.

Table 3.3 Diagnosis of Subordinate Resistance and the Means
             of Influence Used to Overcome It

Means of Influence	Diagnosed Cause of Poor Work			
	Simple Problems			Complex Problems
	Employee Lacks Motivation	Employee Lacks Ability	Employee Lacks Discipline	Combinations of Poor Attitudes, Discipline and/or Lack of Ability
Discussion	Yes	No	Yes	Yes
Extra training (expert power)	No	Yes	No	Yes
Ecological control	No	No	No	Yes
Legitimate power	Yes	Yes	Yes	Yes
Coercion	Yes	No	Yes	Yes

It can be seen that, as the supervisor's diagnosis of what was causing the subordinate's poor performance changed, so too did the means of influence that were used. For instance, when the supervisor believed that the employee's problem was due to poor attitudes, the supervisor used persuasion and informational modes of influence. The supervisor's concern was to find out the reasons for the subordinate's poor attitudes and, if possible, to persuade him to change. If, however, the supervisor attributed the subordinate's poor performance to a lack of ability, then persuasion was rarely mentioned. Rather, the supervisor invoked his expert powers and devoted time to retraining his subordinate.

If the problem shown by a subordinate was complex, with elements of lack of ability and discipline, and poor attitudes, then supervisors increased the number of different means of influence directed toward the subordinate. Apparently, when the supervisors believed that several factors were causing the employee's poor performance ("He could never learn to do the simplest jobs, and on top of that he was always shooting off his mouth"), then the problem was considered more difficult to deal with. Accordingly, more powers were invoked to overcome this added resistance. For instance, 76 percent of a sample of Navy supervisors invoked two or more means of influence (e.g., increased training and change of jobs) when their subordinates manifested complex problems. When the subordinate evidenced a simple problem, however, only 41 percent of the Navy supervisors invoked two or more means of influence. This difference was statistically reliable beyond the .01 level.

A further finding was that, when faced with complex problems, supervisors exercised power by ecological control. That is, significantly more workers were moved to a new job or work shift when their problems were complex rather than simple. The supervisors apparently reasoned: "If he's causing so much fuss on this job, let's try him somewhere else." A moment's reflection will convince the reader that this means of exercising power is not limited to harassed supervisors facing strong resistance. In schools, pupils who are considered intractable by teachers are transferred out of class, while ecological control is exerted over criminals by sending them to prison. In all instances the diagnosis of being hard to influence leads to the temptation to shift the person to a new environment considered more likely to overcome these resistances.

Here we have evidence that powerholders adjusted the kinds of influence they brought to bear to fit what they believed to be the reason for the target's resistance. If the target's resistance was seen as caused by poor attitudes, then persuasion was one of the favored means (coercion was also favored in such cases). If the resistance was seen as caused by a lack of ability, then expert power was used and little time was wasted trying to persuade the target to improve his performance. If the target was seen as manifesting a variety of problems simultaneously, then the powerholder increased the pressure for change by invoking several different kinds of influence. Simply put, as resistance increased, additional means of influence were brought to bear on the target person. And among these was an attempt to move the target person from his present environment.

These findings are consistent with the notion that the use of power involves an active cognitive search which consists of two stages. First, we see that the powerholder diagnoses the causes of the resistance. He says to himself, "The reason X is acting so badly is that. . . ." Second, the powerholder searches for the best means of influence available to him for dealing with this resistance. That is, he says, "Well, if that's why he is doing so poorly, then I'd better do this."

While this process has been illustrated in terms of work settings, it is not difficult to see how a similar search pattern might operate elsewhere. Thus, a parent whose child gets into continual mischief during the summer vacation must decide whether to promise him some benefit for good behavior, sit down and reason with him, send him to summer camp, appeal to his love for his parents, or threaten some kind of punishment. The process of choice will be actively guided by what the parent decides is causing the mischief in the first place.

Limitations to Rational Calculations

There are several reasons why powerholders may not be able to select the best means of influencing a target person. Most obviously, the powerholder may not have available the proper means of influence. For example, a supervisor may not have the authority to promise a pay raise, despite his recognition that he will be able to influence his employees to produce more if such means are used. Related to this reason is the problem that arises when the use of one means of influence may prevent the powerholder from using a second means, despite the powerholder's recognition that the use of the second means would be more appropriate. Thus for example, if one uses coercion on occasion, it becomes difficult then to switch to the use of persuasion. Researchers who have studied the use of power in penal systems point out that therapy programs in prison tend to be unsuccessful because the prisoners tend to be coerced into entering such programs.

The inhibiting effect that the use of one means of influence has upon the use of a second means is also illustrated in the complaints of social caseworkers that their control of the power to grant or withhold welfare money tends to weaken their ability to provide counseling and guidance to their poverty clients. In effect the poor are unwilling to communicate socioemotional problems to a caseworker because of the possibility that some careless revelation about themselves may cause the caseworker to withdraw funds. While many caseworkers would prefer to influence their clients through counseling, they are unable to do so because they also influence the same clients through the use of money. Similar problems have been noted by supervisors in industry who are expected to influence both task attitudes and socioemotional attitudes of their employees. It has been reported (Reed 1962) that subordinates are not willing to openly communicate problems to the supervisors because of the employees' fears that revealing negative information about themselves will reduce their chances for promotion. In both of these instances, the possession of strong economic means prevents the powerholder from using other means despite his recognition of their usefulness for exercising influence.

A second limitation to choosing the appropriate means of influence occurs when a powerholder simply misdiagnoses the causes of the target's resistance and applies the wrong means of influence. Thus, a teacher might threaten to discipline an inattentive student unless the student's behavior improved. The same teacher would rapidly change tactics if it were discovered that the cause of the student's inattention was a hearing loss. Then, perhaps, the student would be moved to the front of the class as a means of improving his attention.

Still another limitation occurs when the powerholder does not consider a particular means of influence as appropriate. For example, open expressions of love as a means of influencing a wife or child are rejected by some men who believe that such expressions are not consistent with their conceived role of manhood. In a different context, Dartmouth College political scientist David Baldwin (1974) has discussed this limitation in terms of the reluctance of government foreign-policy planners to seriously consider other nations in any terms but coercive military power. He points out that:

> students of international politics are so preoccupied with negative sanctions, threat systems, and military force that they have painted themselves into a conceptual corner which has little room for non-military factors, positive sanctions and promise

systems. It is not surprising, therefore, that the recent *International Encyclopedia of the Social Sciences* included an article on military power potential but none on economic power potential. At a time when military power is losing utility in international politics and economic power is gaining utility, this omission is especially unfortunate. [p. 395]

Lack of Ability or Lack of Motivation?

Powerholders usually diagnose the causes of a target person's resistance into one of two groupings. Either the resistance is attributed to the fact that the target person is inept and lacks ability, or to the fact that the target person has deliberately chosen to refuse to comply. In this second instance, the label of "poor attitude" or "lack of motivation" is used. Thus resistance is attributed by powerholders to either the fact that external forces are controlling the target person ("He wants to help but simply doesn't know how") or to internal forces within the target person ("That s.o.b. could do it if he wanted to help out"). The distinction between internal or external forces tends to be critical for understanding the powerholder's choice of influence tactics. In subsequent chapters we will provide data which show that if the powerholder attributes the target person's resistance to internal factors (choosing to resist) then the powerholder will decide to invoke stronger means of influence to overcome this resistance than if the powerholder attributes the target person's resistance to external causes.

Here I wish to consider briefly the question of what kinds of information powerholders use when deciding that the target's resistance is due to either internal or external forces.

University of Wisconsin social psychologist H. Andrew Michener and his colleagues (John Fleishman, Gregory Elliot, and Joel Skolnick [in press, 1975]) have used concepts derived from attribution theory to help explain this decision. Michener et al. have proposed that the powerholder's judgment is based upon four bits of information: (*a*) the difficulty of the demands placed upon the target person; (*b*) the known ability of the target person; (*c*) the extent to which the target person seems to be trying; and (*d*) whether the target person's performance improves or not. In a test of this proposal, Michener found that powerholders attributed a target person's poor performance on an experimental task (solving anagrams) to external forces or, lack of ability, when the task was known to be difficult for most people, when the target person had a prior history of ineptness in solving anagrams, when the target person signaled that he was trying as hard as he could, and when the target person's performance improved over time, even though it never quite reached the level expected by the powerholder. Powerholders attributed the target person's poor performance to a lack of motivation when the opposite of the above four bits of information were communicated to the powerholder.

In short, the process by which powerholders diagnose the causes of a target person's resistance to influence has its own logic. Basically the powerholder attempts to reach a diagnosis by comparing the target person's current behavior with past behavior. Inconsistencies between current and past behavior are considered due to deliberate resistance when the powerholder knows that what has been requested is within the capabilities of the target person. Under these circumstances it is not unusual to hear powerholders justifying their selection of influence tactics in terms of the target person's poor attitude, hostility, or lack of motivation.

Summary

This chapter has examined how powerholders convert inert resources into actual influence. The basic proposal is that the decision to convert resources into influence is guided by an active cognitive search for the best means of making this conversion. This search involves two distinct stages. In the first the reasons for the target person's refusal to comply are diagnosed. The second stage involves selecting that means of influence considered by the powerholder as most likely to overcome the diagnosed causes of resistance.

It has also been suggested that there are stable linkages between the diagnosed causes of a target person's resistance and the particular means of influence that are chosen. If powerholders attribute the target person's resistance to external forces over which the target person has no control ("I'm trying, but I just can't seem to do it"), then the influence techniques chosen involve training and expert knowledge. In essence these techniques serve to restore self-control to the target person so that he can comply in future interactions.

When powerholders attribute the target person's resistance to internal forces under the control of the target person ("I refuse"), then the influence techniques chosen involve discussion and persuasion, at least initially. If, however, discussion fails, then power-holders are tempted to invoke stronger means of influence to overcome what they believe to be deliberate resistance. These stronger means of influence involve the use of both rewards and punishments. Chapters 4 and 6 will examine in more detail the circumstances under which these last two means of influence are used.

Finally the chapter has briefly surveyed sources that restrict the powerholder's selection of the appropriate means of influence. These sources include the fact that often influence tactics are not available to a given powerholder because of his position in an organization, because he does not recognize that it is legitimate to use some influence tactic, or because he has misdiagnosed the reasons for the target person's refusal and simply has chosen the wrong means of influence.

4

The Decision
to Use Rewards

If powerholders use rational calculations when invoking such bases of power as persuasion, expertise, and ecological control, it surely is to be expected that careful thought will be used when considering promises and rewards. This can be traced to the fact that there are costs associated with the successful use of rewards that are not associated with, for example, the use of expert knowledge or persuasion. Promises obligate the powerholder to respond with a reward if the target complies; the powerholder must pay up if he is to retain his credibility.

It is a commonplace observation that, despite the costs involved, rewards and promises are continually used in day-to-day social relations. Aside from their use to increase the benefits to persons who have shown exemplary and meritorious behavior in the past, rewards and promises are mainly used to change the behavior of target persons who are unwilling to comply with simple requests from the powerholder. From Skinnerean psychology to managerial pay policies it has been found that the judicious use of small rewards frequently produces large returns to the powerholder. Behavior is shaped by rewards, and motivations are increased in anticipation of being reinforced. One of the strongest findings of experimental psychology is that target persons respond with compliance when rewards are used. Given the strength of rewards for influencing others, a question that remains to be answered is, why aren't rewards used more often?

Let us begin our search for an answer by asking whether there are identifiable circumstances under which powerholders decide to use rewards. Stated in terms of the idea of "treatment of choice," we ask what kinds of diagnoses of the causes of target resistance lead to the conclusion that rewards should be used.

David Baldwin (1971) has proposed one answer to this question by theorizing that the decision to use rewards is reserved for instances in which the target person's resistance is seen as strong and the powerholder doubts his ability to overcome this resistance. We can restate Baldwin's proposal in terms of the powerholder's subjective expectations of being able to influence a target person: *Rewards are most likely to be used when the powerholder has low expectations that simple persuasion will overcome a target person's resistance.*

If the calculations of the powerholder reveal that only a little urging is needed to overcome the target person's resistance, then the powerholder will be unlikely to couple this urging with some offer of a tangible reward. Thus, politicians will promise very little to the voters in districts that always vote for him but will promise anything in exchange for votes in districts that are not "in his pocket." Similarly, the history of international aid programs suggests that more aid tends to be given to countries that were former enemies than to those that were former allies. In both instances, the use of rewards appears associated with low expectations of successful influence through simple persuasion.

In the following sections of this chapter we will review published instances of the use of reward power and examine whether the "expectancy rule" (rewards are used when powerholders hold low expectations that simple persuasion will cause compliance) is consistent with these published reports.

Before proceeding with this review, however, it is necessary to distinguish between the use of rewards for purposes of philanthropy and the use of rewards as a means of exercising power. If this distinction is not made, then it will be possible to find many instances in which rewards are distributed on bases other than expectations of successful influence.

Philanthropy, altruism, generosity, and charity, as Shopler and Bateson (1965) point out, describe situations in which a typically powerful person, often at some sacrifice to himself, helps someone else who is relatively weak. I believe it makes little sense to describe these acts of charity as power acts, despite the fact that in them powerholders give rewards to target persons. What is missing in them is the fact of the more powerful person wanting something from the person receiving the charity. In its purest form, the act of charity involves no power needs, nor are there any target resistances to be overcome by it. As a result, one may expect that forces other than rational calculations (e.g., norms of social responsibility) are involved in the decisions to distribute rewards for charitable purposes. This distinction should be kept in mind in the discussion that follows on the use of reward power. The discussion will be limited to those instances in which the powerholder: (*a*) has access to rewards that the target person desires, (*b*) and wants the target person to carry out some behavior (*c*) that the target person normally does not want to do.

Perceived Similarity and the Use of Rewards

There is a widespread folk saying that suggests one should reward friends and punish enemies. If these recommendations were applied to power relations, it would follow that rewards should be used more frequently with target persons who were liked than with those who were disliked.

A moment's reflection, however, suggests that this use of influence is not consistent with the general rule that rewards are used when expectations of successful influence are lowest. We surely should be more optimistic about our chances of influencing friends than about our chances of influencing enemies. Accordingly, we expect that, when power is involved, rewards will be used more with disliked than with liked persons. Further, we expect that rewards will be used more with dissimilar than with similar persons. This is because we tend to assume that persons who are similar to ourselves will be cooperative and moved by the same forces that move us. To the extent persons differ from us, however, we have no way of understanding their motives. And the intuitive conclusion is that we have to work harder to make them cooperate.

There are relatively few studies, unfortunately, that have directly examined the frequency with which rewards are used among liked and disliked (or similar-dissimilar) target persons. Furthermore, of the few studies in this area most are based upon the use of bargaining games, in which two opponents of relatively equal power bargain with each other using promises and threats. Tedeschi, Schlenker, and Bonoma (1973) have reviewed the various research studies that have been done in this area and concluded that there is good evidence that liked target persons are seen as more cooperative than disliked persons in bargaining games. However, a study in this series by Schlenker and Tedeschi (1972) found no support pro or con for our belief that disliked persons would be offered more rewards in exchange for cooperation than would liked persons.

Positive support for the prediction, however, has been reported in several studies where superior-subordinate relations were involved.

In a study by Baker, Demarco, and Scott (1975), volunteers were asked to act as supervisors of workers who were either sighted or blind. Actually, the workers, by agreement, did equal amounts of work, whether they were sighted or blind. The supervisors were told that the project was funded by a company which used both sighted and blind workers. The work involved filling bags of marbles in front of TV cameras so that the workers' performance could be monitored by the supervisors.

As supervisors, the volunteers were given the power to award ten-cent pay raises every two minutes to any worker, if they chose to do so. The question that was examined in the study was whether more rewards were given to blind than to sighted workers. The results were that the supervisors awarded three times as many pay raises to the blind workers as to the sighted workers, although both sighted and blind workers did equally good work. These results support the idea that rewards would be invoked more frequently to influence dissimilar others. While there are many other possible explanations for this outcome (for example, feeling sorry for the blind workers), we favor the interpretation that the supervisors held lower expectations of successfully influencing these blind workers because of their handicap. As a result more rewards were promised and used as a means of encouraging them to expend extra effort and so to keep up with the sighted workers.

While the Baker et al. study revealed the predicted relation between the use of rewards and similarity of target person and powerholder, it can be argued that liking for the target person may not have been directly involved. A study by Banks (1974), however, directly investigated the use of rewards among liked and disliked target persons. Liking was experimentally created through a variation of the attitude similarity-dissimilarity technique (cf. Byrne 1961) in which subjects are told they share a similar outlook on life with the person they are to be paired with. As in the Baker et al. study, volunteers were assigned to the role of supervisor, with the job of monitoring the performance of trainees. Power to reward was provided the supervisors in the form of money that could be allotted to the trainees in order to encourage good work.

The findings were that significantly more rewards were given to dissimilar trainees than to similar trainees. Instead of rewarding those they liked, the supervisors gave more rewards to those they disliked. This finding can be interpreted to mean that the supervisors had low expectations that the dissimilar target persons would continue to perform at a satisfactory level if the supervisors relied upon simple persuasion. Thus, rewards were more frequently invoked to prevent performance from falling off.

What is needed at this time is research that directly examines a powerholder's expectations of successful influence in relation to the use of rewards with similar and dissimilar target persons. While the above-cited studies by Banks and by Baker et al. are consistent with our "expectations rule," there are still alternate explanations for the findings that need to be ruled out. Until such additional studies are done, the speculations present in this section should be labeled as interesting but untested hypotheses.

Status, Reputation, and Ingratiation

A continuous theme in the literature of Western civilization is that of a hero seeking to define himself through his relations with other people. To be an outcast is tragedy. To lose one's reputation is sufficient cause for war. To win love is divine. We cannot fail to respond with intense interest to accounts of a hero's journey through life with its tragic, noble, and often funny encounters.

In the social sciences, as in literature, there is an intense interest in trying to account for people's persistent urge to be liked and accepted by others. This urge has been studied from many vantage points. We ask, What determines romantic love? Why do persons comply with the opinions of someone they like? Why the necessity to win affection and love?

For some social scientists, the gaining of love and admiration from others is not only seen as a desired end in itself but represents a way to increase one's power over others. Power, says Mott (1970), is access to the pooled energy of many, and Hobbes has written, "to have friends is Power: for they are strengths united." Thus, it is possible to view the urge to relate in positive ways to other persons as one manifestation of a drive for power. Indeed, Tedeschi et al. (1971) recently argued that an important element in understanding interpersonal relations is the assumption that people seek to be consistent in their behavior so that they will be liked and trusted and, accordingly, so that they can exert influence more easily.

If power is involved in the pursuit of friendship, then our expectancy rule should hold concerning when rewards will be used. As a powerholder perceives that the target person views him with indifference or worse, one should expect an increased reliance upon rewards by the powerholder as a means of overcoming this resistance.

While no direct evidence is available on this point, there is considerable biographical material detailing the behavior of persons attempting to rise in society which supports this view. In general, persons desiring to gain new and more prestigious friends spend large amounts of money for parties, presents, and gifts to charity regardless of the objective costs involved. Cleveland Amory (1960) and other observers of society in this country have described in detail the lavish parties given by persons with newly obtained wealth who wish to be admitted to equal standing with those already high in society. In these instances, the spending of large amounts is done solely to change for the better the indifferent or negative attitudes of persons considered of higher status. In line with the arguments presented in this chapter, it is assumed that our social climber does not believe that he will be freely welcomed as an intimate friend. His expectation is that simply asking for friendship will not be enough to overcome the indifference of the higher-status target persons. Hence, stronger means of influence must be used.

Of course, we do not need to examine the drama of attempts to rise in society among the very rich to find instances of this kind of use of rewarding power. At a day-to-day level, presents are frequently given by persons attempting to win the affections of another. Candy, flowers, jewelry, and expensive and inexpensive knicknacks are continually used by lovers who doubt their affection is reciprocated and who wish to influence for the better the opinions of their heart's object.

One concern of powerholders when rewards are invoked for this purpose has to do with the permanence of the social relations that are established. Despite the cynical observation that money can buy anything, observers in the social sciences continue to advance compelling reasons to doubt this belief. For instance, Raven and Kruglanski (1970) argue that the use of sanctions such as rewards are not likely to produce permanent changes in the attitude structure of target persons, at least immediately. Rather, when rewards cease to be applied, there is a high probability that the target person may revert to his original attitudes and behavior.

Similar arguments concerning the lack of permanent social change produced by using rewards can be derived from the resource exchange theory of Foa and Foa (1975). Using this theory, one might argue that the exchange of a material resource, such as money, for an affectional resource, such as love and friendship, is psychologically out of balance and, hence, not likely to endure. Centuries earlier, Machiavelli similarly warned the Prince that the use of reward powers, or "liberality" as he called it, would not guarantee that the Prince would be perpetually held in high regard by his followers. After first warning the Prince that attempts to gain the affection of others through "liberality" might over time exhaust his resources, Machiavelli went on to cite the temporary effects of gaining status through the use of rewards and concludes:

> it is much safer to be feared than loved, if one of the two has to be wanting. For it may be said of men in general that they are ungrateful, voluble, dissemblers, anxious to avoid danger, and covetous of gain. *As long as you benefit them, they are entirely yours*; they offer you their blood, their goods, their life and their children . . . when the necessity [for making sacrifices] is remote, but when it approaches they revolt. And the Prince . . . is ruined; for friendship which is gained by purchase, and not through grandeur or nobility of spirit, is bought but not secured. . . . And men have less scruple in offending one who makes himself loved [in this way] than one who makes himself feared.

For love is held by a chain of obligations which, men being selfish, is broken whenever it serves their purposes; but fear is maintained by a dread of punishment which never fails. [p. 90]

Despite such warnings, there is continual documentation from books, public media, research, and everyday observation that persons are willing to dispense rewards in order to change a target person's appraisal from indifference to avowed admiration. While not direct evidence, this kind of use of material rewards is consistent with our "expectancy rule."

So far we have talked about conscious efforts by powerholders to influence the opinions of target persons by using material rewards. There is another variant of this use in which the powerholder is made the victim of his desire for admiration. In this variation, powerholders are influenced to dispense rewards in exchange for flattery from subordinates. The decision to dispense rewards in this instance is based, not on a deliberate effort to win another's affection, but upon needs that powerholders tend to be unaware of. For instance Rogow and Lasswell (1965) have described one type of political leader who willingly exchanged the material resources of his office for flattery. Similarly, in business organizations, it has long been recognized that "buttering up the boss" is a royal road to organizational advancement and success. In exchange for flattery, managers seem willing to grant promotions and higher pay. In these kinds of instances it is doubted that the expectancy rule operates. If asked, managers would claim that they were seeking no ego gratification from their subordinates and that any added pay that was given out was awarded on the basis of the subordinate's loyalty to the company. In short, ingratiation tactics can be viewed as part of the tactical behaviors of those who have few resources.

In summary, to the extent that a powerholder's aim is to increase his social standing, or to improve his reputation, or to make friends of those who are indifferent to his existence, he will be tempted to dispense rewards. If the expectancy rule is correct, the decisions to use rewards in these instances should be accompanied by the belief that the target persons would not change their evaluations for the better by simply talking to the powerholder. The problem here is that the powerholder's sense of worth may be built on shifting sands. As Machiavelli warns the Prince, the powerholder can exhaust his resources in exerting this kind of influence and subsequently lose the friendships he sought in the first place.

Rewards at Work

In his book *Pay and Organizational Effectiveness*, Lawler (1971) listed the many kinds of valued outcomes that employees associate with their pay. Most obviously, money is instrumental in satisfying needs for security and physical well-being. In addition, pay may provide the person with bench marks for evaluating his own worth. Lawler reports that a broad spectrum of psychological motives including esteem, autonomy, and self-actualization have at one time or another been found to be correlated with the amount of pay the person receives. For a fair majority of persons, what one "gets" represents what one is worth.

Despite the central relevance of pay and other material rewards in our society, there have been surprisingly few attempts to examine what influences managers to grant or withhold pay increases. Perhaps the lack of interest in this question arises from the textbook idea that rational managers distribute pay in proportion to the employee's productive contribution to the business establishment. Simple reflection should tell us, however, that these rational considerations are not the whole story. There are many social and psychological forces acting on the manager to lead him to ignore the productivity of the employee. These forces range from the number of persons available for hire, to the financial state of the business, to such subtle psychological forces as the presence of ingratiating employees who exchange flattery for money.

In the next three sections of this chapter we will examine the social-psychological conditions that have been associated with a manager's decision to award higher pay as a means of influencing the behavior of his employees. It will be argued that money is used by managers when they anticipate that at some future time an employee may be unwilling to comply. *Money as reward is used to prevent the occurrence of resistance rather than to eliminate present resistance.* Thus, we modify the expectancy rule to read: rewards are most likely to be used at work when the powerholder has low expectations that the target person will continue to comply in future interactions. The following sections will examine this expectancy rule in terms of the organizational climate in which pay is given, employee motivation, and the social context in which performance is judged.

Organizational Climate

Cartwright (1965) has observed that the organizational climate in which pay is administered will affect a manager's decision about the use of pay. Basically, the organizational climate operates in this way by influencing the manager's assumptions about what motivates employees to work hard. In an *autocratic* organizational climate there exists a general belief system that employees require surveillance and cannot be trusted to work independently. The very fact that there are strict rules and regulations, a continual surveillance of the employees, and a strict hierarchical control of behavior produce the belief among managers that their employees are motivated by outside forces, that is, the managers' orders and influence. Since this is the assumption, it follows that managers will not place too much reliance upon means of influence such as discussion. Use of this form of influence assumes that employees are in charge of their own behavior and that rational discussions are enough to produce compliance. Given these low expectations of successful influence through discussion, there is a great emphasis placed in autocratic climates upon the establishment of strong sanction systems. Most faith is placed in "objectively based pay systems that tie pay to hard criteria such as quantity of output, profits, or sales, and thus require a minimum of trust" (Lawler, 1972, p. 277).

In democratically run business organizations there is a deemphasis upon surveillance, supervisory control, and upon rules and regulations. Rather, the emphasis is on shared decision-making activities in which employees are given the power to make decisions about their own work loads and effort. One consequence of this kind of democratic climate is that managers come to believe that their orders will be carried out willingly and at the discretion of the employee. The employee is seen as freely choosing to do the work properly rather than being compelled to do so by the manager's promises and threats. An interesting observation of Lawler is that democratically run organizations tend to place less emphasis on money and more on psychological forms of return to employees. These psychological forms of return tend to focus on allowing employees more autonomy and opportunities to do meaningful and creative work.

This kind of emphasis is consistent with the expectancy rule derived from Baldwin's hypothesis of an inverse relation between expectations of successful influence and the use of rewards. This rule asserts that reward power is most likely to be used when the powerholder assumes that the target person is actively opposed to accepting influence. As expectations of successful influence go down, the probabilities of a decision to use rewards go up. Since managers in democratically run organizations tend to believe that employees are self-motivated and do not have to be forced to work with either a carrot or a stick, their expectations of being able to exert influence successfully through discussion should be higher.

While I know of no data on this point, what has been said here suggests the curious prediction that pay should be lower in democratically than autocratically run organizations. This is because managers should rely less on such means in the former than the latter organizations. In any case, my point is that one can expect variations in the use of pay within business organizations that can be traced to the kinds of assumptions managers make about employees' motivations. In turn, these assumptions can be traced to the collective values of management which form a part of the organization's psychological climate.

Employee Performance and the Decision to Reward

From Baldwin's proposal we might expect that managers would reward employees doing unsatisfactory work. This is because in these instances expectations of successful influence are lowest. In the previously cited field studies by the present writer (Kipnis and Lane 1962; Kipnis and Cosentino 1969) concerned with supervisors' attempts to elevate subordinates' poor performances, no mention of rewards was made by supervisors as a means of influencing their employees to do better work. Indeed, it would be difficult to locate many managers who attempt to correct incompetence with pay raises. Organizations do not encourage the use of rewards as a means of changing the performance of noncompliant workers. Such a use of power might be viewed as a "bribe" and, hence, as being illicit. Furthermore, having to honor a promise to reward a worker who has previously annoyed a supervisor by his poor work may in fact be personally distasteful, and would certainly anger satisfactory workers.

We have found generally that pay raises, promotions, favorable performance reviews, and the like are used either to maintain a target at some acceptable level of performance or to encourage the target to exceed this level. For instance, in a laboratory simulation of work (Kipnis and Vanderveer 1971), subjects in their role as managers were provided with the power to reward their workers with pay increases if they so chose. It was found that most rewards were given to superior performers, next most to average workers, and the fewest rewards were given to inferior workers. This finding is hardly surprising and merely confirms the commonplace observation that good work is usually rewarded more than bad work.

Exchange theorists might also view this finding as support for the belief that notions of equity regulate human exchanges, since management tends to match the employees' input of effort with appropriate outcome levels of money. From the perspective of power relations, however, one might suspect that the added money awarded the superior worker was not used by the managers merely to reward past performance. Rather, I suggest that the managers had one eye to the future and used rewards to insure that the output of the superior workers would continue at high levels. As a general rule, rewards serve in the mind of the powerholder as a means of preventing entropy, that is, of preventing the performance of well-motivated workers from decaying to some unacceptable level. Thus, promises and rewards are used by managers to overcome *anticipated* resistances, rather than *actual* resistances, by workers.

It follows from this conclusion that superior work per se is not likely to be often rewarded if management is confident that the employee is programmed to remain at this high level without interference from outsiders. Praise and encouragement tend to be substituted for money in these instances. It is only when uncertainty is associated with the employee's performances, when management suspects for example that the employee's high level of performance may soon fall off (the employee may hint of taking another job), that serious consideration is given to awarding higher salary.

The Rewards of Loyalty When Rebellion Is Near

In our research in work settings we have found that the use of pay as reward was sharply influenced by the amount and kind of resistance managers were experiencing from their employees. When employees were all performing satisfactorily, rewards were doled out sparingly. When some employees expressed poor attitudes about the work and reduced their output, then managers increased the number of pay raises given to the remaining satisfactory employees. Presumably these raises were given to prevent their satisfactory employees from joining the ranks of the malcontents.

This conclusion is based upon several industrial simulation studies (Goodstadt and Kipnis 1970; Kipnis and Vanderveer 1971; Fodor 1974), which found that the presence of noncompliant employees, who deliberately refused to obey a manager's orders, increased the number of pay raises given by managers to workers who did accept orders. In the absence of these noncompliant employees, the number of pay raises given out to employees was significantly reduced.

We may illustrate this process with the findings from the Kipnis and Vanderveer study. In this particular study, business majors were appointed as managers of a simulated business and required to direct the work of four employees. The managers were delegated the power to give pay raises if they chose to do so. In one condition (labeled "poor attitude"), one of the four workers deliberately refused to follow orders, while the remaining three workers did satisfactory work. In a second condition (labeled "control condition"), all of the workers did satisfactory work. Table 4 shows the average number of pay raises given by managers to the three compliant workers in these two conditions. Table 4 also shows the managers' evaluation of the three compliant workers' performances at the end of the work sessions. These evaluations were based upon the managers' rating of each worker or four 11-point scales that were summed into an overall evaluation score. Since the amount of work in this study was regulated by the experiments, the reader should understand that the performances of the three compliant workers in both the Poor Attitude Condition and the Control Condition were exactly the same. Hence, any difference in managers' use of rewards toward these three compliant workers could be safely attributed to the presence or absence of the defiant fourth worker.

It can be seen that the same compliant performance evoked more pay raises and higher performance evaluations when the manager experienced resistance from the fourth worker than when no resistance was shown. These differences in pay raises and perform-

ance evaluations were statistically significant. The explanation offered by Vanderveer and myself was that the presence of noncompliant workers provided the managers with new standards for judging
the worth of compliant workers. The managers were suddenly reminded of how bad things could be if all the workers, rather than
just one, decided not to comply. The presence of a militant who
challenged authority provided a new baseline for evaluating the
behavior of the loyal workers.

Table 4.1 Evaluation and Average Number of Pay Raises Awarded by
Managers to Three Compliant Workers

Condition	Number of Pay Raises Given to Three Compliant Workers	Performance Evaluations of Three Compliant Workers
Fourth worker expressed defiiance	4.0	32.0
Fourth worker expressed *no* defiance	2.1	26.9

It should not be thought that these findings are restricted to
simple, contrived laboratory situations. A recent doctoral dissertation by my student Ronald J. Grey (1975) provided strong evidence that supervisors in "real life" similarly increase the number
of rewards they give to compliant workers as the number of noncompliant workers they direct increases.

Grey's research was carried out among supervisors of clerical
workers in a large insurance company. Fifty-nine supervisors were
asked to evaluate each of their employees. The supervisors directed
units of varying size, ranging from three to twenty-six female employees, with a median of eleven employees. The data collected
consisted of the supervisor's summed evaluation of each of their
employee's performance on six factors: quality of work, quantity of
work, consistency of performance, ability to follow instructions,
ability to learn unit procedures, and a rating of the employee's
overall worth to the company. In addition the supervisors were
asked whether they would recommend the employee for promotion
and for a pay increase. Finally records of actual pay increases for
the previous year were obtained from company files. This last bit
of reward data was incomplete for many of the employees, and

the actual amount of the pay increase was only partially controlled by the supervisor, thus rendering actual pay raises somewhat suspect. Nevertheless, this information, coded in terms of the percentage of salary increase for the prior year, was included because of our interest in the distribution of rewards.

The major problem for Grey was to obtain information on the number of compliant and noncompliant employees working for each supervisor. In the prior experiments it had been possible to program workers to act in a compliant or noncompliant manner. Thus there was no problem of how to measure the existence of compliance. It had been put there or taken away by the experimenter. Grey measured the number of compliant and noncompliant employees working for each supervisor by including the following question on each employee's evaluation form that the supervisor filled out:

If this individual has a basic weakness, is it due to:
(check one answer)
—Lack of ability
—Poor attitude
—Both a lack of ability and poor attitude
—This individual has no basic weakness

The proportion of inept subordinates working for a supervisor was calculated from the above form by first determining the number of employees working for each supervisor who were rated as lacking ability. This number was then divided by the total number of employees in the supervisor's unit. In like manner the proportions of poor-attitude employees and complex-problem employees were computed. Finally the total proportion of noncompliant employees was obtained by summing the above three indices of noncompliance (% inept + % poor attitude + % complex). Through this procedure, information was obtained about the proportions of employees who resisted their supervisors' orders due to external reasons (lack of ability) or due to internal reasons (poor attitudes). In addition, information was available on the total numbers of employees who resisted their supervisors' orders, regardless of the reasons involved. Supervisors reported, on the average, that about one-third of their employees resisted their orders for reasons of attitude or ability. This figure ranged from a high of 70 percent for one supervisor to a low 0 percent for nine supervisors who said that none of their employees had any weaknesses.

In short, through this method of measurement Grey had a count on the number of noncompliant employees and the number of compliant employees working for each supervisor. Compliant employees were all those employees whom the supervisor said had "no basic weaknesses."

At this point the reader may object that the measures of noncompliance used in the study were subjective and were based solely upon the biased judgment of the supervisor. In part, the objection is correct. Whether or not a given employee was in fact inept or held poor attitudes, as measured by objective standards, was not known. However, such information is not relevant in terms of the objectives of the research. Supervisors' perceptions of these conditions are, for all intents and purposes, their reality. Since they use these perceptions of their employees to decide upon the distribution of rewards and punishments, we must, like the employees, accept these judgments as having some claim to validity in their own right.

The basic question was the extent to which supervisors would distribute rewards equally or unequally to their *compliant* workers. Grey's hypothesis was that the distribution would be unequal; that compliant employees working for a supervisor who had many noncompliant employees would receive more rewards than compliant employees who worked in units that contained few or no noncompliant employees.

Table 4.2 shows the data to test the hypothesis in the form of correlations between the proportion of noncompliant employees working for a given supervisor and the supervisor's average evaluations of the remaining compliant employees. Positive correlations mean that the larger the proportion of noncompliant employees in a given unit, the more favorable the evaluations given by that unit's supervisor to compliant employees.

As examination of table 4.2 reveals that one can predict quite well a supervisor's evaluations of compliant employees by simply knowing the proportion of noncompliant employees in the supervisor's work unit. In particular, the greater the proportion of employees seen by a supervisor as manifesting poor attitudes, the more likely was the supervisor to recommend compliant employees for promotion and pay raises, as well as to give them higher performance-evaluation ratings. The proportion of inept employees appears to have less influence on the supervisor's judgments, although this proportion does carry some slight weight.

Table 4.2 Correlations between the Proportion of NonCompliant Employees in a Work Unit and Evaluations of Compliant Employees

% Noncompliant employees in the work unit	Evaluations of Compliant Employees			
	Performance Evaluations	Recommended Promotions	Recommended Pay Raise	Actual Pay Raise
1. % Poor-attitude employees	.30**	.32**	.33*	.25*
2. % Inept employees	.23*	.15	.09	−.02
3. % Complex problems[a]	—	—	—	—
4. % Total non-compliance (1 + 2 + 3)	.50**	.48**	.32**	.21*

NOTE: All correlations are partial r's, adjusted for the number of noncompliant employees in the unit, and tenure, sex, and age of the rater and ratee.
[a]Only 2 percent of the employees were rated as complex problems—hence correlations were not computed for this group.
**significant beyond .01 level; *significant beyond the .05 level.

If one disregards the reason for the noncompliance and simply adds up the total proportion of noncompliant employees in a given unit, the findings become even stronger. I am tempted to suggest from these findings that if one wishes to curry favor with the boss, a sure means is to plant several truculent, hostile employees in the unit (the more the better), and then hasten to assure the boss of one's loyalty. One should be deluged with riches.

Returning to the original argument of this section, the data from these several studies are seen as consistent with our expectancy rule. In this instance it would appear that the presence of large numbers of employees who resist a manager's influence serve to lower the manager's expectations that the remaining employees can be counted on to maintain satisfactory performance. Increasing the amounts of rewards, in the form of recommendations for promotion and so on, is seen as a way of helping to guarantee the future loyalty of those who still remain compliant.

By analogy, if a father has all dutiful and compliant sons, his evaluations of their worth might tend to be less favorable than if one of his sons has proved to be a continued disgrace. Under these circumstances his remaining sons would be appreciated far more intensely. Indeed, the father might increase the amount of benefits given to the remaining sons as a means of preventing them from following the example of the disgraced son. Or, to give another example, in the late 1960s, when political dissent was most active, the silent majority was most praised by supporters of the Vietnam War. Thus, the powerholder can be expected to actively use his available resources to promise rewards to his supporters when peril threatens from without or within. As mentioned before, rewards tend to be used by powerholders to prevent the decay of satisfactory performance. Any forces that arouse suspicion that loyal followers are soon to be subverted also serve to increase the powerholder's attraction to invoking rewards.

Summary

In this chapter we have examined the powerholder's decisions to use rewards in relation to his beliefs concerning the amount of resistance liable to be shown by the target person. Following Baldwin's view of when rewards are used, we have suggested that, as expectations for successful influence decrease, the powerholder is tempted to use stronger means of influence. These stronger means tend to take the form of rewards or punishments.

One conclusion reached in this chapter is that rewards are used when the powerholder wishes to secure the good will of the target person or when the powerholder has some doubts that existing compliance by the target person will continue. The implications of this expectancy view need to be worked out in considerably more detail, however, than has been provided here. In particular, study must be given to the situational forces that help shape the powerholder's expectancies, as well as to the personal characteristics of the powerholder, as these also influence expectations of successful influence. Chapter 6 provides considerably more detail concerning the forces shaping decisions to use coercive power. The paucity of research dealing with this issue in relation to the use of rewards, however, precludes discussion of that aspect of the subject at this time.

5   Coercive Power

Of all the bases of power available to man, the power to hurt others is possibly most often used, most often condemned, and most difficult to control. The absence of coercive power creates insecurities, but its presence terrifies. Our feelings about coercion are mixed, similar to those of a ten-year-old looking under his bed for "spooks." He hopes they're not there, but suppose they were! Fascination with coercion is reflected in such disparate events as the enormous popularity of films depicting violence and aggression to the reading of the Old Testament, with its focus on the horrific forms of coercive power used to punish transgressions. Many persons receive great comfort from reading that God used plagues, famines, diseases, and death to crush his enemies. Indeed, I think that the ambivalent feeling held by many toward Christ can be traced to his message to renounce coercion and love those who do you harm. To this day those who truly accept this message are considered naive, if not half-witted.

While the art of coercion has not advanced much since Christ's time, its use is perhaps more widespread today and its expression takes more forms than in past times. Let us briefly consider the many ways in which coercive power may be expressed. First, the state relies on its military and legal resources to intimidate nations, or even its own citizens. Businesses rely upon the control of economic resources. Schools and universities rely upon their right to deny students formal education, while the church threatens individuals with loss of grace. At the personal level, individuals exercise coercive power through a reliance upon physical strength, verbal facility, or the ability to grant or withhold emotional support from others. These bases provide the individual with the means to physically harm, bully, humiliate, or deny love to others.

In this chapter, we will discuss some reasons why people may be tempted to invoke coercive power. As with other bases of power, the use of coercion can be viewed as being a complex function of (1) an aroused need, (2) access to resources which have the potential to be used coercively, and (3) restraining or inhibitory forces acting on the powerholder. Within this framework we will also discuss the possibility that, as the reasons for invoking coercion change, so too will the ways in which the powerholder views himself and his target.

While these reasons can be viewed in terms of the expectancy rule that was discussed in Chapter 4, we shall delay discussion of coercion from this vantage point until Chapter 6. It suffices to say here that the picture of the rationally calculating powerholder fits all of the various reasons for choosing coercion described in this chapter except that of anger. In this instance one frequently finds that little thought has been given to the act of doing harm.

Definition of Coercive Power

Tedeschi, Smith, and Brown (1972) define coercive power as the use of threats and punishments to gain compliance with the powerholder's demands. This definition is consistent with our more general definition of power motivation, but here the means of influence used to induce compliance are considered noxious. While Tedeschi et al. do not state from whose point of view the threats and punishments are considered noxious—that is, the powerholder's, the target's, or an outside observer's—we will consider the point of view of the powerholder. That is, if he *thinks* he is invoking a threat or a punishment, we will call the means of influence coercive.

Because of this emphasis on the powerholder, little will be said about the effectiveness of the use of coercive power in securing a target's compliance. This is because we must know what the target feels about the threatened sanctions before we can tell if the threats and punishments will produce their intended effect. For example, a banker's threat of foreclosure may be viewed as rewarding by a homeowner whose house is in complete disrepair and who is looking for an excuse to move into an apartment. In this instance the banker's threat only strengthens the homeowner's resolve not to pay. There is general agreement that the motivations of the target, and how much weight he gives the powerholder's resources, need to be understood before statements can be made concerning the likelihood of successful use of coercion (French and Raven 1959; Thibaut and Kelley 1959).

The burden of attempting to predict when threats and punishments will achieve intended consequences is a task that may be beyond the ability of social science, except in very limited and contrived situations. This is because the use of coercive power tends to have both immediate and long-range effects. While the immediate effects are predictable, if one has sufficient information about the target, the long-range effects of the use of coercion appear almost unknowable because the use of coercive power generates resistances in the target (Brehm 1966; French and Raven 1959) that may be far stronger than any present initially. Frequently, the perception of threat generates aid from bystanders, who, out of sympathy and moral outrage, join ranks with the target to help thwart the powerholder (Stotland 1959). A good example of this inability to predict the outcomes of the use of coercive power may be found in the *Pentagon Papers,* which documented the early stages of America's entry into the Vietnam War. Repeatedly, steps were taken by military planners to increase military pressure on North Vietnam as a means of causing the early collapse of its efforts in the South. Projects such as Operation Rolling Thunder were devised in which American use of force, including bombing, would periodically escalate until the North Vietnamese gave up. Despite optimistic predictions about the outcome of this use of force, the war actually escalated and intensified—the exact opposite of what had been predicted. The bombing may have strengthened, rather than weakened, the enemy's resolve to resist.

Alfred Adler (1956), in an article written in 1918-19, commenting on the Russian Revolution, made similar observations on the uncontrollable and unpredictable effects of the reliance on coercive power:

The struggle for power has a psychological aspect. Even where the welfare of the subjugated is intended, the use of even moderate power (of a punitive kind) stimulates opposition everywhere, as far as we can see. Human nature generally answers external coercion with a countercoercion. It seeks its satisfaction not in rewards for obedience and docility, but aims to prove that its own means of power are the stronger. The results of the application of power are apt to be disappointing to both parties. . . . Those who are excluded from power lie in wait for the revolt and are receptive to any argument [P. 456].

It is, thus, more manageable and perhaps more important to understand what tempts the powerholder to use threats and punishments than to understand when these threats and punishments will achieve their intended effects. We will describe some of the more important reasons for the use of threats and punishments, ranging from the angry aggressor seeking revenge, to the analytic government policy-maker calculating the costs and benefits of engaging in war. The reader may note that in only one of the instances that we shall describe does the desire to inflict harm figure as a major reason for invoking coercive power. We see no reason to assume that aggressive and malicious intent are always associated with the use of coercive power. In most instances the use of coercive power, when viewed from the vantage of the powerholder, represents an attempt to increase chances for obtaining some desired effect, one which less harsh means of influence are considered unlikely to achieve.

The Use of Coercion for Aggressive Purposes

The first reason why individuals seek out and use coercive power is that they have a desire to punish and harm others for real and imagined wrongs. In this case the power need of the powerholder is oriented toward forcing the target into a negatively valued region so that the target will experience pain and suffering. Of all the various reasons why coercive power is employed, this one has received the most attention from psychologists.

Many observers of human behavior have argued that underlying aggressive behavior of this kind is an instinctual apparatus that propels humans into violent encounters with other (Lorenz 1966; Freud 1957). Furthermore, recent physiological research dealing with the brain's functioning has uncovered findings that are not inconsistent with this contention; it has been shown that older areas of the brain contain regions that control the expression of aggression. Both in animals and humans, electrical or chemical stimulation of the hypothalamus and associated regions of the brain elicit aggressive responses, which appear to be coordinated in humans with thoughts of inflicting harm to others (Moyer 1971).

To think of doing injury, however, is not the same as actually to deliver noxious stimuli to another person. In terms of our model of power usage, the inclination to do harm is only the first step in this process. Before this inclination may be translated into behavior it must first be determined if the angered individual possesses appropriate resources that can be converted into coercive means of influence. Does he possess weapons such as guns or knives? Is he physically stronger than the target, so that he may assault him? Does he possess a "poisoned" tongue to belittle and insult him? Can he withdraw emotional support as a means of doing harm? Lacking such resources, the individual may be forced to "turn the other cheek" and swallow his anger, or he may perhaps secretly turn his efforts to developing appropriate resources and thus eventually be in a position to openly aggress (Gurr 1970). But in any case, the expression of aggression must be contingent upon the availability of appropriate resources.

As an aside it should be noted that psychologists concerned with the study of aggression have paid little attention to how persons without resources react to provocation. Most of the experimental studies in this area have provided subjects with appropriate resources (for example, the power to administer electric shock to the target) and have examined the circumstances under which subjects will convert this resource into coercive power. Thus we lack information about the cognitive transformations that must occur within angered subjects when they do not have the resources to act coercively. Dollard et al. (1939) have suggested that organisms displace their anger onto weaker targets in these instances, but this suggestion has not been the central focus of present-day research. Studies of poverty cultures by modern anthropologists suggest that one common reaction among those lacking resources is the development of forbearance and patience in the face of provocation and the adoption of an "Uncle Tom" orientation toward power. Animal studies also support this suggestion. For example, studies of apes in their natural habitat (Washburn and Hamburg

1968) reveal that weaker apes, when provoked by the more dominant and stronger members of the group, respond with a repertory of placating acts (fondling the scrotum of the stronger ape) rather than with aggression. A lack of means, in this case superior physical strength, serves to inhibit an ape's open aggression.

Institutional Power Used for Aggressive Purposes

Attempts to use coercive power to satisfy aggressive needs are not limited to personal actions, such as physical assaults and the like. To the extent the angered party has access to *institutional* resources, such as political patronage or the right to hire and fire employees, he will be tempted to use these instead of personal resources. A good example of this is found in Swanberg's study (1961) of the life of William Randolph Hearst, the influential newspaper publisher. Swanberg reports that Hearst frequently invoked his institutional powers to avenge personal affronts. From about the years 1917 through 1930, Hearst very much wanted to be nominated by the Democratic party for the presidency of the United States, and, if not that, for the governorship of New York State. These ambitions were continually blocked by Alfred E. Smith, one of the heads of the Democratic party, who had similar ambitions and publicly charged that Hearst was a liar and worse. In anger and retribution, Hearst ordered his many newspaper editors to print only information that would damage the reputation of Smith. Thus Smith was described in all Hearst papers as a "corrupt lackey" of various business interests. At one time, a story charged that Smith was personally responsible for the starvation deaths of young children in New York City because, as a servant of the milk lobby, he refused to lower the price of milk. Pictures of wan, starving children were featured prominently. Similar virulent newspaper articles continued to appear from the 1920s to the 1930s, none of them particularly true. According to Swanberg, Smith was on Hearst's "sh-t list" and was to be treated accordingly.

Other instances in which angered individuals have invoked their institutional resources for purposes of retaliation can easily be found. Albert Speer (1970), a close associate of Adolph Hitler before World War II, reported in his memoirs that a night club comedian, Werner Fink, made fun of Hitler's passion for architecture. Hitler, who was particularly sensitive to any personal criticisms, was infuriated and immediately retaliated by ordering Fink sent to a concentration camp.

In these instances, we have accounts of individuals invoking their institutional powers to seek retribution because of anger over personal insults. The process is difficult to detect because it is covered over with justifications that make it seem as if the individual were only attempting to further the goals of the institution by his coercive actions. Yet the same physiological processes may be involved in the decorticated cat angrily clawing and hissing at an imagined enemy as in the case of the offended publisher printing tales about his enemy. The availability of institutional resources in combination with this anger, however, can produce more destructive and long-lasting consequences.

Security and the Perception of Danger

Little needs to be said about this second reason for seeking and using coercive power. Enormous amounts of time and energy are spent by individuals, businesses, and nations in developing means to protect themselves from dangers, real or imagined. The arousal of fear tends to take priority over any of man's contemplated enterprises.

When fear is aroused, one of the first strategies of most persons is to attempt to mobilize greater force than the potential attacker. Unfortunately, the successful mobilization of means of defense does not necessarily alleviate fears, and often may intensify them. This is because, once armed, individuals become overly sensitized to danger signals. The very presence of means of defense continually signals how unsafe the environment is.

An interesting study by Mulder and Stemerding (1963) illustrates this tendency of people to mobilize resources when faced with threat. In this particular study independent shopkeepers in small Dutch villages were informed of the possibility that a large American-type supermarket was to move into their village, with the strong likelihood of wiping out the smaller shops. The reaction of the shopkeepers was to organize into militant groups, who collectively would possess the resources needed to block the threat. Further, the shopkeepers elected as leader the most militant person among them, suggesting that given sufficient resources the shopkeepers might move from a purely defensive posture to what is called, in military terms, "a defensive first strike," in which safety is secured by eliminating the sources of fear.

It is important to note that, unlike in the first reason offered for seeking coercive power, fear rather than anger is the main emotion involved here. The power need involved is to eliminate through the use of threats and punishments the danger signal originating from the target.

Ego Needs and Sense of Strength

A third reason why people seek to control and use coercive power is to satisfy ego needs related to a sense of worth. In our culture weakness is a pejorative term. It is a feminine trait, perhaps not even valued nowadays by many women. Strength on the other hand is a positively valued male attribute. The young boy is admonished by his parents to fight back and not to be a sissy. The desire to build up one's personal sense of worth by increasing one's physical strength is catered to by a whole industry. Beginning some time in the 1920s and continuing to this day is an enormously successful magazine campaign offering young boys a series of lessons in "dynamic tension," as a means of increasing their physical strength. The burden of the argument is that "97-pound weaklings are ashamed of themselves, tend to be humiliated by bullies, and usually must settle for second best."

Thus we see that, as the result of this cultural linking of strength with self-esteem, individuals come to seek the potential to harm others or actually to harm others as a means of reaffirming their own sense of worth. The envious Iago appears to have had no other motivation for his destruction of Othello than an inner rage that the Moor was more respected than himself; thus, to destroy Othello was to reaffirm the worth of Iago. While I know of no direct evidence on this issue, it appears that paradoxically, self-esteem and perhaps mental health are improved to the extent that the individual believes himself to be stronger than those of higher status.

Raven and Kruglanski (1970) have extended this argument in a discussion of the views of Frantz Fanon, the black psychiatrist and implacable enemy of colonialism. Fanon argued that only the use of coercion and violence would free the colonized from their ingrained feelings of inferiority. In essence, the use of violence becomes a cleansing force, ridding the colonized of their habitual deference and bent knees.

Why should the use of violence produce these beneficial effects among the downtrodden? Raven and Kruglanski argue that only through the use of violence can an individual be sure that he, rather than others, is in control of the situation. These authors point out that if an individual attempts to influence others through gentle means, such as persuasion and pleading, one cannot be sure that any subsequent changes in the target were in fact due to the individual's personal influence. Change accomplished through coercion, on the other hand, can clearly be attributed to the action and the power of the influencing agent. The influencing agent knows that he is effective, that his threats caused people to respect and to listen to what he has to say. In an experimental study on this point Kite (1965) found that when a powerholder used threats to change another's behavior he attributed these changes to his personal influence, whereas when rewards were used to change behavior, changes were attributed to the personal motivations of the target of influence. Similar findings have been reported by Kipnis (1972) and Berger (1973), who both contrasted a variety of "strong" means of influence (pay raises or pay decreases) with persuasion and found that, when the powerholders used "strong" means of influence, they were more likely to believe that they had caused the target's subsequent behavior. In short, persons who have doubts about their own effectiveness appear to be drawn to the use of force to compensate for their feelings of weakness. An unlikely kind of psychotherapy, to say the least!

An Illustration from the State Department

It should not be thought that the association of coercion and self-esteem can only be detected in personal relations. The use of force as a way of affirming a nation's self-esteem has been a constant theme in history. The German people prior to World War II responded readily to Hitler's arguments that the country must rearm as a way of erasing the past humiliations of World War I. In a long, revealing article dealing with policy-makers during John F. Kennedy's time as president, Richard Barnet pointed out that esteem was accorded to those who advocated the direct use of violence. According to Barnet:

Some of the national security managers of the Kennedy-Johnson era, looking back on their experience, talk about the "hairy chest" syndrome. The man who is ready to recommend using violence against foreigners, even where he is overruled, does not damage his reputation . . . but the man who recommends putting an issue to the U.N., seeking negotiations, or "doing nothing," quickly became known as "soft." To be soft, that is, unbelligerent, compassionate . . . is to be irresponsible.

Bureaucratic *machismo* is cultivated in hundreds of little ways. . . . The most important way . . . [it] manifests itself is in attitudes toward violence. Those who are in the business of defining the national interest are fascinated by lethal technology. . . .

To demonstrate toughness, a national security manager must accept the use of violence as routine. . . . The man who agonizes about taking human life is regarded by his colleagues at the very least as "woolly" and probably something of an idealistic "slob." Thus the critics of the Vietnam escalation never raised the issue that "taking out" great areas of Vietnam, a euphemism for killing large numbers of Vietnamese, was wrong. Their arguments were invariably pragmatic—bombing doesn't work, don't get bogged down in a land war in Asia—or they relied on the torturer's idiom: keep the victim alive for later. When we asked one of the most strategically placed doves in the State Department why the moral issue was never raised, he replied that such a discussion "would be as if from another world." [P. 55]

Elsewhere in the article Barnet assumes that the policy-makers' stress on violence in order to prove their own "toughness" may have been a unique occurrence due to the fact that only power-hungry men seek high government positions; hence the "hairy-chested" syndrome found among the policy-makers probably reflected their unique inner drives. The implication of Barnet's remarks is that ordinary men on the street might be less ferocious in that situation. On the contrary, we suggest that the attiudes of the government security managers reflect the shared cultural values of most people in this country. Thus when asked to make decisions which ultimately reduce to winning or losing, letting others "push" one around or not, the culturally acceptable decision is clear: "Don't be a sissy, act like a man."

Material Gain

So far we have been discussing reasons for using coercive power which arise out of emotionally based needs such as anger, fear, and envy. In these instances heightened emotionality of a negative sort appears to impel individuals to seek out and use violent means. Here we consider a reason why people use coercion that has much less to do with emotionality. This reason is concerned with using coercive power as a means of obtaining a greater share of the good life. Doing harm to a target, protecting oneself, or raising one's self-esteem are secondary in this case to the desire of the power-holder to enrich himself by inducing the target to give up some valued commodity. Buss (1971), speaking from the framework of aggression theory, has labeled this reason for using coercive power "instrumental aggression."

The importance of this motivation for using coercive power is suggested by Walster, Berscheid, and Walster (1973), who observe:

> A basic aim of most persons is to seek maximum rewards at a minimum cost for themselves. Theories in a wide variety of disciplines rest on the assumption that "Man is selfish." Psychologists believe that behavior can be shaped by the careful application of reinforcements. Economists assume that individuals will purchase products at the lowest available price . . . [and] politicians contend that "Every man has his price." [P. 151]

Where does power fit into this view of man as attempting to minimize costs? Quite obviously the answer is that with power the individual can force a target to give up a valued commodity with a minimum of cost to the powerholder. The robber with a gun can force people to "stand and deliver" and the business manager with a large financial reserve can cut prices until his local competitors are driven from business. Thus, even if a person is without malice, fear, or envy of his fellows, we might still expect him to seek and use coercive power as a means of satisfying this basic need of minimizing costs. One should note that, considered in this way, our view of power is similar to that of Hobbes's definition of power as "one's present means to obtain some future apparent Good." Lacking present means implies the absence of future benefits, an outcome, according to Walster and her colleagues, that would be distasteful for "selfish" man. Centuries ago Xenophon clearly saw the relation between access to resources, in his case military force, and the ability to maximize gain, when he attempted to persuade his army of ten thousand not to disband but to march back together to Athens from their wars in Asia Minor. Xenophon argued:

"One of the results of our power is the ability to *take* what belongs to the weak." To disband was to lose this base of power and as a result pay dearly for any food, clothing, or shelter that was obtained while returning home individually.

Institutional Use of Coercive Power for Gain

An interesting illustration of the use of coercive power for material gain is provided by Ida M. Tarbell's (1904) account of the early history of the Standard Oil Company and its founder, John D. Rockefeller. Although perhaps dated by now, since the process of economic consolidation among the major industries has been completed for several decades, her account is of interest since it reveals how motivation for gain and the availability of coercive means of influence combined to favor Rockefeller and Standard Oil's growth. It is clear from the story that Rockefeller, far from experiencing regret for what he did, felt fully justified in his behavior, at best perhaps viewing his vanquished business opponents as somewhat stupid.

The story begins with the availability of unexploited resources in the United States that could provide the basis for wealth, if one could figure out how to use them. In the northeastern region of the country, from Pennsylvania through Ohio, a thick oily substance variously labeled "rock oil," "seneca oil," and "petroleum" oozed from the earth. It was a curiosity and something of a nuisance to those who sank wells for water and for salt-water layers from which salt might be distilled. By 1850 a few enterprising souls were bottling the oil as a medicine. Kier's Rock Oil was sold in eight-ounce bottles and was advertised as both a liniment and also as a cure for cholera, liver complaints, bronchitis, and consumption when taken internally. Then George Bissell, a graduate of Dartmouth College, was told that this oil just might be better than coal oil or whale oil for use in lamps. The enterprising Bissell leased a farm in Pennsylvania near Titusville, where the oil collected in pools, and sent a sample to Professor Silliman of Yale University for analysis. Basically the question was, Could money be made from this stuff? Professor Silliman slowly heated the rock oil, and with each increment of heat new and commercially profitable products were refined out of the crude oil—illuminating oil, which provided more light than the best whale or coal oil available, paraffin for candles, grease and lubricating oil for ma-

chinery, gasoline and kerosene. Perhaps 10 percent of the rock oil
was waste product.

The good professor concluded his report: "In short your company have in their possession a raw material from which by simple
and not expensive processes they may manufacture very valuable
products. Nearly the whole of the raw product may be manufactured without waste."

And so the race was on. Edwin L. Drake, a railroad agent, was
sent out by Bissell to drill for oil on Bissell's property. After some
preliminary misfortunes due to the weather and hauling heavy
equipment over wilderness trails, Drake successfully brought in the
first well in 1859. By 1869 over a thousand wells were successfully
producing. Refineries were set up both in the oil regions and in the
cities of Cleveland, Philadelphia, Pittsburgh and Newark. Buyers,
both in America and abroad, eagerly bought the refined oil for
lighting and lubrication. Prices reached as high as twenty dollars
a barrel, as Professor Silliman predicted. The problem was that
the enormous flow of oil reduced the price in a short time to less
than a dollar a barrel.

By the early 1870s, several oil refinery owners, including John
D. Rockefeller (who owned a medium-sized refinery in Cleveland),
saw the answer to the problem of price. The refining of oil must
be limited to only a few refiners, acting as a single company. In
turn production could be controlled and prices maintained at a
high level. The key was the railroads. If they could be convinced
to give secret and substantial rebates to one company when trans-
porting the oil to New York, then that company would be in a
position to undersell all others and drive them from the market.

In 1872, only twelve years after the industry began, Rockefeller
and the Standard Oil Company, in conjunction with several other
oil refineries, signed a secret agreement with Thomas A. Scott of
the Pennsylvania Railroad, and Jay Gould of the Erie Railroad,
which provided substantial rebates on all oil shipped by the company. Not only that, the railroads agreed to give Rockefeller a
rebate on all oil shipped by independents. From the railroads'
point of view, the agreement would provide them with continuous
traffic in oil, with a guaranteed price that would not fluctuate with
variations in supply and demand. For Rockefeller the agreement
allowed his company to sell oil at a price far lower than that of
any other oil refiner in Cleveland. Here, then, Rockefeller had

developed a base of power which he was not long in using coercively.

Once armed with his ability to sell cheaply, yet with enormous profit, Rockefeller approached other refiners and asked them to turn their refineries over to his appraisers. In his rather dry style he advised his competitors: "I will give you Standard Oil stock or cash as you prefer for the *value we put on your refinery.*" Initially many refiners objected, since the price placed on their businesses by Rockefeller's appraisers was low. Mr. Rockefeller was regretful but firm. "It was useless to resist—if they persisted they would certainly be crushed."

Miss Tarbell relates that these tactics reached a point where a proposal from Mr. Rockefeller was certainly regarded popularly as a little better than a command to "stand and deliver." "The oil business belongs to us," Mr. Rockefeller said. "We have facilities; we must have it. Any business concern that starts in business, we have sufficient money laid aside to wipe him out." And people believed him.

Under the combined threat and persuasion almost the entire independent oil interests of Cleveland collapsed in three months time. Of the twenty-six refineries, at least twenty-one sold out. From a capacity of 1,500 barrels of crude oil a day, Standard Oil rose in three months to 10,000 barrels.

This illustration contains many of the elements of our description of the power act. Mr. Rockefeller's goal was the control of the oil refinery business. Not unnaturally, this goal met resistance from other refiners that initially blocked his plans. Once Mr. Rockefeller had secured an agreement with the railroads, however, he rapidly accrued a base of power, in the form of excess capital, which could then be used to intimidate his rivals. Note that what is missing in this picture is restraining force. Simply put, there was none of any consequence. The main restraint in this instance would have been government laws regulating interstate commerce. As these had not yet been enacted by Congress, what was left was the potential restraint exerted in the form of moral indignation by those forced from business, or Mr. Rockefeller's own personal values against doing business in this way. Neither served—leaving Mr. Rockefeller free to invoke threats and sanctions to satisfy his wants.

Role Involvement

Perhaps the most perplexing and pervasive reason why coercive power is used in our society originates in the involvement of persons in their organizational role. Instances of this use of coercion are easily cited and cover a wide range of institutional experiences. Teachers assigning failing grades to students, supervisors firing or demoting their employees, mortgage bankers ordering the foreclosure of homes or businesses for nonpayment of debts, mothers hitting their children because they have been "naughty," soldiers obeying the order "Fire!" German civil servants assiduously working to develop the means of carrying out the order to "finally settle the Jewish question" in Nazi Germany—all these are examples of the use of coercive power by individuals acting as agents for a larger institution. And in all instances, if you ask "Why?" the answer is the same—a bland or apologetic "I had little choice. It's part of my job."

It is important to note here that the needs of the person invoking coercive power are based neither upon emotionality nor upon the need to gain materially from the act. While emotion might be present, and the individual might stand to gain from his act, basically the motivations arise from the desire of the individual to further the goals of the institution by doing his job properly. Thus if his job involves the potential of doing harm to others, the more dedicated and involved the individual is in his work, the more likely he will be eventually to do harm to others.

There are several points to be made in conjunction with this reason for the use of coercive power. The first is that there are demand characteristics associated with institutional roles that appear to deprive the involved individual of voluntary will. The role occupant justifies his behavior in terms of such words as "should," "obliged," "ought," "required," and other imperatives. In a sense the individual is trapped by his own loyalties to legitimate authority, so that he finds it almost impossible to ignore its demands. Adolph Berle (1967), in speaking of the demands placed upon individuals given access to institutional powers, puts the surrender of voluntary action in this way:

> One of the first impacts [upon assuming office] is realization that the obligations of power take precedence over other obli-

gations formerly held nearest and dearest. A man in power can have no friends, in the sense that he must refuse to the friend considerations, that power aside, he would have accorded.

This form of compliance presents complex problems to the outside observer, when the compliance leads the individual to carry out acts which the larger society would consider illegal or immoral. For instance, in the early 1960s, managers of leading American corporations were convicted of entering into illegal trade agreements to limit competition in the sale of electrical generating equipment. Those who suffered from this act were of course the citizens of the communities that purchased this equipment, who had paid a higher price. What is of interest was that managers of these corporations were not acting to increase their personal wealth by committing this illegal and coercive act but apparently felt compelled to act in this manner to further the goals of their companies (Fuller 1962). In their view the requirement that each company should compete for contracts by submitting sealed bids interfered with one of the key elements of their jobs, the development of stable pricing procedures needed for long-term planning. Far better for the managers of the various companies to agree to take turns in submitting low bids, so that a safe level of return could be assured for all companies.

Involvement in one's role, then, appears to be a partial key to understanding the use of institutional power for coercive purposes. The well-socialized employee does what he must to further the aims of his organization, despite the fact that these actions may involve doing harm to others. What leads to such involvement? Cyert and MacCrimmon (1968) have proposed that involvement in organizational roles occurs where there is a high degree of compatibility between the person's self-image and the role requirement of his job. Further, according to these authors it is necessary for the person to experience a high degree of need fulfillment. In other words, when "what I want to be" and "what I am doing" are congruent and satisfying, then the individual becomes absorbed in his institutional role and willingly carries out those behaviors that will forward the aims of the organization, despite the fact that these behaviors may involve coercion.

An illustration of this process is provided in a *Harper's Magazine* interview with Daniel Ellsberg (Terkel 1972), who discussed how a congruence between self-concept and role requirements controlled the behavior of policy-makers in the Pentagon and the State Department during the Vietnam War. "It was like electricity coursing through their veins," Ellsberg stated in describing how these officials enjoyed their work. "In fact, the speed of decision-making, flickering from one part of the world to another—a weapons system to be decided upon, or one set of decisions about force levels, or big wars, or little wars—from moment to moment gave their lives an electric excitement to which they were clearly addicted and which they could not imagine living without."

Ellsberg then wisely comments on how these satisfactions could only be obtained by an unquestioning "knuckling under" to all decisions. He says, "The course of power however could only be theirs if they stayed in line, if they toed the mark and remained [unquestioning]. An [adverse] judgement by their bosses could lose them access to that flow of information in minutes, if they made the wrong move. They would not be invited to the next White House meeting. They would no longer be in it, be part of it." Further commenting on this role involvement, Ellsberg speaks of the dilemma of George Ball, undersecretary of state, the number-two man in the State Department, who privately opposed American involvement in the war in Vietnam but publicly testified in its favor in front of Congress. Ball, in justifying this behavior years later, stated, "After all, we're just hired hands of the president." Ellsberg concludes by observing, "These men have a self-image of powerlessness except as loyal servants, not of the Constitution, not of their countrymen, not of humanity, but of the men who hired them."

This of course is the dilemma that persons of conscience experience in carrying out their role obligations. To admit that one has the freedom to obey or disobey jeopardizes the rewards and satisfactions obtained at work. Better to assume that one does not have a choice and either ignore private doubts or transform them into convictions as to the correctness of the institution's course of action.

There are, however, complexities here which are not completely explained by invoking the concept of role involvement. There are many instances in which there is little compatibility between the individual's self-image and his institutional role-requirements, as for example the drafted army infantryman, and yet these role occupants still feel obliged to carry out what are perceived to be legitimate role demands.

Milgram (1963), in his well-known studies of obedience, has most extensively treated this problem in psychology and provided some insight into the feelings of those involved in carrying out distasteful role activities. In its most general form, the problem according to Milgram may be defined thus: if x tells y to hurt z, under what conditions will y carry out the command of x and under what conditions will he refuse? Basically what Milgram found was that most persons in the role of y carried out the orders of x to harm z, despite their complete abhorrence of this activity. Obedience to the demands of legitimate authority, the experimenter in this case, in conjunction with their acceptance of their role, compelled persons to act in ways they considered personally distasteful. As Milgram says, "With numbing regularity, good people were seen to knuckle under to the demands of authority and perform actions that were callous and severe. Men who are in everyday life responsible and decent were seduced by the trappings of authority, by the control of their perceptions, and by the uncritical acceptance of the experimenter's definition of the situation into performance of harsh acts."

Basically what is implicated here is the influence of the early socialization process which stresses above all else obedience to parental and school authority and, as Milgram suggests, produces a national character structure which experiences *greater* difficulty in defying authority than in harming others. Support for Milgram's suggestion that compliance to authority is a well learned trait for many of us is found in a nation-wide opinion survey conducted by Kelman and Lawrence (1972). In response to the question, "What would most people do if ordered to shoot all the inhabitants of a Vietnamese village suspected of aiding the enemy, including old men, women, and children," 67 percent of a cross section of the American public said that most people would "follow orders and shoot." Half of those interviewed said that they would do so themselves.

In addition to dramatically showing us how the demands of a given role may override personal convictions and morality, Milgram has also identified in his research some circumstances under which the role occupant may defy orders and refuse to invoke coercive power. These circumstances included: (*a*) distance from

the target—the more remote the target was from the role occupant, the more willing was the role occupant to harm the target;
(*b*) the arousal of a norm of responsibility through observing
others in similar roles refusing to inflict harm; and (*c*) the close-
ness of authority to the role occupant. As surveillance of the role
occupant by an authority figure decreased, obedience also sharply
dropped. This finding appears to distinguish between those who
Cyert and MacCrimmon have labeled as either role-involved or
not. While both may carry out the orders of their superiors to
inflict harm on others while their superiors are present, non-
involved persons are more likely to desist in the absence of surveillance.

Absolution and Role Behavior

Let us turn to another problem related to the use of coercion
as part of the job. One may ask what are the mechanisms involved
that allow people in their institutional roles to carry out behaviors
that they would personally condemn if performed by others outside the institution. We have already suggested the answer to this
problem in Chapter 2 by pointing out that most people believe
that the institution grants them absolution for their acts. Since
the individual believes that he has no choice but to obey, he also
sees himself as not responsible for the suffering he has caused.
Edgar Wallace, in a short story called *The Treasure Hunt*, expresses this view when the hero—a Mr. Reeder—a diligent and
relentless police officer, finds himself the target of anger and
hatred by those he has caught and sent to prison. "Mr. Reeder
in so far as he could resent anything, resented the injustice of
being made personally responsible for the performance of a public duty," wrote Wallace.

It is important to note that not only does the individual absolve himself of blame, but society in general does not condemn
an individual who uses coercive power in the service of a legitimate institution. Even when the role occupant exceeds or abuses
his authority and uses excessive coercive means of influence, most
persons are willing to absolve the role occupant of any personal
guilt. For instance, in the previously cited national survey by
Kelman and Lawrence, most Americans considered the conviction of Lieutenant Calley, commander of the American troops
at My Lai, to be too harsh. Almost two-thirds believed it was

unfair to hold Calley *personally* responsible for what occurred in the line of duty.

Thinking about Coercion

Except in the case of accidental infliction of harm, the use of coercive power for all the reasons given in the previous pages involves anticipatory planning and reflection. We have to decide why we want to deliver noxious stimuli to the target person. Not only that, our reasons must be justifiable. To inflict harm on another person is not a matter of indifference to the harmdoer, the target person, or to society. Ordinarily the justifications involve some statement about one's own intentions and some statements about the behavior of the target person.

It has been suggested by several social psychologists (Lerner and Simmons 1966; Walster and Berscheid 1967) that harmdoers tend to justify their acts by placing the blame for the acts upon the victim. That is, in cases where the harmdoer does nothing to provide restitution, he will describe the victim as "stupid," "deserving punishment," and so on. And in this way the harmdoer absolves himself of responsibility for the victim's suffering. Memmi (1965) has observed a similar rationalizing process among French colonizers in explaining their treatment of the Tunisians.

This section will amplify on these views and attempt to show how the powerholder's justifications for his acts of coercion may vary as the reason for using coercion varies. I have attempted to describe the powerholder's thoughts prior to the use of coercive power and after the coercion has been successfully used. The reader should be aware that there is little direct evidence to support the validity of these presumed thought processes. What is written here is given as a means of sketching in the range of questions one should ask about coercive power rather than definitive answers.

Table 5.1 provides an analysis of the reasons and thoughts involved in the decision to use coercion. These reasons have been broken down into statements of: (*a*) the initial emotions experienced by the powerholder, (*b*) his justifications for the proposed coercive act, (*c*) a statement as to whether the powerholder desired to harm the target person or had some other rea-

Table 5.1 Thoughts Prior to the Use of Coercion

Powerholder's Thoughts and Feelings	Reasons for the Use of Coercive Power				
	Aggression	Security	Self-esteem	Material	Role Behavior
a. Initial emotion	Anger and rage	Fear	Envy	Greed	Annoyance to anger (?)
b. Personal justification	The target made me suffer.	The target is a source of danger.	I have to show I am better.	The target has something I want.	The target violates role hebavior.
c. Desire to harm target person	Yes	Secondary to desire to protect self	Little or none	Little or none	Little or none
d. Evaluation of target person	Personality, abilities, and character of target are devalued.	Fear will exaggerate target person's potential for harm-doing.	Perhaps grudging respect	Target seen objectively but as a depersonalized object.	Perception varies with role involvement

son in mind for using coercion and, (d) how the powerholder saw the target person prior to the use of coercion.

It can be seen in table 5.1 that the profile of hypothesized thoughts varies considerably according to the powerholder's reasons for using coercion. That is, the intensity of the emotions involved, the concern for the target's well-being, and the perceptions of the target all are seen to vary according to the reasons that are involved in the initial decision to use coercion. Thus, for example, if aggression is the reason for using coercion, it is suspected that the worth of the target person is devalued considerably. If the desire for material gain is the reason for using coercion, however, then the powerholder should evaluate the target person as objectively as possible in order to understand his strengths and weaknesses. At the same time, the powerholder should view the target person as a depersonalized object, since any positive feelings might interfere with the use of coercion.

In table 5.2 we have charted the thoughts of the powerholder after he has successfully used coercion. Now he has achieved his goal by force, and in some way must justify to himself the consequences of his acts. We have charted the dimensions of the powerholder's thoughts in terms of his: (a) feelings and emotions after successfully using coercion, (b) his concern for the target person's discomfort, (c) the extent to which the powerholder is willing to state that he was responsible for his acts (did the powerholder believe that he was forced by outside agents to inflict harm, or did he believe that the use of coercion was based upon his own decision?), and (d) how the self-esteem of the powerholder may be raised or depressed by the successful use of coercion—that is, does the powerholder like himself better, or worse, or just the same as a result of causing harm.

Here again we see that the powerholder's thoughts about himself and the target person will vary as a function of the reasons for using coercion in the first place. For example, we speculate that the powerholder's self-esteem may be raised after having revenged himself on a disliked target person but be depressed after using coercion as part of his role obligations. Thus Milgram (1963) reported that participants in his forced compliance studies were depressed after being required by their role to inflict harm, whereas Berkowitz (1971) suggested that persons enjoyed committing ag-

Table 5.2 Thoughts after the Successful Use of Coercive Power

Powerholder's Thoughts and Feelings	Reasons for the Use of Coercive Power				
	Aggression	Security	Self-esteem	Material	Role Behavior
a. Subsequent emotions	Satisfaction	Relief	Satisfaction	Satisfaction	Relief to depression (?)
b. Concern for target's suffering	Enjoyment of his pain and suffering	Little or no concern (?)	Sympathy for target (?)	Contempt to sympathy (?) for target	Sympathy (?)
c. Does the powerholder feel responsible for his acts?	Yes	No, use of coercion attributed to outside forces. "I had to protect myself."	Yes	Yes	No, powerholder feels obliged to invoke coercion.
d. Self-esteem	Elevated	Perhaps lowered	Elevated	No change (?)	Depressed

gressive acts, although he has not presented clear evidence on this point. Finally, some support for the speculation that powerholders devalue the worth of a target person after using coercion for material gain is given by a laboratory study done by T. P. Cafferty and S. Streufert (1974). In this study, the authors examined the attitudes of group members after they engaged in competitive actions. It was found that group members who chose to aggress against the opposing group members, and were the victors, rated their opponents less favorably than equally victorious group members who did not choose to aggress in order to win.

We close this final section by noting that the relation between coercive power and the reactions of the powerholder to his own acts is not yet entirely clear. Thus the reader should view the suggestions given here as tentative. Additional research and study is needed to understand just what happens to a powerholder's views of himself and his target when he is continually involved in the use of coercive power.

Summary

In this chapter we have reviewed five reasons why people seek out and use coercive power. The first three are based mainly upon emotional feelings of the powerholder, in that what is primarily sought from the target is relief from unpleasant feelings, whether of anger, fear, or envy. Thus, the powerholder does not gain in any material sense from successfully using power. The fourth reason that has been reviewed, however, is based upon the aim of extracting some desired commodity from the target which the target is unwilling to give freely. Finally, the last reason discussed is concerned with how an individual's involvement with an organization may oblige him to inflict harm on others who appear to be interfering with the proper functioning of the powerholder's institution.

While we have discussed each of these potential reasons for using coercive power as if they were independent of each other, in practice a powerholder may have several overlapping reasons for deciding to use coercion. From Barnet's description of the behavior of national security managers, one could infer that, if asked why coercion was used, the reply would be that it was done in the interests of national security, not, as Barnet implies, because of a desire to maximize one's manliness.

It has also been suggested in this chapter that differing psychological processes relating to the powerholder's own emotions, as well as his perceptions of the target, can be used to distinguish among the five reasons for using coercion. Much research, however, remains to be done to verify our tentative statements concerning these processes.

6   On the Use of Coercive Power

The previous chapter described various reasons why people seek out and use coercive power—anger, safety, self-esteem, material gain, and institutional involvement. We have described some of the circumstances which arouse these reasons, as when insults provoke anger. This chapter considers in greater detail the calculations of a powerholder when deciding whether to invoke his resources in a coercive manner. In some instances it will be found that strong emotions are associated with the powerholder's judgments, and in other instances rational judgments will have the upper hand and there will be little evidence of emotionality. Of course, from the point of view of the target person, this distinction may not be particularly enlightening since his pain and suffering will be the same in either instance. Nevertheless, from the viewpoint of understanding and perhaps controlling coercion, the distinction is critical.

The major topic to be encountered in this chapter will center on the role played by thought in the decision to harm others. The reason for this emphasis is that discussions of emotional versus cognitive control of coercion in psychology have been particularly one-sided in favor of emotional causes. Books concerned with the problem of angry aggression (our first reason for using coercive power) continue to appear in large numbers. As a result, the implication for many is that being angry, upset, or frustrated are the critical factors. As we shall see, the use of coercive power is frequently guided by rational calculations, with little or no emotion involved.

Kaufmann in his book *Aggression and Altrusism* (1970), presents somewhat similar views concerning the importance of cognitive factors as determinants of aggression. In Kaufman's view, cognitive factors enter the scene at several points. First, the individual learns from his culture when it is proper openly to aggress. Second, the individual learns who are the target persons one can attack in safety; that is, one may attack weaker persons, those of equal or lower social status, but not children, those who are stronger, old people, and so on. Third, citing the research of Schachter and Singer (1962) on the cognitive labeling of emotions, Kaufmann argues that the same feelings of physiological upset may be equally interpreted as anger, happiness, or relief, depending on the label attached to these body feelings. If a person attaches the label "I am angry" to these bodily feelings, then aggression may occur. However, if he interprets the same bodily feelings as due to heightened feelings of euphoria, then aggression will not occur. Thus, the cognitive labels attached by the person to his own bodily feelings help to determine whether or not he will openly aggress.

Cognitive Factors in the Use of Coercive Power

We begin by noting that in most institutional settings powerholders possess a range of means of influencing a target. Hence, they are not limited to punishment only. Managers at work, for instance, can do many things to change their subordinates' work behavior. They can use persuasion, offer rewards, provide extra training, or even shift their employees to new jobs or new work shifts. Thus many options exist for powerholders at work in addition to forcing employees into negatively valued regions by threatening suspension, poor performance evaluations, pay deductions, and firing. If a range of means of influence is available, questions may be raised about the point at which each powerholder decides that more gentle means are not sufficient and that harsher means must be invoked.

In Chapter 3 it was suggested that the powerholder's decisions concerning power were based upon a twofold process of first diagnosing the causes of the target's resistances and then selecting the means of influence that, in his view, was most likely to overcome this resistance. It is reasonable to suggest that the same process occurs in the decision to invoke coercion. Furthermore, it is suggested that expectations of successful influence are closely allied to this decision in a way that parallels the decision to use reward.

Raven and Kruglanski (1970) have offered the generalization that the powerholder anticipates the possible effectiveness of each of his bases of power and avoids using those which he believes will be ineffective. How, then, are variations in anticipations associated with the use of coercion? One answer provided by psychologists Barry Goodstadt and Lawrence Hjelle (1973) is that, as the powerholder's expectations of successful influence are lowered, he is increasingly tempted to exert more pressure upon the target person by invoking coercive means of influence. Milder forms of influence are used when the powerholder believes that the target person is not completely resistant to change.

The reader will, of course, recognize the above statement as our expectancy rule stated in slightly different form. Goodstadt and Hjelle's generalization about coercive power and its use, though independently derived, is remarkably similar to David Baldwin's already cited views on the use of reward power. In both instances, promises and threats are seen as used when expectations of succesful influence are lowest. *Combining the two views, then, leads to the generalization that sanctions, whether positive or negative, are most likely to be invoked when expectations of successful influence are lowest.* Positive sanctions appear to be preferred when the powerholder wishes to retain the good will of the target person or when the powerholder anticipates that compliance is likely to drop in the future. Negative sanctions appear to be preferred when the good will of the target person is less involved and the influence attempts are directed at changing some behavior rather than maintaining it.

If we accept this analysis as it pertains to coercion, then the question becomes: What causes the powerholder to become gloomy and doubt his ability to effect change in the target? Here we will review evidence suggesting that the behavior of the target, the social setting in which the influence is attempted, and the personal characteristics of the powerholder all contribute significantly to lowered expectations of successful influence and to the subsequent decision to use coercion.

The Behavior of the Target

Whenever coercive power is deliberately used, it is almost inevitable that this usage is justified by blaming the behavior of the target. As Kaufmann points out in his book *Aggression and Altruism* (1970): "The target or stimulus has been shown to be of considerable importance in the elicitation of aggressive behavior. We know from everyday experience that some people just seem to be asking to be punched in the nose, whereas others elicit meekness from even the most notorious bully" (p. 55). Recently, a new area of inquiry, victimology, suggests that it is possible to predict who will be a target of violence, based upon the earlier behavior of the victim. It has been reported that a fair majority of homicide victims have as violent an earlier background as their murderers. Thus, as Kaufmann suggests, some people seem to invite nastiness.

Clearly, the attitude and behaviors of the target person toward the powerholder are implicated in the use of coercion. The question is, Just what does the target do that provokes these assaults? Or, in the language of this book, what does the target do to lower the powerholder's expectations of successful influence? Goodstadt and Hjelle (1973) offer the answer that, *when a target's resistance to inflence is attributed to motivational causes ("I refuse") rather than to a lack of ability ("I can't"), powerholder's expectations of successful influence are lowest, and their reliance on coercion is greatest.*

This distinction returns us to the issue of the powerholder's diagnosis of the causes of the target person's noncompliance. It was suggested in Chapter 3 that if the powerholder attributed the target person's resistance to internal causes, or a lack of motivation, then he also believed that the resistance shown was deliberate: that is, that the target person had freely decided not to comply with the wishes of the powerholder. If, however, the target's resistance was attributed to a lack of ability, then the powerholder was more likely to believe that the target person was not in charge of his own behavior and, consequently, was not deliberately resisting.

It was also reported in Chapter 3 that the powerholder was more likely to *discuss* change with the target person if it was believed that resistance was deliberate. Suppose, however, that such discussion fails and the target person persists in his deliberate resistance. It seems clear that the powerholder's expectations for successful influence must drop considerably. Stronger means of influence must now be tried. In contrast, when considering involuntary resistance, I would argue that powerholders remain optimistic for far longer periods of time. In these instances, if one form of training does not work, the powerholder will invoke other forms rather than immediately considering harsh means of influence.

Several studies have tested the implication of this expectancy view of when coercive power is invoked. In one study I asked 103 managers employed in state government and in private industry to read eight case histories of employees doing substandard work. In four of these case histories, the cause of this substandard work was attributed to a lack of ability; in the other four, it was due to motivational causes. For instance, in one of the case histories, an employee was described as "being uneven in performance following a promotion. He had a series of minor accidents with his new equipment, the quality of his work was low, and he appeared tense and nervous." In a second instance, an employee's job performance was also described as uneven. "At quitting time he sometimes tried to leave early, he laughed off mistakes, and if you asked him what the problem was, he said that people were picking on him."

Managers were asked to assess the probability of their being personally able to correct each of these subordinate's performances. In addition, managers rated how desirable it would be to invoke coercive means of disciplining the employee (bawling out the employee, threat of suspension, letter of warning, firing).

It was found that managers, at a statistically reliable level ($p < .01$), consistently rated at lower odds the chance of their being able successfully to influence the employee's behavior when the employee lacked motivation to work than when he lacked the ability to work. That is, the managers said that they personally would have a good chance of improving the performance of an employee who was inept in his work. Managers did not think their chances were very good, however, if the employee had a "chip on his shoulder" or generally lacked motivation to work.

It was also found that the managers recommended the use of coercion far more often among employees who lacked motivation than among those who lacked ability. Here again these differences in recommendations were statistically reliable beyond the .01 level. Threats and actual use of force in the form of firings were reserved for the employee who *would* not perform, rather than for the employee who *could* not perform.

Finally, of interest in the present context was the finding that regardless of the reason for the employee's poor performance, if managers rated themselves as having low expectations of being able to correct the worker's performance, then the managers endorsed the use of coercion. The correlation between the managers' rating of their expectations of being able to improve the employee's performance summed over all incidents and the managers' endorsing the use of coercion summed over all incidents was −.41. The lower the expectations, the more coercion was recommended.

In a laboratory simulation of work, Barry Goodstadt and myself (1970) also demonstrated, via experimentation, that more coercion was invoked when the target person was seen as deliberately resisting the orders of a powerholder. In this simulation study, college business majors were appointed as managers of a manufacturing organization and asked to direct the performance of a group of workers. The managers were provided with a range of institutional means of influence (power to grant pay raises, to shift workers to a new job, to train, to deduct pay, or to fire). It was left to the managers to decide which, if any, of these means would be used. The experimental manipulation involved the programming of one of the workers to perform at substandard levels. In one condition, the reason for this poor performance was ascribed to the ineptness of the worker, who passed notes to the manager saying such things as: "I'm trying, but I can't seem to get it." In a second condition, the same poor performance was ascribed by means of the worker's notes to a lack of motivation, e.g., ("this job is horrible"). It was found that more managers threatened to deduct pay, or actually deducted pay, or fired the worker, when the worker's poor work was due to a lack of motivation than when the poor work was due to ineptness. Similar findings from experimental studies have been reported by Rothbart (1968) and by Michener and Burt (1974).

Finally, in the previously mentioned field study among first-line supervisors (Kipnis and Cosentino, 1969), it was found that 63 percent of the supervisors who attributed their worker's unsatisfactory performances to a lack of motivation, poor attitudes, or discipline used coercive means in attempts to alter this behavior. Among supervisors who attributed their worker's unsatisfactory performance to a lack of ability, only 26 percent invoked coercion. It appears to be a safe generalization that more workers are fired for poor attitudes and lack of discipline than for a lack of ability.

Police tactics and expectations of successful influence. So far we have examined in business settings the generalization that low expectations of successful influence determine the decision to invoke coercion. As we have seen, the perception that the target person is deliberately refusing to comply is far more likely to cause low expectations than the perception that the target person's resistance is involuntary. A final illustration of this linkage can be found in a study of factors causing police officers to arrest offenders for disorderly conduct (Kipnis and Misner 1974). This is a violation that allows police enormous discretionary powers for deciding how to respond, since the laws defining what behaviors constitute public disorder are vague. For instance, a boisterous drunk in a quiet residential street is likely to be approached very quickly by a police officer. The same behavior in a night club district would probably be ignored. In short, the police officer must use his own judgment by assessing the extent of the disturbance and whether or not passersby are being sufficiently disturbed for him to take action. Aside from ignoring the situation, the police officer may attempt to persuade the offender to stop acting in a disorderly manner by making his presence known, by using physical force, or by actually making an arrest.

To examine what guided police officers' decisions to make an arrest, thirty police officers of a large city were asked to describe the most recent incident in which they arrested a male offender for disorderly conduct, that is, an incident in which coercive power was actually used. Another twenty-eight police officers described a similar incident, but one in which they decided not to arrest the citizens. In addition to describing the incident, the police officers described its background in terms of the number of passersby, whether the officer was alone or with a partner, time of day, whether the offender was drinking, and whether women were present. These questions were asked since informal discussions with police officers suggested that these circumstances could influence the officers' decisions. In fact, many of these background factors did influence whether or not an arrest was made. It was found that a citizen was more likely to be arrested for disorderly conduct if he had been drinking heavily, if there were women watching, and if there were at least eleven or more passersby. Assigning a score of 1 to each of these three context factors if they were present, and a score of 0 if they were absent, resulted in a biserial correlation of .59 with the decision as to whether or not to make an arrest. In short, the decision to use coercive police power was highly predictable from certain background information.

The next question examined was in what way these background factors influenced the decision to make an arrest. Why should the presence of women, for instance, influence the police officers' judgments? To examine this question, the actual nature of each of the fifty-eight incidents was examined by means of content analysis. This analysis found that neither the kind of incident (domestic fights, traffic violation, street corner disturbance), nor the presence of initial violence differentiated when an arrest would be made. What clearly determined this decision was whether the offender continued to resist the police officer's orders to stop being disorderly. As resistance and concurrent threat of violence grew, the probabilities of an arrest increased sharply. If the citizen quieted down, and in some form complied with the police officer's persuasions, then the incident terminated without arrest. In short, as the police officer's expectations of successful influence were lowered by the willful resistance of the citizen, the officer was increasingly likely to increase the amount of pressure placed upon the target by the use of harsh means of influence.

Let me illustrate by presenting, verbatim, two of the police accounts, the first ending in an arrest when the citizen refused to comply, and the second in no arrest when compliance was obtained. In both instances, it may be noted that the police officer was faced with personal threat. Wilson (1968) has stated in *Varieties of Police Behavior* that the maintenance of public order exposes the police officer to physical danger and that his reactions to this potential danger need to be taken into account in understanding his "working personality." This would suggest that when the police officer believed that his personal safety was involved, he would be more likely to arrest the citizen than when no such perceptions were involved.

Incident of Arrest: My last arrest for disorderly conduct occurred about three weeks ago in which a male became loud and boisterous on the corner of a very busy street. The people waiting for the bus became very uneasy at the male's behavior. He entered a restaurant, causing several patrons to leave. I identified myself as a policeman, at which time I observed a razor in his hand. I asked him to drop the razor and he refused. I had to disarm him and place him under arrest. I felt as though I couldn't talk or reason with him.

In the next incident, although the potential for danger was equally present, the citizen finally complied, thus ending the incident. The reader should note the police officer's tactical use of threats, that is, using a public address system, and his attempts to "cool off" the situation by simply waiting, rather than continuing the confrontation.

Incident of No Arrest. "I was writing a traffic summons for an illegally parked vehicle, when a man came out of a bar in front of my location and asked me if it was for him. When I told him yes, he began to give me a hard time, and said that the Police Department stinks, that when you need a cop they're never around, said that he would tear the summons up, and that giving him a ticket made me feel good. I told him that I was working on a complaint, that he should stop causing a camotion [sic], and go back into the bar. After this he became louder and said he wouldn't leave. I then notified radio for a wagon over the P.A. system, so he could hear it, and waited outside of my vehicle. He then at this time walked back into the bar."

Toch (1970) has reported similar findings in his analysis of police assaults. In 266 out of 444 incidents of such assaults, violence occurred after the assaulter had expressed verbal resistance to the policeman's orders and the officer had continued to press his case. Toch summarized his findings by stating that "the most frequent sequence we encountered begins with an order or request by the officer, which elicits a contemptuous response from the citizen. The sequence repeats itself and ends [with violence] a number of steps later, in some instances, after a notification of arrest, in others, without it."

How do these findings on resistance fit with the observation that the presence of women, bystanders, and excessive drinking were associated with the decision to arrest? Presumably, women, drinking, and an audience served as disinhibiting forces (Berkowitz 1971) which encouraged the continued expression of hostility and defiance. Brown (1968), for instance, has reported that restraints against the expression of aggression are lowered when previously angered persons are made aware that others have witnessed their humiliation. Issues of "machismo" then complicate the situation for both police officer and the citizen. To give in while an audience, and especially women, are watching would be inconsistent with the citizen's and perhaps the police officer's conceived role of manhood. Both parties are unwilling to "lose face," and antagonisms escalate as the target of arrest refuses to stop what he is doing. The forces acting on the police officer are even more complicated. In addition to concerns about his public image, he is obliged by his role to maintain public order. This he must do through a process of applying increasing pressure on the citizen for compliance with his request to cease being disorderly. If resistance continues, he must in fact make the arrest.

Taken together, the findings from these various studies are consistent in showing that an appointed leader's choice of coercive means of influence is based upon the belief that the target's resistance is willful and voluntary. In turn, this perception reduces expectations of successful influence and generates the conviction that harsh means of influence are necessary to obtain compliance. We have illustrated this process in terms of research studies at places of work and among the police. It is to be expected that similar findings would obtain in such disparate settings as international relations and family quarrels. It is not surprising that the most frequent explanation given by the parents of "battered" children for hitting the child is that the child would not listen to reason and do as he was told. As we shall go on to show, these lowered expectations of successful influence are frequently not based upon reality but upon extraneous social influences which distort the powerholder's evaluations of the intentions of his target. Let us turn now to a second condition that will influence a powerholder's expectations of successful influence—the setting in which influence is exerted.

The Social Setting

Many will argue that there is nothing surprising in being told that powerholders use coercion when they believe that strong and deliberate resistance has been encountered. What is of interest, however, is that the powerholder's expectations can also be shaped by a wide variety of social influences that have nothing to do with the target's behavior. Under stress, for instance, the powerholder may miscalculate the amount of resistance that is being shown by a target. A worker's misunderstanding of a poorly communicated order may be taken as evidence of calculated insolence by an overworked executive. A teacher who has been told that a new student is hostile is far more likely to perceive deliberate resistance in any mistakes made by the student.

In short, the target's behavior is only one factor that may affect the powerholder's expectations of successful influence. Three major environmental sources have to date been identified as influencing expectations of successful influence. These are the extent to which persons control the potential to harm each other; the setting in which power is exercised; and the number of persons to be influenced.

The possession of coercive means. It has already been mentioned that the possession of resources serves to arouse new needs within the powerholder. The possession of excess amounts of money, for instance, expands the range of experiences the individual wants to encounter. Travel, gifts to others, the development of rich tastes in food and clothing become new goals as money becomes available. Little real thought may be given to these experiences in the absence of money.

Access to resources that can be used coercively also appears to arouse an "itch" within the individual to actually punish others. The writer, on occasion, has listened to conversations between gun owners speculating on the amount of human tissue damage that could be caused by the use of various kinds of bullets in their guns. I have also spoken with owners of large, violent dogs who were looking forward to the day when they would be sufficiently provoked to unleash their dogs, with instructions to attack. Throughout history, the development of military weapons is associated with pressures to act aggressively. While those who lack such means may "turn the other cheek," this conciliatory gesture is far less likely to happen when powers of a coercive kind are possessed. Recognition of this fact has been recorded throughout history. Thucydides reported, for instance, that the Athenian generals justified their invasion of the neighboring island of Melos in 416 B.C. by arguing that a rule of nature is that "those with power should rule where they can"—that is, power demands to be used.

Deutsch and Krauss (1960) have provided evidence that the possession of power to harm others transforms what was essentially a benevolent relation into a hostile one. In their research, it was found that persons with the advantage in terms of the control of coercive power became tempted to demand more than an equal share of the available outcomes. Such demands inevitably produced resistance and counterattacks from targets, who resented being subjected to exploitation. Other studies (Tedeschi, Lindskold, Horai, and Gahagan 1969) suggest that, even when the weaker party agrees to compromise, those who possess the capability to inflict harm tend to ignore these peaceful overtures. Why compromise, asks the strong party, when small threats can bring in a larger share?

A field study within industry by Kipnis, Silverman, and Copeland (1973) provides further evidence on how the control by two parties of coercive means served to escalate conflict and the use of coercion. This study compared the influence modes used by supervisors in unionized and nonunionized companies. The presence or absence of a union in an industrial organization can be viewed as a measure of the relative power held by management and labor. In the absence of a union, the balance of power is held by management since it can deal with each employee separately. The presence of a union, however, tends to equalize power between the two parties. Hence, it is of interest to see how management uses power in these two settings—one in which an employee's potential for resistance was low and one in which this potential was high. From what has been said so far, it might be expected that management would use more coercion on a day-to-day level in situations where the potential for resistance was high.

To test this idea, supervisors working in both union and nonunion plants described incidents in which they corrected the performance of their employees. The analysis of the incidents focused on what was done to correct the employee's performance in each of these two settings.

Two findings emerged that are of interest with reference to the use of coercive power. First, supervisors of union employees reported that they encountered more instances of poor attitudes and an unwillingness to work by their workers than did supervisors of nonunion employees. Second, supervisors in union plants reported using more coercive power than those in nonunion plants. That is, supervisors of union workers reported a greater frequency of using threats and reprimands, reducing the employee's privileges, and evoking administrative punishment such as written warnings and suspensions. Seemingly, the presence of unions approaches a situation of bilateral power in which subordinates can actively resist the demands of their supervisors by reason of union support. From the supervisor's point of view, however, this resistance is viewed as reflecting deliberate attempts by subordinates to defy their authority. Hence, the reports of more poor attitudes on the part of work ers in union companies. In this climate, the supervisors may come to doubt that even simple suggestions will be freely carried out. As a result, they are rapidly drawn to threats and actual punishments as a means to back up their orders. Their threats replace simple persuasion as the preferred power tactic.

Many will argue, of course, that the possession of coercive means does not necessarily lead to exploitative and aggressive behaviors and that what has been said so far is too pessimistic. The power-holder, it is argued, may act in all innocence as "the peacekeeper" of the world, stockpiling weapons in order to prevent aggressive actions by others. The problem as I understand it is that while each peacekeeper, or several peacekeepers acting together to establish a balance of power, may have no intent to do harm, the very fact that they possess coercive means makes them objects of distrust. Sooner or later, the possessors of coercive power will fiind themselves drawn into confrontation with others, if for no other reason than that the weaker parties are anxious to eliminate the advantage the peaceholders have over them.

To the extent that these attitudes of mistrust are communicated to the powerholder, he in turn will soon view others with caution. Both the local bully lording it over the neighborhood and the policeman patrolling the neighborhood to maintain public order can never be sure that they will not be subjected to a defensive "first strike." As of the writing of this chapter, for instance, the newspapers have reported that India has developed its own nuclear bomb. And so now the major powers must lower ever so slightly their expectations that India can be easily influenced in international relations.

A final reason why the possession of coercive means of influence makes it difficult to maintain harmonious relations is that the powerholder frequently suspects that others dislike him. Such beliefs were found by Berger (1973), who provided some persons with power to reward and others with power to punish. Those who controlled coercive means felt that target persons disliked them, regardless of whether or not they actually used their coercive means. It is obviously difficult to hold friendly feelings toward persons one suspects of disliking oneself.

In short, providing powerholders with coercive means of influence escalates conflict. For one thing, the possession of coercive means tempts powerholders to use such means in order to maximize outcome for the self. Furthermore, the possession of coercive means encourages the belief that others are unfriendly and will not freely comply with one's persuasions. These beliefs, in turn, further encourage the actual use of coercion by lowering expectations that persuasions will successfully change the target person's behavior.

Competition. The manner in which rewards are distributed in a given social setting can also be expected to affect decisions concerning coercion. Quite simply, to the extent persons must compete for valued outcomes, reliance upon coercion should increase. Karl Marx, for instance, viewed the emerging capitalist system of the nineteenth century as forcing different strata of society into open conflict. Because the economic system was subject to periodic collapse, Marx foresaw that increasing numbers of workers would be unemployed, that these workers would be forced to compete with each other for scarce jobs, and that they eventually would have to fight owners for an equitable division of the wealth. Thus, the very nature of the capitalistic system, in Marx's view, would foster revolution by the workers. The critical factor that distinguishes this form of conflict is that persons are forced to invoke coercion by a social system that determines the form in which required goods and services are distributed. Personal predilections to harm others are not particularly important in this context.

Deutsch (1969) has focused attention among psychologists upon the consequences of this struggle for scarce resources. In Deutsch's view, competition between persons occurs under two circumstances. The first is when individuals cannot agree on the *means* to achieve some agreed-upon goal. Both parents may want their son to obtain good grades in school, but the husband wants an hour of study set aside each day, while the wife argues that the son should decide for himself when to study. Here the competition is in terms of ideas which allow for compromise and accommodation of each to the other. Thus, disagreement does not necessarily have to involve power relations of a harsher kind. Both parties can, if they have respect and affection for each other, reach an agreement without either party experiencing loss.

A more fundamental conflict occurs when the goal region is in dispute, as, for example, when the husband wants the son to concentrate on sports and the wife wants him to concentrate on grades. More formally, Deutsch has stated that competition occurs when the movement of person A into the goal region blocks the movement of person B into this region. If the Acme Company is awarded a contract for $1 million, then the Bolt Company does not get the contract. If students are in a class where grades are based upon a normal curve, then Jane's grade of A lessens Mary's chances for an A. These zero-sum social settings clearly encourage the use of coercive means of influence. The powerholder knows that simple discussion will not convince the target person to let the powerholder be the first to enter the goal region. Of course, this does not mean that relations will always be overtly hostile. Everyday observations suggest otherwise. Rather, a competitive social structure discourages community interests and feelings that allow people to stand together in times of stress. Hence, when persons strive for the same valued outcome, a competitive structure encourages the belief that a solution can only be of the type imposed by superior force.

Such a readiness to use force becomes all the more evident in situations that have not developed strong restraints governing the use of power. This may be particularly true in international relations, or in certain businesses which have typically been guided by a "dog-eat-dog" philosophy. Underlying this process of overt use of power is the gradual transformation of emotional attitudes toward the other, brought on by competition. Further, at a cognitive level, competition generates a firm conviction that the other party will not willingly compromise or accept influence. Thus, the joint action of emotional antipathy and lower expectation of successful influences set the stage for the introduction of harsh means of influence.

Number of target persons. So far, we have suggested that the possession of coercive means of influence and the setting in which power is exercised may both change a powerholder's expectations for successful influence, independently of the actual behavior of the target person. A third aspect of the social setting that can influence the use of coercion has to do with the number of target persons subjected to influence at the same time.

Typically, this problem is referred to in personnel management literature as the problem of "span of control." While top-level business managers may have from three to five persons directly under their control, one encounters instances in which a first-line foreman may have as many as two hundred employees working for him. A consequence of this large number of subordinates is that the appointed leader has very little time to spend with any one employee. Further, the appointed leader may have only the slightest idea of what each person is doing. Thus, he is placed in a position where good work may go unrewarded and poor work may not be corrected. Not too surprisingly, under these circumstances one finds that appointed leaders are attracted to the use of a strict system of controls. Among the features most favored are those that allow continuous monitoring of each individual's performance and that rely heavily on threats of punishment for rule infractions. Evidence for this process has been reported in several studies (Goodstadt and Kipnis 1970; Kipnis, Silverman, and Copeland 1973). In these studies it was found that more coercive means of influence were used by supervisors who were overburdened by the requirement that they supervise large numbers of men. As a supervisor's span of control increased, so too did his reliance on rules and punishments for controlling the behavior of subordinates. Although no direct evidence is available, I suggest that appointed leaders who are required to direct the behavior of large-sized groups would, if asked, express more doubts about their ability to control subordinates through simple persuasion than would leaders given only a few persons to influence.

The paradox involved here is that, from a design point of view, it is economically desirable to organize large numbers of persons into single units; whereas, in terms of psychological comfort, such organization is disastrous. This point tends to be recognized most immediately by appointed leaders who view their work in terms of socioemotional goals. Such leaders resent being forced by the situation to impose coercive rules on those they must direct. Thus, we find teachers continually agitating to reduce the size of the classes they teach and social caseworkers similarly arguing for a reduction in their case load. These persons recognize that, if they cannot give individual attention to their charges, then their very goals of encouraging individual growth will be blunted. Harshness and disciplinary emphasis will replace more gentle means of influence.

To summarize, there are numerous *situational* circumstances that decrease the powerholder's expectations that his influence attempts will be successful. Here we have mentioned some of the more important of these, ranging from the possession of coercive means which tempt the powerholder to demand more and also convince him of others' dislike, to the kinds of social structures in which power is exercised. In competitive structures where rewards are distributed in such a manner that sharing is precluded and a "winner takes all" philosophy prevails, individual powerholders come to believe that others will not freely give way to the powerholder. Under these circumstances, the powerholder may view his alternatives as either using force or not competing at all.

Individual Differences in Expectations of Successful Influence

Even casual observation will convince most observers that there are individual differences associated with the use of coercive power. People who doubt their own competence as a source of influence may be more likely to see others as resisting their influence when, in fact, such resistance may not exist at all. Thus, expectations of successful influence can be changed by not only the behavior of the target or by the social setting in which power is exercised, but also by the powerholder's past history. Recall, for instance, Webster's wonderful cartoon portraits of the Timid Soul, who in one sequence suffered in silence when a fellow passenger on a crowded bus stepped on his toes. The Timid Soul was both afraid to complain and afraid to ask the fellow passenger to move. Psychological studies have provided evidence that, in situations in which it is only possible to influence others by relying on personal powers of persuasion, persons low in self-esteem and self-confidence do not attempt to influence others (French and Snyder 1959; Hochbaum 1954). These timid persons' needs remain unsatisfied because they are not willing to forcefully argue for what they want.

What happens, however, when these same timid persons are given access to a range of institutional means of influence? Do they remain passive? Do they do the work themselves rather than order others to do it? We have not found this to be the case. While still not relying on persuasion, less confident powerholders remain active by relying extensively on their institutional means of influence. Moreover, less confident officeholders are rather rapidly attracted toward harsher means of influence, involving administrative punishments. Kipnis and Lane (1962), for instance, asked Navy noncommissioned officers to indicate to what extent they would use each of five different means of influence to correct the behavior of a troublesome subordinate. These means ranged from discussing the problem with the subordinate to placing the subordinate on "report." Placing a subordinate on report is a first step in the Navy's official disciplinary proceedings. Each noncommissioned officer also indicated the extent to which he was confident he could carry out his leadership duties in seven areas dealing with the technical and human-relations aspects of leadership. It was found that noncommissioned officers who stated they had little confidence in their leadership abilities recommended placing troublesome subordinates on official "report" more often than did confident noncommissioned officers. Furthermore, less confident leaders stated they were less willing to hold face-to-face discussions with the subordinate.

Similar findings have been obtained by Goodstadt and Hjelle (1973) in a laboratory study in which persons who perceived themselves to be either subjectively powerless or powerful (using Rotter's locus-of-control measure) were given access to a range of means of influencing a target. This range of means included the power to reward, to shift persons to new work environments, to persuade, to use expert power, and to punish. Those who saw themselves as weak and powerless chose to invoke punishing means of influence far more frequently than persons who perceived themselves to be powerful. Persons who believed they were powerful attempted to produce change in the target person through persuasion.

Thus, we see that when a person feels of little worth, he or she will be strongly attracted to harsh means of influence, if they are available. Underneath this behavior is the belief that gentle means of influence will not work since no one "respects me enough to do what I say if I only ask."

This conclusion is of considerable interest in extending existing writings on the relation between subjective feelings of powerlessness and violence. That is, it has generally been recognized that persons without resources are most prone to participate in violence. Ransford (1968), for instance, in interviews about the Watts riots found that subjective feelings of powerlessness were related to a willingness to participate in further riots. In these interviews, 41 percent of the respondents who scored high on a scale of powerlessness expressed a willingness to engage in riots, compared to 16 percent of those with low powerlessness scores. In a similar manner, the Kerner Report on civil disorders (1968) stated that "the frustration of powerlessness has led some Negroes to the conviction that there is no effective alternative to violence as a means of achieving redress of grievances." What is of interest in Goodstadt and Hjelle's research is the conclusion that, even if given a range of means for influencing other persons and thereby having their objective powerlessness reduced, persons who have a long history of experiencing a lack of power will still choose destructive forms of influence.

The explanation for these findings appears to be that chronically low self-confidence, or feelings of powerlessness, reduces a person's expectations that he can influence others through persuasion or other more gentle means of influence. Subjectively, the odds of being able to influence others appear to shift to the difficult end of the scale as feelings of self-worth decrease.

Thus, the suggested relationship is that low self-confidence produces low expectations of successful influence, which in turn lead to a greater reliance upon the use of coercion. Some correlational evidence in support of this chain of relations was found by myself in a questionnaire study of power usage, completed by 103 managers in state government and private industries. This study was described at the beginning of this chapter and involved managers' reading descriptions of ineffective employee performance, rating the probable odds that they could personally correct the problem and also rating the extent to which they would use coercion as a means of dealing with the ineffective performance. In addition, managers completed a scale that measured their own self-confidence in their abilities as managers.

It was found that managers who had low self-confidence also said that the odds were poor that they personally could correct the ineffective performances described in the questionnaire. The correlation was .39 between ratings of self-confidence and ratings of expectations of successful influence.

The question may now be examined as to the relative importance of both confidence and expectations in determining the use of coercion. The model proposed here suggests that confidence should affect expectations of successful influence, which in turn should affect the decision to use coercion. In support of the model, the correlation between confidence and endorsement of the use of coercion was $-.27$ ($p < .01$), while the correlation between expectations and coercion was $-.41$. Clearly, expectations were more directly related to the use of coercion than was self-confidence. This pattern of correlations is consistent with the belief that cognitive evaluations play a central role in the use of coercion.

One implication of these findings is that people who are passive and timid in day-to-day life tend to be transformed into the most severe of taskmasters when given access to institutional means of influence. They bring to their work a history of failure to influence others through persuasion and other gentle means of influence. Once armed with the authority to invoke coercion, however, and now required to influence others who work for them, passive persons very soon learn to use authority harshly. Interestingly enough, Raser (1966) reached somewhat similar conclusions in a biographical analysis of the personalities of totalitarian and democratic political leaders. Totalitarian leaders were more insecure in private life and lower in self-esteem. Certainly, Albert Speer's (1970) portrait of his relations with Hitler fits very well with Raser's description. Speer describes many incidents in which Hitler avoided personal confrontations with his close associates and, if in conflict with them, overcame their resistance through harsh and punishing means rather than through discussion. Force, then, as the psychiatrist Fanon suggested, seems the main means by which the power needs of those who, by nature or by circumstances, are passive can be satisfied.

Liking for the target person. Another individual-difference factor affecting a powerholder's decision to use coercion is whether the target person is liked or disliked. There is a growing body of evidence which shows, not surprisingly, that harsh means of influence are invoked in attempts to influence a disliked or distrusted target person (Banks 1974; Michener and Burt 1974; Michener and Schwertfeger 1972). One immediate explanation that comes to mind for this finding is that powerholders use threats and punishments because they enjoy seeing the target person suffer. Because they dislike the target person, they may wish to hurt him as well as to make him comply. Further, as Michener suggests, since powerholders do not wish to maintain affectionate relations with people they don't like, the choice of coercion tends to guarantee that the relationship will not be preserved.

In line with the main argument of this chapter, I would suggest that another explanation for the use of coercion with disliked targets is that powerholders doubt their ability to persuade under these circumstances. Powerholders may assume that their dislike is reciprocated and as a result expect the target person to resist their influence. Thus the desire to punish may not be the only reason for using coercion with those whom we dislike. Instead, lowered expectations of successful influence may be an important instigator. Banks (1974) has amplified this argument by stating that when we dislike somebody we tend to assume that any resistance shown by the disliked other is a deliberate act of free will, while similar resistance from someone we like is attributed to uncontrollable forces in the environment. And as was pointed out earlier in this chapter, the perception of deliberate resistance to our requests produces lowered expectations of successful influence and increases our attraction toward coercive forms of influence.

Prejudice against minority groups illustrates very well this process of power use. While no direct test of the relation between prejudice, expectations, and the use of coercion has been done, one study (Kipnis, Silverman, and Copeland 1973) did investigate whether more coercive power would be used by white supervisors among black employees than among white employees. This possibility was suggested by the congressional hearings held in 1972 concerning race riots on Navy ships. A charge raised at this hearing was that black sailors received harsher punishments than white sailors for the same offense. Similar charges have been made concerning punishments meted out to black and white convicts (Levy and Miller 1970). White guards, it has been reported, were more punitive with black convicts than with white convicts.

The results of the Kipnis et al. study were similar in that coercive means were found to be used more often to influence black than white employees. That is, black workers were suspended or fired more often than white workers for the same infractions. When this information was reported to the company at the end of the study, the supervisors involved denied any malicious intent. Rather, they justified their behavior by arguing that black workers were less dependable. Since the analysis of the incidents reported by the supervisors revealed that the problems attributed to black subordinates were no different in kind or severity from those attributed to white subordinates, it seems probable that prejudice acted in this instance by affecting the supervisors' expectations of successful influence. The same problem manifested by a black subordinate was perceived as more difficult to correct than when manifested by a white subordinate.

Similarity and the use of coercion. Related to the concept of prejudice, but not necessarily sharing the strong emotional antipathy of prejudice, is the perception that someone differs from us in some important way such as religion or political beliefs. It was already mentioned in Chapter 4 that when dissimilar target persons *complied* with a powerholder's demands, they were given more rewards than similar target persons. The proposed explanation for these added rewards was that powerholders doubted that dissimilar target persons would continue to voluntarily comply without being provided with added incentives.

Consider now what happens when dissimilar target persons do not comply. Clearly, powerholders should be very pessimistic that any simple requests they make will be enough to overcome the target person's resistance. "They are not like me at all," thinks the powerholder, "why should they care about me or do what I want them to do?" With these kinds of thoughts, especially when it is not important to the goodwill of the target person, it is but a small step to decide that coercion must be used to overcome resistance.

The hypothesized tie-in between perceived dissimilarity, noncompliance, and the choice of coercive means of influence can be illustrated by findings of the present writer concerning power relations between men and women at work. In this investigation, the decisions by male and female managers to use coercive power with employees of the opposite sex were examined. Even in today's climate of changing sex-role attitudes, most women see themselves as different in important ways from men, and vice versa. Given these assumptions of differences, it seems likely that in situations in which men and women must continually influence each other there should be more reliance upon strong means of influence when resistance does occur. At work then, one might expect man-

agers to use coercion more often with employees of the opposite
sex than with employees of the same sex when resistance to the
manager's orders is expressed by the employee.

The data to test this hypothesis were drawn from the previously
mentioned questionnaire study in which 103 managers in state
government and private industry read case histories of employee
noncompliance and rated the extent to which they would use coercion as a means of changing for the better an employee's ineffective
performance. What has not been mentioned before is that there
were two forms of the questionnaire. In one form the ineffective
employee was described as a woman and in the second as a man.
The questionnaire contained eight incidents of ineffective performance, so that it was possible to have, in counterbalanced form,
half the incidents describe female employees and half male employees. Of the 103 managers completing the questionnaire, 32
were female and 71 were male. Thus it was possible to examine
whether the manager recommended more coercion when the ineffective employee was of the same sex or of the opposite sex.

Table 6.1 shows the average endorsement of coercion made by
male and female managers when dealing with same sex or the opposite sex employees. The higher the score the greater the endorsement of coercion.

Table 6.1 Endorsement of the Use of Coercion by Male and
Female Managers

	Male Managers (N = 71)	Female Managers (N = 32)
Male employees	11.98	13.36
Female employees	13.73	12.87

While the differences in ratings appear small, they follow the
predicted pattern. Male managers endorsed more coercion with
female employees, and female managers endorsed more coercion
with male employees.

The statistical analysis (of variance) of these findings revealed
a significant relation between the sex of the manager and the sex
of the employee ($p < .01$). Male managers endorsed significantly
more coercion for females than for male employees (means of
13.73 vs. 11.98). While the female managers endorsed more coercion for the opposite sex (means of 13.36 vs. 12.87), this difference was not statistically reliable.

The next question that was asked was whether managers had lower expectations of successful influence when required to change the behavior of a problem employee of the opposite sex. Subjective expectations were measured by asking each manager to rate the probable odds that they could personally correct the problem being shown by the employee. An analysis of these ratings revealed that male managers rated the odds as poorer when attempting to influence female employees than when attempting to influence male employees. The reverse of these findings were true for female managers. However, the statistical analysis of these ratings of subjective expectations yielded only marginally significant results ($p < .10$), thus leaving unproven, in this instance, the mediating role of expectations of successful influence.

Drawing back from the data, we can ask whether the findings of more reliance upon coercion when attempting to influence the opposite sex tell us anything of interest about relations in general between men and women. One suggestion is that the greater the emphasis on differences between the sexes, the more likely are both parties to assume that the other is irrational. That is, each assumes that the other must be cajoled and pushed and forced into compliance. "I am reasonable, but he or she is stubborn. Talking will do no good." With these assumptions of differences between the sexes, simple discussions tend to be avoided and stronger means are sought. Perhaps Professor Henry Higgins best illustrates these lowered expectations of other sex's reasonableness when he sings in *My Fair Lady*:

> Why can't a woman be more like a man?
> Women are irrational, that's all there is to that
> Their heads are full of cotton, hay, and rags,
> They're nothing but exasperating . . . vacillating
> . . . maddening . . . hags.
> Why can't a woman be more like a man?
> Men are so honest, so thoroughly square. . . .
> Oh, why can't a woman be more like a man?

With these thoughts in mind, it is not surprising that Professor Higgins spends so little time in quiet discussion with his "fair lady."

Sequential Use of Coercion

The concluding section of this chapter now turns to another issue in the use of coercion. This is the temporal sequence to be followed by the powerholder when he is deciding which to use first: coercive means or milder forms of influence.

Throughout this chapter it has been emphasized that anger and hostility do not have to be considered the primary instigators of the use of coercion. Rather, the decision to invoke coercion frequently arises from the powerholder's calculations concerning the best means of inducing compliance. The distinction here has to do with the timing of the delivery of coercive stimuli to a target. When angry and seeking revenge, the powerholder may immediately seek to invoke whatever harsh means are available in order to punish the target. The sequence has been described by Berkowitz (1971) as one of arousal, followed by disinhibition and the immediate evoking of coercive means. Despite the fine old Elizabethan observation that "revenge is a dish that is best eaten cold," most angered persons prefer immediate retaliation. In contrast, most officeholders whose power needs originate in their institutional roles prefer to use coercion as a last, rather than first, resort. The goal of the institutional powerholder is not, strictly speaking, to punish the target but to make him change his behavior in order to further institutional objectives. In the absence of emotional arousal, the decision to use coercion arises from calculations concerning the best means to induce compliance. Since there are far less costs involved in the use of persuasion, training, or ecological changes, as compared with threats, these less costly means will almost invariably be tried first. Exceptions to this generalization exist, of course, such as the previously mentioned less confident or prejudiced officeholders, who were drawn rather rapidly to harsher means.

Some evidence that evoking harsher means of influence will be deferred until more gentle means have been exhausted is available from the previously cited experimental study of Goodstadt and Kipnis (1970). In this study, the focus was on how subjects acting as managers used various power tactics to influence the performance of a worker who had been programmed to perform poorly. This study had six work periods during which the output of the workers was brought in to the managers. Thus, it was possible to examine the means of influence invoked by managers during the first three work periods and the last three work periods.

During the first half of the experiment, the preferred means used to influence the performance of the below-average worker were:

(*a*) ecological control (assigning new jobs), (*b*) expert powers, and (*c*) threatening to deduct pay from the worker's salary. During the last half of the experiment the preferred means of influence involved: (*a*) actually deducting pay from the worker's salary, (*b*) threatening to fire the worker, and (*c*) actually firing the worker. This progressive trend toward reliance on harsher means was less for the worker who was inept than for the worker whose poor performance was based upon poor attitudes. However, since the outputs of both types of worker had been programmed to stay below average, an increasing reliance upon coercion was apparent for both types.

Thus, given the availability of a range of means of influence, I suggest that there will be a progressive scaling of means from less harsh to most severe. University instructors will usually first discuss and give extra instruction to a failing student before assigning a failing grade; managers will assign new jobs, counsel, and train before recommending suspension; and diplomats prefer to "jaw, jaw, jaw" before proceeding to "war, war, war." Underlying this progression, presumably, will be declining expectations of successful influence and the concurrent attraction to strong means of influence.

Summary

The basic assumption that has been examined in this chapter is that all forces that reduce an individual's belief in his own effectiveness also serve to increase the individual's attraction to coercive means of influence. Among the forces that may reduce the powerholder's belief in his own effectiveness are:

a) The perception that the target person is deliberately, rather than involuntarily, resisting influence.

b) Environmental forces such as the kinds of influence means available to the powerholder, the structural arrangements for reward allocation, and the number of target persons to be influenced at the same time.

c) The temperamental and characterological makeup of powerholders, as these determine powerholders' beliefs about their own personal effectiveness and the kinds of people that they see as similar or different than themselves.

7   Inhibition of the Power Act

It was suggested in Chapter 2 that there was a region of inhibition that the powerholder must successfully navigate before he could exercise influence. The necessity for assuming the existence of this region of inhibition arises from the fact that we could not otherwise explain the many instances in which the powerholder appears in complete control of events and individuals and yet takes no further action.

Understanding the forces leading to the inhibition of behavior is one of the two fundamental tasks that have engaged the attention of behavioral scientists, the other being the understanding of the forces leading to the arousal of behavior. Inescapably, the stance one takes in regard to the question of restraint has political overtones. The laboratory finding, for instance, that punishments will deter aggressive behavior so long as the punishments are feared cannot fail to cause speculation as to how to use this information to control behavior on a larger scale.

The humanist, the radical, and the romantic have the fixed idea that the individual must be free to realize his own potential, that the human spirit is distorted by repressive institutions and laws. At all levels of society a continual acrimonious dialogue goes on between those representing the forces for individual freedom and those representing the forces for restraint. Sometimes the debating parties change sides, as when the strong "law and order" representative argues that there should be no laws restraining the conduct of businesses. Despite these occasional role changes, however, the issue of how much restraint and how much freedom society can afford to allow its members is a source of continual debate. Hence the input of research findings from the social sciences is bound to add fuel to any ongoing controversies.

Basically the issue pivots around a set of assumptions made about human nature. If it is assumed that each person has the potential to develop to God-like dimensions, if nurtured properly by society, then freedom from restraints which distort this growth seems the answer to the debate. If one believes, however, that humans left to regulate their own behavior would soon destroy themselves in frantic efforts to maximize their own outcomes, then social restraint is the answer.

Freud in particular saw little possibility of man being able to control urges to use power for selfish goals. In a long letter written in response to a question from Albert Einstein concerning the possibility of ending war, Freud stated his view that the instinctive impulses of man were almost impossible to control. Even when man banded together into a community and established laws to regulate the excesses of violence, sooner or later inequities entered into the law, as one person gained an advantage in power over his fellows, and thus excesses of behavior continued to occur. Toward the end of his letter Freud pessimistically concluded:

> The upshot of these observations . . . is that there is no likelihood of being able to suppress humanity's aggressive tendencies. In some happy corners of the earth, they say, where human nature brings forth abundantly whatever man desires, there flourish races whose lives go gently by, unknowing of aggression or constraint. This I can hardly credit. I would like further details about these happy folk. The Bolshevists, too, aspire to do away with human aggressiveness by ensuring the satisfaction of material needs and enforcing equality between man and man. To me this hope seems vain. Meanwhile they perfect their armaments, and their hatred of outsiders is not the least of the factors of cohesion among them. [1964, p. 77]

It should be noted that Freud, despite his deep pessimism concerning man's fate, acknowledged the possibility that limits could be placed on man's aggressive nature through the development of culture and correlated changes in man's genetic makeup. On the cultural side he foresaw the slow growth and strengthening of the intellect, which would eventually master instinctual life. Freud included in the role of intellect the growth of ethical values which would allow humans to realize the unworthiness of aggression. On the genetic side, Freud assumed that, through a process of evolution, aggressiveness as an inherited trait would become less dominant. Aggression, that is, would have less survival value for the individual as man's technology began to produce enough for all.

These are changes in man's nature that Freud saw as happening in some distant future. When the world of power is considered today, however, many observers would favor the view that curbs should be placed upon behavior rather than more freedom should be granted. Everyday events seem to point to the fact that we are surrounded by power usages that are insufficiently restrained. To our great despair the values of "take" appear far stronger than the values of "wait."

Nevertheless, there *are* forces that strengthen the value of "wait" even if at times they appear very weak. These forces, I believe, operate in one of two ways in limiting the use of power. The first is by reducing the individual's need to seek goals that require the use of power. The second is by requiring the powerholder to use different means of influence than he would have chosen in the absence of restraining forces. Each of these two methods of restraint will be illustrated in the following pages.

Physiological Inhibition of Aggressive Power

People vary greatly in the extent to which they are willing to invoke coercive forms of power against others. Some retain an innate gentleness that restrains their actions, despite the fact that they encounter many provocations. For these people the idea of doing harm invokes feelings of anxiety and guilt (Hare 1968). The very thought of hurting others is troublesome. Some have argued (Clark 1971) that, if one could inject this spirit of pacifism into our political and military leaders, a personal distaste of hurting others would then cause them to trip the decision in favor of peace when faced with a choice between war or peace. Strangely enough, there is some evidence that the spirit of restraint and gentleness in man is at least in part a function of complex biochemical and neurological factors. Further, there is emerging a psychotechnology concerned with learning how to control biological impulses to do harm to others.

There are several sources of research supporting this contention. It has been known for some time that persons characterized by aggressive and violent acts have abnormal EEG brain patterns, in terms of spiking and excessive slow-wave patterns (Knott and Gottlieb, 1944; Gottlieb, Ashby, and Knott 1946). These findings extend to children. In 1938, Jasper, Solomon, and Bradley, for instance, found that there were definite abnormalities in the EEG patterns of children who since infancy were irritable, hyperactive, and aggressive, or who had a short attention-span, and whose behavior and mood varied unexplainably from time to time.

Studies of brain functioning have confirmed these early findings and have also revealed that there are neural systems which when active appear to be directly associated with aggressive behavior. Thus one possible control of aggressive behavior that has been suggested is by interfering with the function of these neural centers. And as is fairly well known at this time, many studies among animals, and occasionally in man, reveal that surgical ablations or incisions in the temporal lobes and posterior hypothalamus will in fact produce reductions in aggressive behaviors.

In addition to evidence of areas that arouse aggressive behavior, there is also evidence, according to Moyer (1971), that there are suppressor systems in the brain serving to inhibit aggressive behavior. These suppressor regions can apparently be activated through direct electrical and chemical stimulation, as well as indirectly through drugs that act on the central nervous system. Delgado (1969) has shown that normally vicious animals can be tamed by the activation of the aggression-suppressor region in the brain by means of radio signals. Bulls raised for fighting have halted their attack at the very last moment in response to a signal from an implanted electrode.

Besides through electrical stimulation or brain extirpation, control over aggressive behavior may be gained through altering the chemical and hormonal factors in the blood stream. It has been known for centuries, for instance, that castration reduces aggressive tendencies in bulls. Blocking the action of the male sex hor-

mone, androgen, through such agents as the injection of the female hormone, estrogen, has been recently suggested as a means
of controlling aggressive behavior.

Along the same line, hyperactive and impulsive children can be
treated through the use of various forms of amphetamine. These
drugs have a calming effect on children such that they become less
aggressive and less loud; in general, they become much more acceptable members of the community (Bradley 1942). Moyer has
suggested that a wide variety of additional drugs have a calming
effect upon man. These range from dilantin, a drug originally used
to control epileptic seizures, to various forms of tranquilizing
agents. Moyer has somewhat facetiously suggested that some form
of calming drug may be routinely added to our milk, or to our
water supply, to make people suppress their aggressive power
needs.

Kenneth B. Clark, in a presidential address to the American
Psychological Association (1972), took note of these possibilities
of using drugs to control powerholders. Man, he warned, is easily
tempted to use social power for self-serving and selfish ends. Out
of existential feelings of fear, weakness, and moral emptiness, originate irrational drives to dominate, destroy, and do harm. In our
time, such irrational drives, combined with the access of political
leaders to great destructive sources of power, has left the world
on the verge of a new age of barbarism. What must be done, according to Clark, is to control and redirect the powerholder in
more peaceful directions.

> Given the urgency of this immediate survival problem, the psy-
> chological and social sciences must enable us to control the
> animalistic, barbaric and primitive propensities in man and sub-
> ordinate these negatives to the uniquely human moral and ethi-
> cal characteristics of love, kindness, and empathy.

But how is this to be done? Clark argues against traditional
methods of moral education as being too slow and uncertain to
control powerful leaders. He says:

> We can no longer afford to rely solely on the traditional pre-
> scientific attempts to contain human cruelty and destructiveness.
> The techniques and appeals of religion, moral philosophy, law
> and education seemed appropriate and civilized approaches to
> the control of man's primitive and egocentric behavior in a pre-

nuclear age. They are in themselves no longer appropriate because they permit too wide a margin of error and a degree of unpredictability that is rationally inconsistent with the present survival urgency. Furthermore, moral verbalizations of the past have been prostituted by the pathos of power; they have been perverted by the pretenses of rationality in the service of inhumanity if not barbarity.

After briefly noting the advances being made in biochemical investigations, Clark points out that we are on the threshold of that "type of scientific biochemical intervention which could stabilize and make dominant the moral and ethical propensities of man and subordinate, if not eliminate, his negative and primitive behavioral tendencies." Clark sees it as a logical requirement imposed on all power-controlling leaders that they accept and use these biochemical pacifiers, once they are developed, so as to block the leaders' own inclinations to make warlike and aggressive decisions. In short, through chemical means, leaders and nations would be internally disarmed.

Space has been devoted to Clark's proposal because it appears to be technically possible in the not too distant future. In our discussion of power usage it was pointed out that the availability of a means of influencing others tempts the powerholder to use this means. Thus it should come as no surprise that the availability of a new technology for controlling behavior through physiological means should immediately lead to a consideration of its use. Further, Clark's proposal illustrates the dilemma for society created by research in the social sciences. Applications of control technology inevitably involve political and ethical concerns of the most fundamental kind. One must clearly work out whether it is in the best interests of society to interfere with the functioning of the central nervous system as a means of controlling the misuse of power—whether the misuse is by violent criminals lashing out with their fists or knives, or by political leaders corruptly using their offices. Recent law suits by civil libertarians attempting to block researchers from experimentally implanting electrodes in the brains of imprisoned criminals, or to carry out actual brain surgery in the limbic region to reduce violent behavior, suggest the immediacy of these concerns. Chorover (1973) has most recently explored the issues involved here and concludes that society stands to lose more than it will gain by these kinds of efforts.

Deindividuation

Restraint of power usage is frequently justified on the assumption that without restraint the powerholder would take more and more for himself, leaving less and less for others. Thus man's tendency to maximize his outcomes is considered a compelling reason for the necessity of restraints.

Still another reason for justifying restraints, to be considered in this section, is that many people appear to experience great pleasure from controlling the lives of others. That is, power seems to unleash in many persons cruel motives to manipulate others, motives the persons had not suspected of existing prior to their control of power. Aside from the explanation that we harbor within us small demons waiting for the right moment to emerge, we must seek an explanation for these tendencies in the range of experiences that humans are potentially capable of enjoying.

In this regard Stanford University psychologist Phillip Zimbardo (1970) has written that there exists within most people "dark forces" that seek to gratify immediately any desire; forces that seek to live for the here and now and to enjoy any action, no matter how antisocial, that provides emotional release and gratification. These forces are most likely to be manifested when the person has lost the restraints produced by self-awareness and is experiencing what Zimbardo and others (Festinger, Pepitone, and Newcomb 1952) have called a state of deindividuation. It is these particular motivational forces produced by deindividuation that appear to be involved when persons experience great pleasure in exercising personal dominance over others. Awareness of self, then, can be designated as a second restraint in power usage. Apparently to lose his sense of identity encourages the powerholder to influence others in ways that society would ordinarily condemn.

One of the key questions for Zimbardo is to identify the circumstances leading to an individual's experiencing deindividuation, or to a lowering of threshold for normally restrained behavior. Zimbardo has theorized that to the extent the individual believes he is not likely to be identified, or that he is in a large group, or that he experiences altered states of consciousness, restraints may be lowered against carrying out acts normally inhibited by various mechanisms of self-control.

Our interest in Zimbardo's analysis comes from its implications for understanding when an individual may be tempted to use resources to satisfy power needs which violate personal or societal taboos. To the extent power may be exercised under conditions of anonymity, for instance, one would predict that the individual powerholder would be increasingly tempted to use his resources in ways condemned by society.

Zimbardo presents an interesting study of this possibility in an investigation of when coercive means are directed against an innocent target. In this particular study, coeds were provided with a machine that could deliver an electric shock (the resource) to a sister coed, located in another room. The rationale for delivering shock was that the experimenters were studying conditioning processes by means of electric shock. *However the decision as to the number of shocks to give over a series of trials, as well as the intensity of shock, was left up to the individual coeds.* Thus, the coeds were in the role of powerholder, with resources in the form of electric shock that they could use to influence the target if they chose to do so.

Zimbardo's prediction was that the coeds would be more willing to exercise coercive power if they were in a state of deindividuation. To establish the conditions of deindividuation, groups of four coeds participated at a time. Half of these groups put on very large lab coats, hoods over their heads, and their names were never used. In contrast, each coed assigned to the individuation condition was greeted by name and given a big name tag to wear, while the importance of her unique reaction was emphasized by the instructions of the experimenter.

The results of this study revealed that deindividuating the coeds had a significant influence on their willingness to invoke electric shock. The total duration of shock was twice as much for the deindividuated coeds as for the individuated coeds. Zimbardo concluded that "under conditions specified as deindividuating, normally mild-mannered college girls shocked another girl almost every time they had an opportunity to do so, sometimes for as long as they were allowed, and it didn't matter whether or not the fellow student was a nice girl who didn't deserve to be hurt" (p. 270).

Zimbardo's theorizing suggests something that perhaps we have known all along; namely, that when power can be exercised without the surveillance of the public, the powerholder will experience fewer restraints against invoking resources than when such surveillance is present. The control of unchallenged power, in itself, probably serves to deindividuate the powerholder. With power the person can protect himself from public scrutiny and from the necessity of justifying his acts. A study by Zimbardo and his colleagues (1974) of prison guards who were given almost unrestrained power over their prisoners clearly suggests that such a process of deindividuation can occur under these circumstances. The prison guards acted in an increasingly brutal manner and, perhaps more disturbing, reported that they enjoyed the master-slave relationships that were evolving.

Costs as a Restraining Influence on the Exercise of Power

It was mentioned in Chapter 1 that theories which view human interactions as the exchange of benefits have been particularly useful for examining problems of conflict and bargaining. An assumption underlying these theories, that may be traced to economics and to reinforcement psychology, is that each of the parties in these exchanges acts to maximize gains and to minimize costs.

From this assumption, one can conclude that a strong restraint upon an individual's decision to invoke resources has to do with the costs that are involved. As Cartwright (1965) points out: "When an agent is deciding whether to exercise influence, it must be assumed that he calculates in some sense the net advantage to him of making an influence attempt" (p. 8). If the results of the agent's calculation indicate that he will lose more than he will gain, presumably the individual does not attempt to influence others. The young lover may be eager to seduce the maiden, but will look elsewhere if the cost of seduction is marriage. Sorenson (1965), in discussing how decisions were reached concerning the Cuban missile crisis during the early 1960s, stated that the overriding constraint in the situation against invoking military power to eliminate the nuclear missiles in Cuba was the possibility that Russia might be forced into war with the United States. Even the decision to impose a blockade around Cuba was viewed by President Kennedy as clearly likely to incur costs to this country in terms of possible increments in Russian countertactics in Germany and the Near East,

In the above instances we have the idea that the powerholder exercises deliberate restraints on his behavior while calculating the net advantage of action or inaction. The seeming rationality of this behavior has persuaded several theorists to explicitly introduce the idea of costs into their discussions of the use of power. Harsanyi (1962) has argued that, without information about what he calls "opportunity costs," the power of various persons cannot be evaluated, nor can it be predicted when they will use power. Costs for Harsanyi, who leans toward the analysis of power in economic terms, are measured in relatively objective ways such as money expended and commitments that the powerholder must make in exchange for compliance.

In psychology, Thibaut and Kelley (1959) have also made the idea of costs and gains a central component of their views of power. Power for these writers is defined in exchange theory terms as the capability of one person to affect another's outcomes. Once again the major restraint upon the decision to exercise influence is the costs that the powerholder may incur. Police, for example, have the power to arrest others, and hence may be considered to have the ability to affect others' outcomes. However there are limitations on the extent to which the police will use this power, which in Thibaut and Kelley's view are a function of the costs involved in making the arrest. To arrest a wandering hobo may incur few costs for the policeman. To arrest the mayor's son for reckless driving is another matter, since the costs for exerting power may leave the officer without a job.

The exercise of power for the rational man, then, becomes a function of costs and benefits. If the results indicate that he will lose more than he will gain, presumably resources are not invoked and power is not exerted. What seems to happen is that concern over costs convinces the powerholder to give up trying for whatever it was that he wanted.

Within the context of laboratory experimentation, several studies have provided support for the notion that, as costs of exercising power increase, the powerholder restrains himself (Tedeschi, Horai, Lindskold, and Faley 1970; Tedeschi, Bonomo, and Novinson 1970; Thibaut and Faucheux 1965; Bedell and Sistrunk 1973). In these studies subjects are given full information about both the gains and the costs of exercising influence. The focus of interest is in noting whether the participants with power do behave rationally, that is, in a way to maximize gains and minimize costs. The answer is that they do, within reasonable limits. Apparently if the powerholder is fully aware of the costs involved in exercising power, he will use a hedonic calculus to determine his actions. If the results are negative he will limit his use of resources.

The reader can easily contrast this source of restraint, which emphasizes the rational and cognitive components of behavior, with the sources previously discussed. In these earlier sources, the individual is propelled unwittingly into postures of attack, withdrawal, or restraint as the result of the activation of neural and hormonal systems, or being provided with anonymity.

Limitations to the Concept of Costs

There can be no doubt that most persons at most times engage in a form of hedonic calculus before taking any unusual action. Knowledge of this calculus is of importance for understanding the acts that a powerholder has taken. Without it we would not be able to understand why some people leap into action and others hesitate. However, there are limits to the usefulness of the concept of costs for predicting some future behavior of a powerholder or for using the projected ratio of costs and benefits in order to determine precisely whether or not to invoke power.

For one thing, emotionality may influence the calculation of costs, as when the powerholder is angry at the target and is determined to do him injury, regardless of the consequences for himself. Brown (1970) found that when outside observers humiliated a subject by criticizing his behavior in a bargaining game, the subject acted more aggressively against his opponent regardless of the fact that such aggression resulted in a loss of profits. Captain Ahab's furious determination to destroy the white whale, Moby Dick, despite the fact that the whale's destruction would cause his own death, is a deeply moving illustration of how emotions and unbounded determination can override a prudent calculation of costs.

Again, the generalizations concerning costs may not hold because the powerholders are simply not in a position to take into account the costs they are liable to incur. In this connection Berle (1967) observed that it is almost impossible to predict the long-term consequences of invoking power. While the immediate costs involved can frequently be computed, the waves generated by power acts tend to take unpredictable courses. Before World War I began, for example, the leaders of the conflicting countries had not the slightest idea of the costs that their countries would incur over the four years of the war. The tremendous destruction of property in France or Russia was not considered much of a possibility, while the loss of lives in the trenches was considered even less likely.

Finally, the generalization concerning costs may be further weakened by the eternal optimism of persons who are highly motivated to achieve some goal. Real costs that may have served as a deterrent are falsified in the mind in order to make the odds of success more attractive. In the mid 1960s when the stock market was expanding, many companies with excess capital became "conglomerates" by buying up the stock of companies in fields unrelated to those of their products (Brooks 1973). The eventual bankruptcy of many of these conglomerates in the late 1960s and early 1970s could be directly traced to the failure of managers to accurately assess the risks involved in these takeovers. Sustained by previous success and driving ambition, these managers simply ignored warning signs indicating that the resources of their own companies should not be used to expand into areas not directly related to their own kinds of business.

The principal conclusion concerning anticipated costs as an inhibitor of the power act is that people do consider costs and benefits when deciding to take action, and this information is most useful in situations when (*a*) full knowledge of the costs are available; (*b*) emotions are not strongly involved, and (*c*) the immediate consequences of the use of power are all that is considered.

Values and Attitudes

Still other social scientists view the problem of inhibition of power in terms of subjective values and attitudes (Berkowitz and Daniels 1963; Leventhal and Lane 1970; Pepitone 1971; Staub 1971; Walster, Berscheid, and Walster 1973). Despite the fact that the individual may gain substantial advantage by invoking his resources, it frequently happens that he inhibits the invoking of resources because he questions the propriety of the act. The need to act in a just manner overrides the temptation to maximize gain.

Frequently persons in power must decide whether to guide their actions by normative values or by a utilitarian estimate of the costs involved in taking some action. Clashes are deep, frequently emotional, and inevitable when persons holding these two views must jointly decide what to do. One side crisply argues for action because the cost/benefit ratio is favorable, and the other side righteously argues for inaction because the power act is unethical. Neither side can understand the other, and an impasse is reached. When Chester Bowles was assistant secretary of state in the Kennedy administration, he found himself almost alone in his opposition to the government-supported invasion of Cuba at the Bay of Pigs. His opposition was based upon deep convictions about the propriety of such acts. His views, of course, conflicted with the more utilitarian values of the majority of Kennedy's staff, who were committed to a tough-minded exercise of power. During this period he entered the following observation in his diary (reported in Halberstam [1973]):

> The question which concerns me about the new administration is whether it lacks a genuine conviction about what is right and what is wrong.
> Anyone in public life who has strong convictions about the right and wrong of public morality, both domestic and international has a very great advantage in times of strain since his instincts on what to do are clear and immediate. Lacking such a framework of moral conviction of what is right and what is wrong, he is forced to lean almost entirely upon his mental processes. He adds up the pluses and minuses of any question and comes up with a conclusion. Under normal conditions when he is not tired or frustrated this pragmatic approach should successfully bring him on the right side of the question.
> What worries me are the conclusions that such an individual may reach when he is tired, angry, frustrated, or emotionally affected. The Cuban fiasco demonstrates how far astray a man as brilliant and well intentioned as Kennedy can go who lacks a basic moral reference point.

Shortly after Bowles made this diary entry he was forced to resign from his position in the State Department.

Some researchers prefer to include the inhibiting effects of personal values as simply another cost factor. In my opinion, this approach is not useful. If all sources of inhibition are labeled "costs," then this concept loses explanatory value. Values and attitudes serve to restrain behavior for very precise reasons; transgressions invoke guilt, shame, and anxiety. These are not the logi-

cal and cognitive variables traditionally associated with the calculations of costs.

How Ideas about Justice Restrain the Use of Power

Ethical restraints on the use of power can be related to at least
two views of justice. The first view is derived in modern-day form
from exchange theory. The emphasis, however, is not on the cost/
benefit ratios each party derives from the exchange but upon the
perceived fairness of the exchange. The question of fair or equitable exchanges was first described systematically in psychology by
Adams (1963) and modified somewhat by Walster, Berscheid,
and Walster (1973). The equitable-exchange model proposes that
most people accept the norm that the rewards gained by each person in an exchange should be proportional to his contributions.
Thus an equitable relationship is one in which a person's outcomes
are based upon his inputs. If person A works harder than Person
B (their inputs), then A should receive more rewards than B (their
outcomes), if they are doing the same work. Simple justice occurs,
in Adam's view, when inputs and outcomes are in balance. This
view of justice can be summed up by saying, "You get what you
deserve."

Many studies have found that people tend to order their lives
and judge how fair situations are in terms of their equity standard.
Thus persons who get less than others of similar skills have been
found to "slack off" (reduce inputs) in order to compensate for
being under-rewarded (Adams, 1963; Adams and Rosenbaum
1962). Other studies of persons in positions to allocate rewards
to both themselves and others show that these powerholders do
not take everything for themselves despite the fact that they are
in a position to do so. (Leventhal and Lane 1970; Pepitone 1971).
Rather, the rewards are distributed in proportion to each person's
contribution. Pepitone (1971) found that college students who
were initially awarded more than they deserved in a two-person
bargaining game with fellow students, subsequently made bargaining decisions designed to redistribute the available rewards more
evenly. In so doing the students reduced the amount of rewards
they received themselves. Despite being in a position of power,
these students exercised restraints that would be difficult to predict
from the simple notion that persons are motivated to maximize
their own gains.

A second view of justice that may restrain the use of power can be called the "equality" model. Most recently this view of justice has been examined in psychology by Lerner (1974). The equality view argues that rewards should be distributed to all persons in a collective equally rather than proportionally to each member's inputs. For example, on many collective settlements in Israel all persons share outcomes equally—the same living quarters, the same food, the same vacations and pay—despite the fact that some do the work of skilled engineers and managers while others do simple, unskilled manual work. Clearly, the individual's inputs in this system are not proportional to his outcomes. While there has been little research in psychology dealing with the ideal of equality as compared to equity, both models could serve to inhibit a power-holder from using resources simply to maximize his own outcomes. In one instance inhibition could originate in the value judgment that "I have not done enough to deserve these outcomes," and in the second instance inhibition would originate in the value judgment "share and share alike."

What evidence is there that either or both of these ethical concepts are taken into account by powerholders? The answer suggested by the available research is that persons in positions of power are most likely to be guided by notions of *equity* rather than *equality*. Apparently this is because the powerholder can allocate more desired outcomes to himself under the first system than the second, but he is still restrained from taking all. Let us examine the basis for this conclusion.

The first set of evidence comes from studies of interpersonal bargaining. These studies provide reasonably strong evidence to support the generalization that, as an individual's resources increase in comparison to others, those controlling greater resources depart from equality by allocating more of the available resources for themselves and accordingly provide the less powerful with a smaller share (Tedeschi, Lindskold, Horai, and Gahagan 1969; Shure, Meeker, and Hansford 1965). In a two-person bargaining study by Tedeschi et al. one group of subjects was given strong power over their opponents and so could determine the amount of money each could earn. In a second condition subjects and opponents had equal power. The not too surprising finding was that subjects in the strong-power condition shared money with their opponents 18 percent of the time, while subjects in the equal-power condition shared 36 percent of the time. In short, the control of superior power tempted the actors to allocate more for themselves.

Departures from equality should not, however, be seen simply as greedy actions by those in power. If this were the simple case, then in the above-cited Tedeschi et al. study those with strong power would not have shared at all. Rather, it is suggested that the powerholder convinces himself that his inputs into a situation, as represented by his superior power, are greater than those of the less powerful, and accordingly he deserves a larger share of the outcomes.

A second bit of evidence suggesting that powerholders prefer equity over equality may be found in studies of pay and morale within industry. University of Michigan sociologist E. Yuchtman (personal communication) asked male and female employees ranging from blue-collar workers to executives whether they would prefer a pay system that gave equal pay to all workers at the same level in the organization, regardless of each worker's ability (equality), or a system of pay that rewarded persons at the same level on the basis of their skills and abilities (equity). The findings were that more executives than blue-collar workers preferred to be paid on the basis of equity. Further, male workers preferred an equitable pay system and female workers preferred an equalitarian system. Quite clearly, persons in positions of power or dominance preferred a system that allowed thêm to maximize their outcomes by using their skills and abilities. Those with less power (blue-collar workers, women) preferred a system that distributed rewards equally. An explanation of these findings, offered by Yuchtman, is that people in power can get more by relying on an equitable distribution of rewards, while people without power can get more by relying upon an equalitarian distribution of rewards.

We started out this section by asking how ethical ideas might restrain the use of power. The reader, however, may complain that from what has been said so far, ethicality is apparently used to rationalize a lack of restraint. I would not subscribe to this conclusion. My conclusion is that, when given a choice between the two fundamental systems of justice that exist in Western society, persons in positions of power would opt for the belief that "each person should get what he deserves" rather than that "all should share alike." This is because, when power is considered an input, those with power can claim more as a simple matter of justice. Thus "share and share alike" tends to be a value system of the have-nots rather than the haves. A matter of some interest which requires exploration in the social sciences is the process by which persons who initially call for equality subsequently adopt a system of justice based upon equity. Studies among children by Lerner (1974) suggest that a lack of cooperative relationship promotes a preference for equity rather than equality. How the control of resources may also promote this shift would contribute further to our understanding of these differing conceptions of justice.

Cultural Climate and Normative Values

Now we may turn to the last source of restraint that will be examined in this chapter. This source originates in the norms of groups, institutions, and society. Without exception, all cultures take pains to teach young children the propriety of using various resources. Through direct and indirect means the child is taught the general range of situations in which it is permissible, even expected, to use power. In a fighting culture such as that of the Sioux Indian, the young child is encouraged to view a wide range of situations as requiring the use of violence and cruelty (Erikson 1950). In sharp contrast, the children of the Saulteaux Indians, people with a peaceful trapping and fishing culture, are taught to react with indifference and gentleness to the same stimuli that arouse the Sioux child to anger. The child then appears to store the information taught by his society, and include it in a repertory of responses that are available for later use. At the appropriate time he may match the situation with the range of responses he has learned, selecting that response which he views as most appropriate. Included here, of course, is the decision as to whether or not it is appropriate to invoke any given resource.

Societies not only teach the young how to deal with power in a direct fashion but teach them indirectly as well in terms of the values and goals that are considered important. Social goals are ordered for the child in terms of their relative importance. When conflicts occur, the child and subsequently the adult will attempt to satisfy those goals considered to have the highest importance. In our society children are taught to value achievement, the accumulation of material wealth, the need to respect others, to be loyal to friends, and to be of help to others if needed. Of all of these values, the one on which middle-class parents place overwhelming emphasis is the importance of individual achievement and accomplishment. In terms of the rewards and punishments, praises and blames, doled out to the child, the vast majority center around success of the child in mastering his environment.

Given this emphasis, it is not surprising that the drive to achieve may place the person in a competitive relation with his fellows. This is because most achievement type situations are defined in this society as those in which one does better than one's peers, whether at school, at play, in business. Thus, when faced with a decision of using resources to achieve, even if such a use might do injury to others, our cultural values would affirm the invoking of these resources as a proper action.

What I am saying is that a cultural emphasis on achievement is quite likely to lead to a lowering of restraints against using power tactics to satisfy this need. The noted sociologist Seymour Lipset (1974) puts the matter this way in discussing the consequences of failure to achieve: "In America what counts is whether you have won the game, not how you have played it" (p. 60). David McClelland, in his book *The Achieving Society* (1961), has reached similar conclusions, I believe, in his analysis of attributes of the Greek god Hermes, whom he compares to the present day high-achievement motivated businessman. One problem with Hermes was that he was dishonest and unethical at the same time as he was highly motivated to achieve. The key question examined by McClelland is whether a high need for achievement tends of itself to encourage humans to use any means available to satisfy this need.

While not answering this question directly, McClelland provides an indirect answer in his conclusion that the driving force of a strong need for achievement underlies the economic growth of nations. The countries mentioned by McClelland as given impetus for growth through the attempts of their citizens to satisfy their achievement needs—the city states of early Greece, Spain during the fifteenth century, and England—all achieved their greatness not only by commerce but also by wars and the cruel exploitation of their weaker neighbors.

While not directly encouraging the use of power for exploitative purposes, societies that give priority to maximizing individual achievement goals apparently invite their citizens to use whatever resources may be available to satisfy this need.

Penalties for Norm Violation

We may conclude that norms, laws, traditions, and values give powerful guidance to when and where resources will be used. While not absolute, these written and unwritten norms serve to form a climate which serves to encourage or restrain the use of resources, even though their use would have been considered completely appropriate in a different moral climate.

A careful reading of history suggests that, when individuals and nations possess a range of resources, they will forgo the use of several of them for no other reason than that the climate of their time prohibits the use of these resources. The decision of President Truman to use the atomic bomb at Hiroshima could only have been made against the background of continuous killing and destruction of World War II. Without this climate of death, the reasons that were offered for this decision (it would save American lives, or a negotiated peace allowing the Japanese emperor tradition to survive would be unacceptable to most Americans) would not have been sufficient to allow Truman to reach a positive decision. Similar attempts to use far less destructive forms of thermonuclear weapons in Vietnam and Korea have been continually restrained, partly, I believe, because of the overwhelming rejection of such means by most Americans.

Not only do moral climate and norms guide the powerholder's choice of means of influence, but they also include the prescription of penalties when they are violated. Michener and Burt (1974) have written that norms serve to limit the use of power if for no other reason than that continued violation of norms by powerholders would serve to provoke revolts against them.

The importance of penalties associated with a powerholder's violations of norms has also been emphasized by Adolph Berle (1967) in contrasting the American attitudes towards war in the 1840s with those held in the late 1960s. The belief in the American destiny in the 1840s encouraged President James K. Polk to provoke a war with Mexico. Polk had a strong desire to secure California, then Mexican territory, for the United States. After an attempt to negotiate a purchase failed, Polk sent General Zachary Taylor to cross the Rio Grande, causing Mexican forces to retaliate. Two weeks later Polk asked for a declaration of war. At the conclusion of the war, by the Treaty of Guadalupe Hidalgo, the United States acquired the territory that is now Utah, Nevada, Upper California, Arizona, New Mexico, and parts of Colorado and Wyoming. As Berle points out: "Power was never more obviously personal than in President Polk's use of it in the Mexican affair. His aim was aggressive, acquisitive, expansionist, and imperialist. *The reader can imagine the editorials, demonstrations, teach-ins, outpourings of wrath had a comparable decision been taken in the year 1969.*" (Italics mine.)

And Berle is right. Military actions in Vietnam, rather than being cheered by the American public as a fulfillment of the American dream of expansion and manifest destiny, cost Lyndon Johnson a second term in office.

Summary

Inhibitions against invoking resources may act in either of two ways. First, they may diminish the individual's power motivations. Thus, taking of the "power pill" (to paraphrase Clark [1971]) may eliminate the ruler's desire to dominate and manipulate others. Second, the individual may have to use different resources than those initially preferred in order to satisfy his needs, as is true in the case of thermonuclear weapons. In this instance, the need remains but the individual must shift to a reliance upon different resources to induce behavior in the target. Both of these inhibitory functions can be observed to be in operation in guiding the powerholder's decisions concerning whether or not to invoke resources. We have perhaps overemphasized this issue in these pages to sensitize the reader to its importance in understanding the use of power. Too frequently in conducting research on power, experimenters design studies which arouse some power need, provide subjects with resources to satisfy this need if they so choose, but do not include any restraints against the use of these resources, which in fact exist in the real world. Thus, the ease with which persons exercise power, particularly of an aggressive, coercive kind, in the laboratory may, in part, be a function of the fact that no inhibitions against using resources were included in the study.

8

Motivation for Power

The problem of man's strivings for power, as Veroff and Veroff (1972) have written, has held a perpetual and pervasive fascination for students of the human race. We are continually perplexed by the vigor of this motivation as it seeks expression in myriads of encounters and transactions. We are troubled at the ease with which forces striving for power seem to overcome so easily the forces striving for community, harmony, and love. Despite the centrality of this issue, and its intrinsic interest, less has been said in psychology about the origins and consequences of power motivations than has been said about, say, the origins of the motive to achieve, or to affiliate, or to avoid anxiety. It may well be that this omission stems from the fact, as Rollo May (1972) hints, that striving for power is in fact striving for self-assertion, self-development, and growth and that there is very little to be said about power motives, per se, except in the context of discussion of striving for competence. From this view, perhaps one can argue that human beings need power as they need air to breathe and that there are no real mysteries to be solved in this area.

The previous chapters provided the reader with various reasons why powerholders might be motivated to use influence or to restrain themselves from using it. Basically these reasons were concerned with motivations that arise out of the situation in which the individual finds himself, such as his role expectations, or the existence of threats to his own safety, and so on. The purpose of this chapter is to examine the more enduring aspects of human strivings for power. The reader should not be surprised to learn that explanations for power motivation overlap and even at times are contradictory. Power has many faces, some ugly, some bland, and some that are considered admirable by all (McClelland, 1969). According to which face the particular theorist chooses, the reasons for striving for power will be viewed approvingly or disapprovingly—as manifestations of man's inborn urge to overcome odds and create new worlds, or as a sick manifestation of childhood traumas that seek expression years afterward.

Power Striving as Neurotic Behavior—"Sick People Seek Power"

McClelland (1969) has made the observation that persons tend to derive great satisfaction in being told that they have high drives to achieve, or to affiliate, but experience guilt if they are told they have a high drive to achieve power. These emotions occur because of the many negative meanings associated with power motives in our culture. To be told that you are highly motivated for power tends to mean, in the everyday view, that you are a sadistic person who derives great enjoyment from controlling the fate of others. Indeed several psychoanalytic theories see power strivings as representing sick, neurotic behavior. The sickness is based upon the fact that the individual seeks power not as a means of achieving goals that require the services of others but simply as a means of controlling others. By controlling others, various psychological needs of which the person is not aware may be satisfied.

Neo-Freudians were among the first to be concerned with the question of power strivings as a manifestation of neuroses. In particular, psychoanalysts such as Alfred Adler, Karen Horney, and Eric Fromm have seen a direct link between the early social development of the child and subsequent strivings for power. In the psychoanalytic view the initial goals of persons with high needs for power are to use this power as a defense against feelings of low esteem and worthlessness. Neurotic strivings for power, as Horney notes, are born of anxiety, hatred, and feelings of inferiority. The normal person's striving for power is born of strength, the neurotic's of weakness.

While the psychoanalytic school has been in agreement in identifying the early socialization process with subsequent adult power strivings, there has been less agreement concerning the specific causes for such strivings to arise in the first place. In Adler's view (1956), power strivings arise out of childhood feelings of weakness. Adler points out that, from the point of view of nature, humans alone are inferior organisms. They are weak and defenseless. These feelings of inferiority and insecurity serve as basic motivational forces that goad people to discover better ways of adapting to their world. At the positive pole, this pressure to survive leads to the development of speech, intelligence, and communal activities. At the negative pole, it leads to strivings for superiority and dominance over others.

Children are particularly vulnerable to feelings of helplessness and dependency. If this general helplessness is burdened by rejecting or brutal parents, or if the child suffers from some physical disability, then in Adler's view the world tends to be seen by the child as enemy country. In fact Adler says that children with physical disability become particularly involved in a struggle for existence that strangles their social feelings. Instead of adjusting to their fellows, they are preoccupied with themselves, their survival, and with the impressions they make on others. One mode of adjustment is for the child to overcompensate for his weakness by striving for superiority. Through this exaggerated compensatory mechanism he attempts to reduce his feelings of inferiority and loss of self-esteem. Here, then, the process of character development begins in the child's attempts to better his chances for survival.

As an adult, this neurotic striving for power manifests itself in continual attempts to prove one's own superiority by outdoing and controlling others. When the world is viewed as the enemy, Adler states, there is a good deal of hostility associated with attempts to outdo and control. The power-striving individual tends to experience satisfaction rather than sorrow and pity if he finds that his actions have caused target persons to suffer.

This early description of the origin of power strivings was correct as far as it went, but it did not cover all the dynamic forces with which the helpless child must cope. Much more than compensatory strivings over physical weaknesses may be involved in the adult's neurotic striving for power. The incompleteness of the statement was one of the reasons for Karen Horney's (1950) more explicit considerations of the meaning of early childhood feelings of rage and hostility in the development of adult behavior. Once again we begin with the defenseless child. Only, in Horney's view, it is not physical disability which serves as the overwhelming threat but the absence of parental love and protection. Her assumption was that the child who does not receive unconditional love and affection develops feelings of anger and hostility which cannot be openly expressed for fear of further antagonizing its parents. Thus the child is faced with the "double bind" of being angry and yet being afraid of being abandoned. Unable to cope with this kind of conflict, the child experiences deep fears and anxieties. And it is the child's efforts to reduce these noxious feelings that produce neurotic life-styles, including the striving for power.

In Horney's thinking, power is sought when the person's anxiety is coupled with the belief that the world is out to take advantage of the person. Here the strivings for power can serve two purposes. First, to be powerful is an assurance against the nagging fears of being helpless and abandoned. No longer does the person have to beg for help—rather, it is up to him to decide whether to help others. Rather than seek advice, which is a form of weakness, he gives advice. Other manifestations of this seeking to appear strong and dominant, according to Horney, are the neurotic person's incessant attempts to make others admire and love him for his beauty, or his intelligence, or his force of character. In short, by one means or another, he seeks to be the master and so bolster his self-esteem and repress the suspicion that he is not worthy.

A second purpose that is served by these neurotic forms of power striving is to allow the adult to express repressed hostility. Hostility takes the form of attempting to dominate others through insults and sharp criticisms. Horney has observed in her clinical practice that, when a patient's conscious motives were to dominate and control others, the patient had continued difficulties in maintaining affectionate relations with others. This is because the goal of power over others leads to a rejection of equality. Loving relations become especially difficult to maintain, unless the person finds a partner who actively enjoys the submissive role.

In practice, the neurotic strivings for power are seen in the person's incessant demands that others obey him, that he receive a greater share than others, and that others restrain from criticizing him. These strivings can be detected in the unhappiness of others who are required to bear the brunt of the neurotic power-striving person's anger, manipulations, and unconscious cruelties.

In the next chapter I will suggest that similar outcomes may occur in interpersonal relations through the continued exercise of power that is not resisted. However, the distinction between the metamorphic effects of power described in the next chapter and those effects described by Horney is that in the second instance the powerholder unconsciously seeks dominance and devaluation of others as a means of reducing feelings of basic anxiety and helplessness. *Rather than being a consequence of exercising power,* dominance and belittlement of others are the very reasons why power is sought by such neurotic persons in the first place.

Political Power and Childhood Deprivations

If we accept the idea that one origin of striving for power is in childhood deprivations, then it is possible to ask how such strivings manifest themselves in adult behavior. A particularly informative illustration can be found in the studies of political leaders by Harold Lasswell. Since this research is consistent with the idea of a continuity between early childhood experiences and subsequent power-seeking in adults, we will examine one of Lasswell's studies (Rogow and Lasswell 1963) in some detail.

The basic question asked by Lasswell is how political power is used and abused once it has been gained. Further, he asks whether there is a relation between the ego needs of political leaders and the tendency to abuse the power of elected office. To provide answers, Rogow and Lasswell analyzed the careers of thirty elected political leaders who in various ways had been involved in political scandal. Of interest was Lasswell's finding that early material poverty, as well as psychological poverty, could produce an adult character structure obsessed with power-seeking. That is, a politician's misuse of power associated with his office could be traced to early childhood deprivations of either a psychological or material kind.

Lasswell divided the thirty politicians into two types according to their early childhood experiences. The first type was called the "game politician." These officeholders tended to come from wealthy families in which they, as children, were either weak or fragile or had fathers who were strict disciplinarians. The image presented here is of children made to feel helpless and unloved by reason of either physical disabilities or tyrannical parents. Striving for political power, then, was seen as a means of compensating for low self-esteem. These politicians saw politics as a "game" that allowed them the self-expression and self-realization they had been denied as children.

Power was sought by game politicians as a means of obtaining prestige, adulation, and a sense of importance. However, game politicians showed no inclination to make money from illicit use of their power. While corruption surrounded their tenure in office, this corruption was tolerated not for personal gain but to win friends by being a party to deals which involved buying and selling political favors. Game politicians regarded the uses and abuses of money in politics as legitimate so long as they promoted the financial interests of their friends. What they received in return was the flattery and admiration of their special friends—ego needs that had been denied them as children.

A second type of politician was labeled by Rogow and Lasswell as the "gain politician." Generally these persons came from poor, immigrant families that struggled continuously for money and food. However, these families did provide the child with love and emotional security. As adults, gain politicians fought their way to power in their neighborhoods, using physical force if necessary, until finally they controlled a local political machine. Rather than prestige, the dominant motive of gain politicians was to make money for themselves and their families. To this end they engaged in payoffs, deals, and provided inside information to the highest bidders. Unlike the game politicians, they cared little for what others thought of them so long as it did not interfere with their moneymaking.

Rogow and Lasswell in summarizing their findings offered the following observations concerning the importance of early childhood experience for the motivations of these politicians.

1. Severe early deprivation may encourage the striving for power and the use of it in corrupt forms as a means of controlling one's environment.

2. The nature of the early deprivation affects the purposes for which power is employed.

3. If deprivation mainly affects the need for love and ego needs, power will be used in corrupt forms for self-aggrandizement.

4. If the early deprivation mainly affects welfare values, power will be used in corrupt forms for material advantages.

Power Striving as a Substitute for Affection

Some people experience strong pleasure in being able to control the fate of others. Haroutunian (1949) has described the pleasure of exercising power as follows:

> To lord it over others is a means of security, freedom, goods, and so on. But it is also a good in itself. A good which can overwhelm every other good dictated by reason and conscience alike. It is strangely gratifying to make people come and go at our bidding, to overrule their minds and their wills, to take away their power, and virtually annihilate them. . . . There is a soul fulfillment in mastery over human beings. There is no pleasure quite like it, and for its sake men have risked every good and done every conceivable evil. It is well to remember these facts and take them seriously. [p. 9]

This enjoyment seems particularly important to people identified in the psychological literature as high in need for dominance (Watson 1972) or as Machiavellians (Christie and Geis 1970). The question to be considered here is whether those who enjoy exercising power for its own sake are in fact the same persons identified by Adler and by Horney as suffering from early childhood deprivations, or is "something more" involved? Several writers suggest that "something more" is in fact involved and that childhood experiences are not enough to account for the subsequent enjoyment of manipulating the lives of others.

This "something more" involves the simple truth that human beings are unable to live in isolation from their fellows. Not only do we need others as a means of evaluating ourselves, in the manner suggested by George Herbert Mead and by Charles Cooley, but also we need others to provide us with emotional support. Human beings alone, deprived of friendship, social relations, and love, yet always aware of their own mortality, may seek power in order to gain by force the love and esteem from others that they cannot obtain freely.

As a result of this need to make contact with one's fellow humans, the striving for mastery over others for the sake of mastery itself may paradoxically originate in man's fear of being estranged from his fellows (Haroutunian 1949).

In its more modest forms this need may be expressed in using the power to reward (as was suggested in Chapter 4) as a means of binding the affection of indifferent target persons. As its extreme this motive expresses itself in such sentiments as the sadistic desire to kill and torment others and in this perverted way, paradoxically, to express one's linkages with others (Fromm 1959).

Thus another source goading human beings to seek power over others originates in feelings of aloneness and emotional emptiness rather than in childhood experiences. The awful chaos that threatens a person who has no emotional ties, who is the perpetual stranger, can be warded off by forcing others, through power, to give that person the love he craves. Further, the very act of forcing others tends to be seen as an affirmation of one's existence. It is no accident that the principal character in Albert Camus's *The Stranger* resorts to senseless violence as a means of affirming his emotional existence, after having remained for a long period emotionally isolated from others. Here and in other works such as his *Caligula* Camus recognized the link between aloneness and subsequent explosions of sadism and violence. Through these acts of domination one affirms one's own existence and one's emotional ties to others. An important derivation from this view of power striving, which we may now examine, is that any arrangement of society that isolates human beings from each other will encourage the development of power motives whose goal is the domination of others.

The extensive writings of Eric Fromm perhaps best express the interdependency between societal arrangements and man's strivings for mastery over others. Human beings have a basic need to receive love, comfort, and companionship, Fromm argues, and it is how these basic wants are met that determines the structure of motives. From a historical perspective Fromm sees man's relations with others as having been drastically altered by the advent of the industrial revolution and the growth of capitalism. In earlier times the individual was "locked" into relations with his primary family from birth to death. The primary ties of family and work provided each person with a sure sense of personal identity and emotional support. The advent of capitalism freed man from these static primary ties. Man's position in society was no longer predestined by birth and family name. Yet paradoxically this very freedom carried with it an enormous price. Now each person by his own efforts had to establish loving relations with others. No longer were these needs to be automatically satisfied by the structure of society.

To make an emotional connection with someone else is difficult to achieve in a modern society in which the emphasis is on "doing better" than others, in which the enormous concentrations of wealth and technology leave each individual with a profound sense of insignificance and lack of control, and in which the concentrations of people in large cities increase each person's sense of isolation from his neighbor. What then? How is the person to satisfy this basic need of relations with others? How is the person to escape from the unbearable position of aloneness and powerlessness?

One solution, among several examined by Fromm, is to force others to provide one with companionship. This solution may be expressed in sadistic behavior, in which the person desires to have absolute and unrestricted power over others. As Fromm says, the individual's feelings of strength are rooted in the fact that he is master of someone else, and this realization may satisfy his desire to commune with others. The pleasure in his complete domination over another person springs paradoxically from the individual's inability to bear aloneness. One can see a striking parallel between Fromm's views of the consequences of social isolation and Zimbardo's description of the consequences of deindividuation. In both instances isolation of self increases the urge to dominate and control others.

Men isolated from their fellows by the norms, customs, and arrangements of society may develop enormous cravings for power as the best means to establish relations with others. They hope to do with power what they have been unable to accomplish with love. And in part they are correct. I have already pointed out that people will flock around a person with power, flatter him, offer him love and admiration, deference and respect, which he so badly wants.

The problem with this solution is that the more power one seeks and obtains, the more one tends, paradoxically, to isolate oneself from others. The powerholder frequently suspects that the respect and admiration he is given is not for his own self but is given in recognition of the power he controls. As a result he may find himself holding in contempt those persons who surround him, considering them as lackeys or worse. The affection received from such persons, rather than satisfying his basic need for love, may in fact make the craving more unbearable. Thus in one sense power may increase suspicion and distrust of others, the very opposite of the original hopes of the person striving for power. Rather than decrease the "abhorrent void within," to use Kenneth B. Clark's (1971) phrase, the isolation of power may increase it, forcing the person, in anger over his failure to make the desired contacts with others, to ever greater attempts to dominate them.

All People Seek Power

So far the reasons offered for striving for power have been entirely negative. In terms of the description of the power act offered in Chapter 2, the individual's motives for wanting to exercise control are concerned with domination for its own sake. McClelland (1969) has suggested that there is another face of power that is not concerned with these dark motives. This face of power focuses on the beneficial reasons why power motives may arise, reasons in which there is no intent to harm or psychologically diminish the other person.

The intent, rather, is to have the means to control one's world. From this perspective survival is seen as the basic motive underlying universal strivings for power. The sociologist Robert A. Nisbet (1970) writes in this regard that control is the conscious or unconscious aim of all human behavior; and that every element of the individual's socialization process is designed to help the individual acquire control over the environment.

People seek power, then, to survive and to control their worlds. This section will examine the origins of this explanation of power motivation. The reader will see that the explanation for a universal tendency to strive for power centers around the fact that human beings seek not only to survive, but to maximize their own outcomes, and in so doing come into conflict with fellow human beings likewise so engaged. As a result power is sought not for its own sake but for aid in the competitive struggle with others. If this conclusion is valid, it further suggests that strivings for power do not originate in an instinctive desire to control and dominate others, as has been suggested by Freud, but as Hobbes suggests, in a pervasive tendency in mankind to satisfy one's appetites. Out of this need comes the pursuit of power.

An interesting derivation of this view is that the more the developing individual is socialized to achieve, to strive, to maintain the uniqueness of his identity, the more likely it is that he will, as an adult, pursue power. In this connection Skinner has argued, in his book *Beyond Freedom and Dignity* (1971), that a society that stresses the importance of self-realization rather than communal goals is bound in the final analysis to force its members into power strivings, since uniqueness tends to be defined in terms of "doing better" than others.

Rollo May (1972), in discussing human growth, also reflects this view: "Power is essential for all living things. To survive, man must use his powers and confront opposing forces at every point in his struggle" (p. 1). To survive, to grow, to create, all persons must pursue power, since without it these positive goals cannot be achieved. In fact May argues that persons who deliberately avoid using power, glorifying in what they consider their own innocence, tend to be the best candidates for mental illness. Such innocence, May contends, manifests itself eventually in depression and self-hatred as the person's own psychological growth is thwarted by his unwillingness to exert influence and in this way affirm his own worth.

The point of May's argument is, of course, that all persons seek and use power for instrumental reasons rather than because they enjoy controlling others. To deny the importance of power, May argues, is to commit onself to continued helplessness. Yet one may ask, why should this be? Given the multitude of technological advances that have made the distribution of food, shelter, and clothing widespread, why is it necessary for humans to evoke their resources and force others to carry out some act? Seemingly, if there is enough for all, enlightened self-interest would suggest that a reliance on "innocence," in May's term, is surely better than a reliance on power. Furthermore, if there is abundance, why doesn't the motive to strive for power wither away in mankind?

Thomas Hobbes in the seventeenth century, writing in *Leviathan*, explained the universal striving of man for power as the logical result of self-interest. Human beings, according to Hobbes, are motivated by appetites, some inborn but most learned from experience. These appetites are incessant and continually change.

Most important, appetites steer man's behavior because, as Hobbes states, "Men desire 'felicity'—that is men desire continual success in satisfying their appetites." Thus in terms of human behavior Hobbes gives us the image of human beings seeking to satisfy a never-ending stream of wants and desires. When one appetite is satisfied, new ones press for "felicity."

Of course the problem is how man shall satisfy these never-ceasing appetites. To answer this question Hobbes turned his attention to an analysis of power. According to Hobbes, "The power of man is his present means to obtain some future apparent good." That is, man satisfies his appetites and achieves "felicity" through his access to power. Power in Hobbes usage, appears to be equivalent to our definition of the control of resources. Power resides in those resources that are needed or feared by others because they are in short supply. Thus power is seen by Hobbes as the extent to which one person's means exceeds those of his fellows:

> The Value or worth of a man is as of all other things, his price, that is to say, so much as would be given for the use of his power; and therefore is not absolute, *but a thing dependent on the need and judgement of another.* An able conductor of soldiers is of great price in time of war, ongoing or imminent, but in Peace not so. A learned and uncorrupt judge is much worth in time of peace, but not so much in war. And as in other things, so in man, not the seller, but the buyer determines the price. For let a man (as most men do,) rate themselves as the highest value they can; yet their true value is no more than it is esteemed by others. [Pp. 151–52; emphasis added]

In other words Hobbes is telling us that the judgment by others of our skills, abilities, and possessions determines the power we possess. In the 1950s, when there were relatively few engineers to service an expanding American economy, engineers had great prestige and power. They could force employers to provide them with large salaries and benefits, by threatening to withhold their services. By the early 1970s, however, many persons had become engineers and consequently the bargaining power of engineers with employers was practically nil. In short, resources can be invoked to achieve intended effects so long as there is a buyer, to use Hobbes's terms. Intelligence provides no special advantage to the individual, when all are equally gifted and bright. Similarly, beauty is no longer a base of power when all are beautiful, and money loses its special advantage for purchasing goods and services when everyone is equally rich.

What determines an individual's potential power? The answer supplied by Hobbes has a particularly modern ring and covers both personal resources (natural power, in Hobbes's terms) and resources originating from society and institutions. Here is a brief excerpt from *Leviathan* which lists some of the many bases of power that can be used to provide satisfaction of man's incessant appetites.

> Natural Power is the eminence of the facilities of body or mind: as extraordinary strength, form, eloquence, and nobility. To have friends is power, for they are strength united. Also riches joined with liberality is power; because it procures friends and servants. Reputation of power is power; because it attracts with it the adherence of those that need protection. Also what quality soever maketh a man beloved or feared of many; or the reputation of such quality is power because it is a means to have the assistance and services of many. [P. 150]

The timelessness of Hobbes's definition of power is shown in a recent discussion in the *New York Times* Magazine (October 7, 1973) on the reason why the American Bar Association can have a major effect on state legislatures. "Its greatest source of power, and the way it is exercised," explained a staff member, "comes from the standing of the lawyers in the community and the state bar association. They are the pillars of the community. They know their Congressmen and Senators personally." In short, the lawyer's "reputation of power is power," as Hobbes said. Power, then, is ultimately whatever gives the person access to the "pooled energy of many" (Mott 1970), so that the powerholder can cause others to carry out acts that will bring him "felicity."

Hobbes's system of assumptions leads to the inevitable conclusion that all persons must continuously strive for power, without ceasing. The reason for this may be traced in propositional form as follows: (1) human beings are driven by a never-ending stream of appetites that must be satisfied; (2) the possession of power is the means by which these appetites are satisfied; (3) power always resides in the possession of commodities or resources that are in short supply; (4) because power resides in those commodities that are in short supply, all persons must continually strive for power if they are to satisfy their wants. If everybody possesses a resource in equal amounts it is no longer in scarce supply and hence cannot be used to satisfy one's appetites; thus one must continually scramble for new resources to keep ahead of others likewise striving for scarce resources; (5) an inevitable byproduct of this power striving is that human beings are forced into conflict with each other in order to obtain effective bases of power. Hobbes states most eloquently these sobering conclusions:

> So that in the first place I put for a general inclination of all mankind, a perpetual and restless desire of Power after power, that ceaseth only in death. And the cause of this is not always that a man hopes for a more intensive delight than he has attained already, or that he cannot be content with a moderate power, but because he cannot assure the power and means to live well which he has present without the acquisition of more.

Thus every one is necessarily pulled into a competitive struggle for resources, or at least to resist the efforts of others to command their resources (Macpherson 1968). Since by definition there can never be enough scarce resources, and all persons have the same wish for happiness, they must necessarily struggle with each other in order to gain power to secure for themselves the future. In answer to our question then as to why technology cannot reduce power strivings, Hobbes would answer that needs are incessant and continually changing. Technology cannot keep up with the continual stream of "appetites" that humans invent and for which they need power to find "felicity." One might conclude from Hobbes's analysis that, to avoid the continual chase after power, one must give up one's appetites, since more power leads to more appetites, which require more power, and so on—a never-ending circle.

We have given this attention to Hobbes's views because they serve as the basis for most modern-day conceptions of the idea that power strivings may be a universal phenomenon, not one limited to the psychologically sick person. However, the basic goal of Hobbes's writings was not to provide a psychological analysis of power striving but to give a political justification of the need for a strong monarchical system. As a result, Hobbes's ideas are at best a combination of psychological observations of man's nature (all persons are driven by appetites) combined with an economic analysis of the problem attendant on the fact that resources become less valuable as they become more common.

Various modern psychologists have adopted aspects of the Hobbesian analysis, although with less emphasis on the pessimistic aspects of power strivings that pertain to the continual struggle to obtain more than one's fellows. For instance, Tedeschi and his colleagues (Tedeschi, Schlenker, and Bonoma 1971) have assumed a universal drive for power in proposing an alternate explanation to dissonance theory.

Basically, the explanation of Tedeschi et al. originates in the finding that the dissonance effect is most likely to occur when people believe that their behaviors are engaged in freely and are not under the experimenter's control. Tedeschi et al. ask why perceived freedom should have this effect. The answer proposed by these writers is that all persons are concerned with the impression they make on others. That is, consistency of words and deeds enhances the individual's own credibility and *enables him to be more successful in influencing others*. For a person to state, for instance, that he likes apples on one day and to say that he hates apples on the next would cause others to be uncertain as to what statements by the person to believe. Hence the impression they have of him might be less favorable. It is this state of affairs that each person wishes to avoid, since everyone intuitively realizes that people trust others who act rationally. If we are distrusted, our goal of exercising power and influence is blocked.

The motive to avoid doing contradictory things, in Tedeschi et al.'s view, can be seen as not arising from an internal experience of psychological tension, as proposed by dissonance theory, but from a calculated desire by the individual to be in the best position to exert influence and power, by presenting a public stance of rationality and consistency. While Tedeschi et al. do not explicitly propose that all persons seek power, their related hypothesis that all persons seek to maintain a consistent public image so as to influence others is clearly in the Hobbesian tradition.

Effectiveness and Power Motivation

Hobbes in his discussion of human appetites makes no distinction between the drives of individuals to secure wealth and material possessions and the drive to obtain self-knowledge and self-growth. Many psychologists, however, view the individual in terms of his strivings to become a mature adult. Less attention is paid to his attempts to gain material wealth. As could be expected, there appears to be a definite relation between the development of power motives and the striving for psychological growth and effectiveness. May, in *Power and Innocence* (1972), explicitly traces this relation. "Man's basic psychological reason for living," he states, "is to affirm himself, to struggle for self-esteem, to say I am, to do this in the face of nature's magnificent indifference." To do this all people must seek power, if only because, without power to command attention, the individual is basically helpless to realize these goals.

May's view of power strivings as a necessary correlate of attempts to achieve psychological well-being is a valuable addition to the literature on this subject. This is because he provides a view of power motives as a potentially positive rather than negative force in life. He stresses the idea that the reasons for seeking power do not have to center around the goal of dominating and exploiting others but can spring from the assertion of one's own individuality. Of course what is missing from May's writings is a consideration of what may happen when all people simultaneously strive to assert their own individuality. In what ways will they come into conflict with each other?

A Hobbesian analysis of such strivings for maturity suggests inevitable conflict as all strive to assert their will against the indifference of nature and human beings. On the other hand, such conflict may promote the attempts by mature persons to learn how to compromise and to turn competition into cooperation.

Some People Seek Power

So far this chapter has contained little empirical data that pertain to individual differences in power striving. Perhaps the strongest contribution to the empirical literature on individual and group differences is based upon the analysis of power imagery in stories, speeches, and fantasy (Veroff and Veroff 1972; Winter 1973). This research is based on the assumption that the greater the amount of power imagery in the verbal and written expressions of people, the greater their need to control and exercise influence.

Before we can examine the research on power imagery, it is necessary to point out that there are two methods of measuring power imagery in use, each yielding very different findings. The first measure, developed by Veroff (1957), can be labeled *fear of power*, and measures a person's desire to be free from the control of others. This motive is most likely to be aroused when freedom of choice is threatened. The second measure, developed by Winter (1973), involves a positive attraction to the use of power. This second measure closely approximates everyday ideas about "power cravings," in that persons with high scores on Winter's measure are described as deriving satisfaction from influencing other perons.

Through the use of these two measures, an impressive variety of empirical relations have been uncovered concerning how power motives are expressed in day-to-day life. With reference to the *fear of power* measure, the findings indicate, as I mentioned, that this motive is most likely to be aroused when self-assertion is threatened. Veroff and Veroff (1972) report that high *fear of power* scores have been found more often, for instance, among black respondents than among white respondents, among educated women more than among educated men—in general among status groups concerned with overcoming their own weaknesses.

These findings can be interpreted as meaning that, when persons are without power, when their goals of achieving psychological growth or material well-being have been blocked, then their conscious motive structure will center around thoughts of power. To have power under these circumstances will allow the individual, at a minimum, as Veroff and Veroff suggest, to be free from the control of others. These empirical findings are consistent with the idea of Alfred Adler that power motives arise as compensations for physical or psychological weaknesses and threats.

Using the Winter measure of power needs, the findings appear more complex for persons who hold high motives to influence others. Basically, however, such persons have been found by Winter to be attracted to situations and things that enhance the possibility of exercising power. Winter has reported that persons scoring high on his measure of need for power tended to buy prestige objects that would cause envy in others, were attracted to occupations where they could exercise influence (teaching, sales), were more likely to run for political office, tried to dominate others in group discussions, and at times drank too much as a means of fantasizing about power. This is, in many ways, a not very attrac-

tive portrait of an individual's single-minded pursuit of power.
While Winter does not provide us with the early developmental
history of those who scored high on his measure of power motive,
the picture that is presented appears consistent with the description of neurotic power-seekers provided by Alfred Adler, Karen
Horney, and Eric Fromm.

The research of Winter has so far not been concerned with an
analysis of the process by which power is exercised, nor does it
tell us what persons with a high need for power think of themselves
or others as a result of continually seeking to exercise power.

Suppose, for example, that persons with high scores on the
Winter measure of power striving were given access to a range of
means of influence (expert power, reward power, coercive power,
and so on). If these power bases could be freely used to influence
targets without costs to these persons, would those with high
power-needs enjoy themselves? Would they be more adept at selecting the appropriate influence mode to overcome various kinds
of target resistances than persons with low power-needs?

Some answers to these questions are suggested by turning to the
results of studies that have employed the Machiavellian scale developed by two psychologists, Richard Christe and Florence Geis
(1970). This scale was specifically constructed to measure the
tendency of some persons to take advantage of other persons.
While a full description of the scale and its uses is beyond the
scope of this book, it suffices to point out that Winter's description
of persons with high need for power and the description of persons
scoring high on the Machiavellian scale appear to overlap considerably. Thus it seems reasonable to extrapolate the findings
from the latter area of research to the former. Studies of persons
classified as Machiavellian personalities have found that when they
were placed in positions of influence over peers (but given no formal means of influence) they invented a variety of verbal influence
modes to use with their targets and enjoyed the chance to fool and
deceive others. Further, those with high Machiavellianism scores
were found to be more exploitive in situations involving the opportunity to gain resources at another's expense. Studies by Banks
(1974) and by Berger (1973) have also found that high scorers
on the Machiavellian scale were less credible in their use of power
and more adept in its use. Thus the available data point to the
conclusion that persons who enjoy exercising control over people

use different power tactics than those who do not enjoy exercising
such influence.

One further point concerning Winter's measure of power motivation. There is still, I believe, a good deal to be learned about what
happens when "power-driven" persons are in situations that allow
a full range of power to be exercised. The research described above
only indirectly touches on the potential explosiveness of such com-
binations. Studies of the presence of power imagery in the speeches
of American presidents (Winter 1973), for instance, suggest that
conflict may be an inevitable outcome of this combination. This is
because the demands of leaders with strong power motives are
never-ending when they have access to unlimited resources. Conflict arises because sooner or later these demands produce stronger
and stronger resistances among target persons or target nations.

So far we have speculated about how persons scoring high on
the Winter measure of power motivation would actually use different means of influence. Similar speculations can be raised concerning the Veroff measure of fear of power. The most likely answer
is that persons with high fear of power needs would be attracted
to the use of threats and punishments as the preferred power tactic.
This suggestion is made because many of the characteristics associated with persons with high fear-of-power scores (that is, persons
deprived of material or psychological resources) appear similar to
those of persons discussed in Chapter 6 who stated that they
lacked self-confidence or who believed that they were not in control of their own behavior. It would appear that what links these
variously described individuals are low expectations of successful
influence and the associated belief that only strong means of influence will cause others to comply.

Summary

The general conclusion to be drawn from this chapter is that all
forces that reduce the individual's feelings of competence, or that
serve to promote new wants and aspirations, increase the individual's motives to gain power. Feelings of weakness in any form, as
Veroff and Veroff note (1972) are associated with high power-
motivations. We have attempted to distinguish in this chapter when
such feelings of weakness attract the individual to seek power for
its own sake and when such feelings do not establish a bond between power and the desire to control and dominate. It has been

suggested that if these feelings of weakness originate from psychological traumas of early childhood or from present alienation from others, then the goal of power motives is most likely to be to dominate and control others for the sake of the control itself. If the feelings of weakness originate from a need to obtain commodities, or to further goals of growth and maturity, then it appears that the goal of power motives will not include the dream of manipulation of others as an end in itself. Rather power will be used as a means of obtaining services or objects that are controlled by other people. Once these services or objects have been obtained, the powerholder's concern with the exercise of influence tends to cease.

9   The Metamorphic Effects of Power

Typically, power acts begin with the presence of needs that are satisfied by convincing somebody else to do something. These acts are commonplace features of day-to-day encounters with friends, loved ones, and strangers. The powerholder may wish to give a party but his spouse refuses, or he may want to buy a new car from a car agency with no down payment, or he may be a supervisor trying to improve an employee's performance, or he may be a parent attempting to influence his child's behavior. These are not dramatic moments in history, but they contain the same elements of the power act that can be found in the attempts of great political leaders to obtain certain rights from other countries. In all instances, the powerholder anticipates, or has found, that a simple request for compliance will be refused. Therefore, he has to decide what additional force he can use in order to get what he wants.

In this chapter we turn to the question of how the taking of action by the powerholder may influence his opinions about the target person and about himself. Suppose he is successful in getting the target to carry out some desired act. Will he like the target better or worse for showing compliance? And will he like himself better or worse for being able to cause behaviors in others? It is clear from the existing literature that one can expect some kind of changes to occur as a result of successfully influencing others (Sampson 1965; Sorokin and Lundin 1959). As was mentioned earlier, these changes can be called the metamorphic effects of power, a term that indicates how the use of resources to influence others can transform the powerholder's views of both the less powerful and of himself.

The major argument of this chapter is that the continual exercise of *successful* influence changes the powerholder's views of others and of himself, regardless of whether the actors involved are, say, a husband who continually dominates his wife or a great political leader who is responsible for the well-being of an entire nation. The transformations are the same in both instances. They are brought about, in my opinion, as the result of ordinary psychological processes that relate to how we perceive and interpret events. Hence, the transformations produced by the successful use of power are not restricted to remote actors holding high office in distant lands.

The existence of metamorphic effects have been recognized from almost the earliest writings of man concerning the use of power. The Greek dramatists were particularly sensitive to the fate of persons who were at the high tide of their power and status. In the plays of Sophocles, for instance, the viewer is confronted with the image of great and powerful rulers transformed by their prior successes so that they are filled with a sense of their own worth and importance—with "hubris"—impatient of the advice of others and unwilling to listen to opinions that disagree with their own. Yet, in the end they are destroyed by events, which they discover, to their anguish, that they cannot control. Oedipus is destroyed soon after the crowds say (and he believes) that "he is almost like a God"; King Creon, at the zenith of his political and military power, is brought down as a result of his unjust and unfeeling belief in the infallibility of his judgments. Sophocles warns us never to be envious of the powerful until we see the nature of their endings. Too often arrogance, bred of power, finally causes its own defeat and unhappy ending.

Thucydides describes this process of transformation quite accurately in his assessment of the state of mind of the Athenians after six years of success in the Peloponnesian Wars:

So thoroughly did their present power persuade the citizens that nothing could withstand them, and that they could achieve what was possible and impractical alike, with ample means, or inadequate, it mattered not. The secret of this was their general extraordinary success, *which made them confuse their strength with their hopes*. [Emphasis added]

Soon after, of course, the Athenian city-state suffered an irreversible decline by voting to continue its wars of expansion.

While it is true that writers of different times have not always seen a powerful leader destroyed, a persistent image in literature and political science, from the earliest times until now, has been that of an individual, virtuous and innocent at the time he assumes power, soon transformed by his own success into, at worst, a tyrant or, at best, an insensitive and immoral person. In the twentieth century, we have seen political leaders (for example, Stalin) who as young men were fired with the idea of bringing freedom and equality to all but who in the end were transformed into the most inhuman of leaders, devoid of feelings for those who originally started them on their march.

It is not necessary to assume that these transformations are restricted to persons exercising political influence. The exercise of power that is only weakly resisted has similar consequences in all domains of human behavior. In their classic account of life in the Indian village of Karimpur during the 1920s, the Wisers (1967) observed the same transformations occurring among agents of absentee landlords—agents who, once appointed to their positions, exploited their fellow villagers. What is of interest is the Wisers' argument that the behavior of these agents was not due to pre-existing character defects but to their control of power and just as important, the *villagers' servility*. The Wisers state this argument as follows:

If you were to take one of the most harmless men in the village and put him in the watchman's place, he would be a rascal within six months. . . . The sense of power and sudden popularity which a man experiences on finding himself an agent of some outside authority is in itself a danger. If he tests the new power and finds that he does not inspire fear, he may be content to perform his duties without further ventures. But if he finds his neighbors easily intimidated, and if his personal ambitions urge him on, he repeats his assertions of power until he becomes a hardened tyrant. [P. 113]

The well-known observation of Lord Acton that "power tends to corrupt and absolute power corrupts absolutely" reflects the idea of these almost abrupt changes in the humanitarian impulses of the powerholder. In this chapter we will attempt to account for these transformations by presenting in propositional form the steps by which power may change the powerholder. First, however, we will examine more closely Lord Acton's concept of corruption in relation to power in order to understand the kinds of changes our model focuses upon. This examination is based in part upon Lasswell's analysis of the various meanings assigned to the term "corruption."

Pursuit of Power as a Life Goal

The first meaning assigned to the observation "power corrupts" refers to the belief that those who gain power tend to value it above all other values and restlessly pursue additional power throughout their lives. This Hobbesian view suggests that the individual is driven by the fear that others may achieve equality with him in power and so deprive the individual of his own power. Ida Tarbell's (1904) study of John D. Rockefeller suggests that Rockefeller could not stop extending his domination over all aspects of business that touched on oil, despite the fact that he was among the most powerful of American businessmen. During the early 1970s, President Nixon seemed to have charted a similar goal for the United States of America in his insistence that the country could not rest until it was "number one" among nations.

The corrupting influence of power, in this view, is that power becomes an end in itself and replaces the Christian value of love, charity, compassion for the weak, and the like. The urge to be "number one" becomes the exclusive preoccupation of the powerholder. When faced with a choice between giving up power or maintaining it by less than moral or legal methods, those with a taste for power choose the second option.

Cartwright and Zander (1968) have suggested that this view of the corrupting influence of power can be placed in the context of modern learning theory by assuming that the control of power allows the individual to gratify appetitive needs more readily. This is because control of power allows the individual to allot to himself more of those things that do indeed provide satisfaction. Because of these need-reduction properties inherent in the control of power, it follows that individuals learn to value power and seek it.

Power as a Means to an End

A second meaning of the statement "power corrupts" refers to behavior of the powerholder that is motivated by a desire for personal gain. When this form of corruption is under examination, one usually finds the powerholder in a position of trust, where he has access to institutional resources or the resources of another person. What seems to happen is that access to these resources tempts the powerholder to line his own pocket. Power is corrupting in this context because it encourages the individual to deviate from the formal duties of a public role as a means of enriching himself or others to whom he owes favors (Scott 1972). In a sense, striving for power in this second usage is only a means to an end, rather than an end in itself. Studies by Rogow and Lasswell (1963) of the gain politician that were discussed in Chapter 8 serve to illustrate these kinds of temptations that are associated with access to power.

Power, Self-Concepts, and Morality

Corruption can also refer to the way in which the control of power changes the powerholder's self-perceptions and his perceptions of others. Sorokin and Lundin (1959), in a review of the behavior and attributes of individuals controlling political and economic power, stated that persons holding great power develop an exalted and vain view of their own worth which inhibits compassion for others. Furthermore, Sorokin and Lundin suggested that powerful persons evolve new codes of ethics that serve to justify their use of power. Throughout history, we find that a special divinity is assumed to surround the powerful, so that they are excused from gross acts such as murder, terrorism, and intimidation. This view has come down through history in several forms. Machiavelli, for instance, argues that it is necessary for a prince to learn how not to be good. That is, the prince must do those things, whether good or evil, that will perpetuate his own power. Likewise, Sorokin and Lundin cite studies of business executives who led double lives morally, with one set of moral values for the office and a second for the home. Sorokin and Lundin, echoing the beliefs of Sophocles two thousand years earlier, assert that the very possession of vast power tends to demoralize the powerholder.

Why should we continually find reference in the literature to the twin themes that powerful leaders develop exalted views of their own worth and that they believe they are exempt from common moral standards? Do these attitudes develop as the inevitable long-term consequence of successfully exercising power? I believe this may be the case.

Examine, first, one possible route by which the control of power may cause changes in how a powerholder sees himself and others. Two related processes are involved. First of all, the powerholder may find himself the recipient of flattery and well-wishing from the less powerful, who are anxious to keep in his good graces. It is quite common for powerholders to receive positive feedback, both true and false, concerning their own worth from persons eager to continue receiving benefits. Anything will do, from simple compliments about style of dress to elaborate testimonial dinners.

In addition, because of the resources they control, powerholders may find that their ideas and opinions are readily agreed with. There is nothing particularly complex in this observation. Common sense tells followers that it will be costly to continually disagree with a powerholder. From fear of power, followers have been known to accept any suggestions from powerholders, no matter how foolish they seem to be. This public compliance may lead the powerholders to believe that their ideas and views are superior to those held by others, when in fact compliance was not based upon the superiority of their ideas but on the superiority of their power. As a result of this deference and flattery, the possibility cannot fail to be raised in the minds of the powerholders that they may be something special.

Indeed, as a result of this continuous stream of positive feedback, it would be strange if changes did not occur in the power-holder's beliefs about himself. He may come to believe that he is an effective and insightful person, whose ideas are superior to others'. In part, this impression of self may be correct, and in part it may be erroneously derived from a continual association with servile followers.

One sign that ideas of personal superiority have become firmly established is that powerholders begin to express irritation if their ideas are challenged. Berle (1967) has suggested that a false assumption of superiority is one of the early causes of a powerholder's decline. The decline occurs because followers hesitate to present true facts that are counter to the powerholder's beliefs. Followers tend to survive by acting as "yes-men." Thus, decisions are made that tend to underestimate the true nature of the opposing forces. The assumption that "I am number one" makes it very difficult to accommodate information that says otherwise. Among recent American presidents, few have included as personal advisors individuals whose opinions diverged in fundamental ways from their own.

That is, American presidents tend to select personal advisors who do not continually challenge policy. Thus corrective feedback is frequently lacking. David Halberstam points out in *The Best and the Brightest* (1974) that the personal advisors of President John F. Kennedy, for instance, had no use for persons such as Adlai Stevenson and Chester Bowles, who might have effectively blocked the decision to escalate the war in Vietnam. Stevenson and Bowles were generally considered too "soft" to be allowed to advise on policy concerned with international relations. Similarly, business executives exclude from their advisors those whose views are "irritating" because they disagree too often with the executives' ideas and decisions.

Perhaps the most extreme example in modern times of this predilection of the powerful to reject information that challenges beliefs in their own infallibility was Adolf Hitler. He refused to use any information that did not agree with his beliefs of the moment. And, worse still, his advisors were fearful to provide him with news that might contradict his beliefs. The military ruin that overwhelmed the German army following its initial successes in Russia arose in strong part from the unwillingness of Hitler's generals to "speak out." Imprisonment and worse awaited those who disagreed with Hitler's judgments.

Changes in Morality

Since unchallenged power brings psychic as well as material rewards, it is not too surprising that those in power wish to maintain this state of affairs. As a result, changes in values and normative beliefs appear to occur as part of the powerholder's attempts to preserve and extend his influence and power. It is a strong person who can willfully decide not to "bend the law just a bit" so as to maintain or extend his own influence.

The kinds of power one controls may determine which commonly held social values will be changed. When Antigone invoked the universal laws of the gods as justification for the need to give her brother a proper burial, King Creon countered with a new set of laws the chief of which was reverence for the city of Thebes and the king's laws and orders. And if newer secular law conflicts with the ancient customs of the gods, then these latter customs must be suspended. Otherwise, there remains the possibility that King Creon's rule may be challenged. Hence, the old values must give way to the new, and the powerholder adopts a moral code consistent with the kinds of power he controls or serves.

In a different context, Galbraith (1967) has said that managers in large corporations are practically forced to make decisions which minimize risk to corporate investment, despite the fact that these decisions violate laws and the general welfare of the public. For businessmen, the morality that develops is designed to protect and extend corporate power and resources.

Albert Memmi (1965) has described a similar process underlying changes in the moral values of French colonists in Algeria during the late 1940s and the 1950s. Faced with a choice of either relinquishing the rich life of the colonist because of moral doubts about the exploitation of the native Algerians or in some way minimizing the issues of morality, French colonists who stayed chose the latter course. Memmi writes:

> For it was not just a case of intellectualizing, but the choice of an entire way of life. This man [the colonizer], perhaps a warm friend and affectionate father, who in his native country could have been a democrat will surely be transformed into a conservative, reactionary, or even a colonial fascist. He cannot help but approve discrimination and the codification of injustice, he will be delighted at police tortures and, if the necessity arises, will become convinced of the necessity of massacres. Everything will lead him to these new beliefs: his new interests, his professional relations, his family ties, and bonds of friendship formed in the colony. The colonial situation manufactures colonists, just as it manufactures the colonized. [P. 56]

In essence, the corruption of power in this usage refers to the fact that commonly held norms and values are ignored by powerholders when such norms and values appear to threaten or restrict the powerholder's use of his resources. Basically, the norms that are changed are those that interfere with the exercise of power.

Power and Perception of Others

A fourth meaning assigned to the idea that power corrupts refers to the belief that powerholders devalue the worth of the less powerful and act to increase social distance from them. Here, then, in my opinion, is the most destructive psychological consequence of one-sided power relationships—the transformation that occurs in how the more powerful see the less powerful. From individuals with both strengths and weaknesses, the less powerful become objects of manipulation with a lesser claim on human rights than is claimed by the powerholder. In Martin Buber's terms, it is the transformation of one person's perception of another from "thou" to "it," from individual to object.

Considering these tendencies to devalue others and to maintain psychological distance, many writers believe that the control of power precludes the possibility of harmonious interpersonal relations. According to Sampson (1965), inequity in power inevitably produces dominance, manipulation and precludes the possibility of establishing truly loving relations. He further states that it is impossible for any human relationship to avoid distortion to the extent that power enters into it. "At minimum," according to Sampson," the deference and compliance shown by the less powerful is seen as a sign of weakness, if not servility" (p. 233).

Why do these transformations occur? What in the power relation suppresses genuine concern for another person's well-being and leads to the development of contemptuous attitudes? There appear to be two possible explanations.

The first reason for the process of devaluation of the target person has been hinted at in the discussion of changes in moral values. It originates in the fact that it is easier to influence others if psychological distance is maintained and emotional involvement is kept to a minimum. This is especially true if the powerholder believes it likely that he will order the less powerful to carry out behaviors that are distasteful. To the extent that the powerholder feels sympathy for the position of the less powerful, he may not want to issue these orders. It is psychologically more comfortable to assume that the target person is not as worthy as oneself. The powerholder can, then, with good conscience, make the target person do things that he would not be willing to do himself. For instance, Memmi records the following accusations directed by the French at the colonized Algerians, all calculated to minimize the Algerians' worth:

> An old physician told me in confidence, with a mixture of surliness and solemnity that the "colonized do not know how to breathe"; a professor explained to me pedantically that "the people here don't know how to walk; they make tiny little steps which don't get them ahead." [P. 67]

Self-interest, then, according to Memmi, is well served by devaluation of the target person and helps explain the variety of wild accusations directed by the French toward the Algerians.

A second reason why devaluation of the target person occurs is more subtle, less dramatic, and yet of greater interest for psychologists. This has to do with the possibility that the very act of successfully influencing causes devaluation of the target person. This possibility appears to be particularly true when the powerholder invokes controlling or strong means of influence that are seen by the powerholder to deprive the target person of freedom of choice. I suggest here that when these strong means of influence are invoked, the powerholder believes that the target person is not in control of his own behavior. Rather, the target person's behavior is seen as caused by the powerholder's orders and suggestions. In essence, the locus of control is seen to reside in the powerholder, who attributes causality for change to himself. "There is no need to make a fuss over his accomplishments," says the powerholder, "he simply did what I told him to do, step by step."

If what has been said here is correct, then the frequency of devaluation of target persons may be far more pervasive than has been thought. Rather than being limited to master-slave relations, it is possible that devaluations occur in any power relationship— teacher-student, dominant husband-subordinate wife—where the powerholder uses influence means that demand compliance, and the target person obeys. The very act of compliance under these circumstances diminishes the worth of any product achieved by the target person in the eyes of the powerholder.

In the following sections I will amplify how the use of power may transform the powerholder's view of himself and others. First, to summarize, I have pointed out that the corrupting influence of power can refer to the fact that:

a) persons acquire a "taste for power" and restlessly pursue more power as an end in itself; or

b) access to power tempts the individual to illegally use institutional resources as a means of enriching himself; or

c) with the control of power persons are provided with false feedback concerning their own worth and develop new values designed to protect their power;

d) at the same time they devalue the worth of the less powerful and prefer to avoid close social contacts with them.

The model of power usage to be presented next will account more systematically for the changes described in (c) and (d), since such changes in intra- and interpersonal perceptions are of direct interest to psychologists.

The Metamorphic Effects of Power—A Model of Change

The model of the metamorphic effects of power contains six elements. These are (1) the resources possessed by the power-holder, (2) the frequency and kinds of influence attempts made by the powerholder, (3) the attributions by the powerholder concerned with who is in charge of the target person's behavior, (4) the evaluation of the target person, (5) the preferred social distance from the target person, and (6) the powerholder's evaluation of self.

In the following sections, each of these components will be examined in terms of the kinds of evidence available to support its inclusion in the model. As an overview, the metamorphic model assumes that the control of resources, in conjunction with a strong power need, triggers a train of events that goes like this: (a) with the control of resources goes increased temptation to influence others' behavior to satisfy personal wants; (b) if powerholders use strong and controlling means of influence to satisfy these personal wants, and compliance follows, (c) there arises the belief that the behavior of the target person is not self-controlled but has been caused by the powerholder; as a result (d) there is a devaluation of the target person's abilities, and (e) a preference to maintain social and psychological distance from the target person; (f) simultaneously the powerholder's evaluation of himself changes so that he views himself more favorably than the target person.

Several points of clarification need to be made concerning the model.

Successful influence and changes in perceptions. First, success moderates the metamorphic effects of power. That is, the metamorphic effects are seen to occur when power relations have been stabilized and the powerholder has generally had his way, as is true, say, in many teacher-student relations, marriage relations, superior-subordinate relations at work, physician-patient relations, and so on. The model is less likely to provide understanding in circumstances where the contending parties are of relatively equal power or where the weaker party is continually and actively resisting the powerholder's influence, as in the case of individuals in the present women's movement or the civil rights movement of the 1960s. Continued resistance forces the powerholder to reexamine more objectively the target person and, as a result, diminishes stereotypes.

Cause and effect—a reciprocal process. The second point is that the metamorphic model is described in this chapter as a unidirectional cause and effect model. For instance, it will be stated that because a powerholder uses strong means of influence he will devalue the worth of the target person. It is equally plausible, however, to expect that there are many situations in which the direction of causality is reversed. In these situations, the powerholder's prior evaluation of the target person determines his choice of means of influence. Chapter 6 contains descriptions of the research of Banks (1974), and of Michener and Burt (1974), which reported that powerholders used stronger means of influence with disliked rather than liked target persons. Gamson (1968) has similarly discussed a reciprocal linkage between a powerholder's trust for a target person and the decision to use coercive power. He has argued that distrust causes the powerholder to use coercion and also that the use of coercion will cause a powerholder to distrust a target person.

In short, there are both logical grounds and some laboratory evidence to support the belief that there are reciprocal processes between the use of influence and the powerholder's conscious representation of himself and those around him. Over time powerholders build up images of target persons in terms of how much resistance to influence these target persons are likely to show and what means of influence are most likely to overcome this resistance and cause compliance. Such continuous exchange of influence and evaluation make it very complicated to unravel the direction of cause and effect, except in those special instances were we have knowledge of the kinds of means of influence available to the powerholders prior to their meetings with target persons, or where we know how much a powerholder likes a target person prior to influence being exerted.

Actually reciprocal interactions between variables are likely to occur in all areas of the social sciences, although they are usually ignored by social scientists. For example, Fleishman, Harris, and Burt (1955) have proposed that managers who are both task-oriented and considerate of their employees are likely to have pro-ductive work groups. It is equally plausible to suppose that in many instances managers behave in both a task-oriented and a consid-erate manner simply because their work groups are already pro-ductive. Thus the productivity of the work group can alter the leader's behavior. Similarly, in studies of parent-child interactions, the general focus is on the ways in which the parent causes be-havior in the child. Yet it is also recognized that the parent's be-havior can be changed in profound ways by the child's influence. For instance, the child can make the parent aggressive, and vice versa. Or, again, it is argued by social psychologists that similarity between two people causes attraction; yet it is equally true that attraction causes people to see themselves as similar.

Unidirectional causality, then, is not a necessary assumption for the metamorphic model. I believe, however, that the more inter-esting features of the model are revealed by stressing the direction-ality of events (the successful use of strong influence, for example, causes devaluation of the target person). For this reason I will begin with the decision of the powerholder to exercise influence and end with the powerholder's evaluation of self and the target person. The reader should recognize however that I view the link-ages between the elements of the model as reciprocal in terms of cause and effect.

Control of Resources

The metamorphic model begins by attempting to specify when a powerholder will attempt to influence a target person in order to gain satisfaction. I propose that such influence is more likely to be tried when the powerholder possesses resources needed by the target person. The relationship between resources and influence attempts can be stated as follows.

Control of resources needed by the target person increases the probability that the powerholder will attempt to influence the target person.

The assessment of the resources controlled by the powerholder is the starting point for the metamorphic model. This assessment may be relatively objective in terms of an independent cataloguing of the powerholder's resources (wealth, beauty, intelligence, charm, strength, and so forth) or it may be done subjectively by the powerholder himself. Over the long run, we expect that the objective and subjective accounts will tend to agree with each other, although we realize that, in the short run, mistakes will be made. For example, a person may assume that he is far more charming and desirable than he is found to be by most persons he is trying to influence. In this instance, corrective feedback will be quickly forthcoming as the person fails to convince others to carry out some action by simply relying on his charm.

Why does the possession of appropriate resources increase the probabilities that the powerholder will take action? I suggest that the possession of appropriate resources raises the powerholder's expectations that he will gain compliance if he exerts influence. That is, the possession of appropriate resources convinces the powerholder that he is likely to succeed if he makes some attempt to overcome resistance. He knows that the target cannot fail to be moved if he invokes that which the target wants. The individual who wants a new car is likely to approach the car salesman and make an offer only if he has money; the therapist who wants to change his client's behavior will do so by invoking his (the therapist's) specialized knowledge; and the love-stricken suitor will gain the love of his lady by invoking his charm and persuasive powers. Lacking the appropriate resources, each of the above actors must remain mute. In short, the combination of some want that requires the services of others and the possession of resources that will be given weight by these others can be expected to produce action, while the absence of either the aroused need or appropriate resources will lead to inaction.

Of course, the relation between the possession of resources and attempts to influence others is not inevitable. Studies of community power, for example, have reported many instances in which the power elite refrained from influencing community issues, despite their personal interest in the outcome (Hawley and Wirt 1968). However, there does appear to be at least a moderate relation between the possession of resources and their use, if for no other reason than that those without resources are less likely to attempt to influence others (Deutsch and Krauss 1960; Lippitt, Polansky, Redl and Rosen 1952; Zander, Cohen and Stotland, 1957).

To illustrate how the possession of resources influences the taking of action, we will describe a recent study by the present writer (Kipnis 1972) in which college students acted as managers of a simulated manufacturing company. The managers were to make sure that the company's products were manufactured efficiently by their workers. In one condition—the power condition—the managers were given a broad range of institutional powers to influence their subordinates' behavior (power to give raises, to deduct pay, to train the workers, to transfer workers to a new task, and to fire the workers); in a second condition—the no-power condition—the managers were given no means of influencing their subordinates beyond telling them that they were the managers. As a result, in this latter condition, the managers could only rely on two bases of power when attempting to influence subordinates—their legitimate powers as managers and their personal powers of persuasion.

The procedure involved having four workers (confederates of the experimenter), who were in a separate room from the manager, work for six three-minute periods. At the end of each three-minute period, each worker's output, appropriately identified, was brought into the manager for checking. All workers were performing satisfactorily, although some were doing better than others. The manager was given an intercom system in order to give direction and advice to each worker, *if he chose to do so.* The power-needs involved in this instance arose from the manager's role, which required that he obtain high production from his employees.

Table 9.1 shows the average number of times that the managers contacted their workers to give them orders and direction. Inspection of this table shows that managers in the power condition made twice as many attempts to influence their workers as did managers with no power (p. < .05). Moreover, it can be seen that the difference in amount of influence attempted by managers with and without power steadily widened. During the first two trials, the difference in number of influence attempts between those with and without power was 1.0; but by the last block of trials this difference had risen to 4.6 influence attempts. In short, the control of a broad range of powers that could be invoked without costs to the managers encouraged the exertion of influence.

Table 9.1 Mean Frequency of Influence Attempts

Managers	Blocks of Trials			Total Number of Attempts to Influence Workers
	1–2	3–4	5–6	
With power	2.1	4.0	8.2	14.3
Without power	1.1	2.3	3.6	7.0

One may ask how influence was transmitted via the intercom. What did the managers have to say to their workers in order to keep production going? As can be imagined, the communications of managers without powers were limited to their persuasive or legitimate powers (praising performance, ordering workers to speed up, goal-setting, and urging workers to try harder). Of interest was the finding that very few managers with power relied on personal persuasion. Out of 198 separate influence attempts made by managers with power via the intercom, only 32 (or 16 percent) relied solely on persuasion. The remainder all included reliance on their delegated powers (promises of raises, threats of deductions, arranging contests between workers for money). Previously in the experimental literature, it had been reported by Deutsch and his associates (Deutsch 1969; Deutsch and Krauss 1960) that the availability of coercive power encourages the powerholder to use it in order to influence a target person. The results shown above suggest that other bases of power in addition to coercion also tempt the powerholder to exert influence.

The Effects of Influence

So far, it has been proposed that the control of resources increases the probability that the powerholder will attempt to influence others. Consider now the next step in the sequence; that is,

how the act of influencing can shape the powerholder's views of the
target person. We begin by examining the problem of "Who's in
charge?"

Let us suppose that a target person complies with a request by
the powerholder. One issue to be examined is whether we can
determine when a powerholder will believe that his influence, rather
than the free will of the target person, was the direct cause of the
target person's compliance. In terms of attribution theory (Kelley
1967) the question is whether the powerholder locates the cause
of compliance within himself or within the target person.

I suggest that the powerholder decides who is in charge of the
target person's behavior by examining the means of influence he
has invoked. When the powerholder uses strong and controlling
means of influence, such as threats and promises, he is more likely
to believe that he has caused the target person's subsequent compliance. If he uses weak means of influence, such as suggestions
and simple requests, the powerholder is more likely to believe that
the target person decided on his own to comply. Both Cartwright
(1959) and Raven and Kruglanski (1970) have discussed this
possibility in their examination of the strength of the power used
and the amount of freedom various power bases allow a target
person.

These ideas can be stated in more formal terms as follows.

*The more a powerholder attempts to influence a target person's
behavior using directive and controlling means of influence, and
this influence, is followed by compliance, the more likely the
powerholder is to believe that the target's behavior is not self-
controlled, but controlled by the powerholder.*

Assume, for instance, that a mother says to her thirteen-year-old
son: "Go to the store and buy a half-gallon of milk." Perhaps the
child ignores the first request but goes when it has been repeated
several times. Then the mother will conclude, quite naturally, that
the son's trip to the store was caused by her requests. Furthermore,
this belief is likely to be reinforced even more if the mother decides to offer to pay her son for the errand. On the other hand, the
mother's belief that she has directly caused her son's behavior is
liable to be weakened if she only says: "Do me a favor, if you have
the time, and go to the store for me" Under these circumstances,

the mother is likely to be uncertain as to whether she exercised complete control over her son. Perhaps it was the son's good nature which made him decide to do the errand?

Raven and Kruglanski (1970) have suggested in this regard that reliance on certain forms of persuasion alone allows the target person a good deal of latitude to decide whether or not to obey. For example, if a powerholder merely says to a target: "Here are the facts; you decide for yourself," the powerholder cannot be certain that his influence per se caused any subsequent changes, since the target has a good deal of freedom to weigh alternatives and choose for himself. Hence, the target's actions could be viewed as relatively autonomous, influenced at best by the powerholder's providing new information.

Restricting the target's freedom of choice, however, by promising to increase his pay in exchange for compliance or, as was done in the film *The Godfather,* making the target "an offer he couldn't refuse" is more likely to convince the powerholder that any subsequent compliance was due to his influence.

More generally, it is suggested *that the strength of any means of influence can be inferred from the dependency of the target on the resources that are invoked.* The greater the target's dependency, the more likely it is that the powerholder will believe the target's subsequent compliance was due to the powerholder's request. Offering food to a starving man in exchange for compliance is a stronger act of influence than offering this food to a man who has just eaten. Furthermore, we believe that powerholders subjectively assign weights to the means of influence that they bring to bear on targets, so that they have a good idea of how much pressure they are exerting. When the powerholder believes that he has brought strong means to bear, then he believes that he is in control. This is especially true if the target changes his behavior in ways that are not consistent with his day-to-day style of life, and the changes parallel those suggested by the powerholder (Kruglanski and Cohen 1973).

Let us now examine several research studies that provide evidence to support the view that reliance on strong means of influence affects attribution of causality. These studies range from those concerned with persuasion and attitude change to studies of attempts to control behavior in marriage relations.

Attribution and Attitude Change

The first study we wish to examine was reported by the psychologist D. G. Dutton (1973) and was an attempt to examine the consequences of using "high-powered" and "low-powered" arguments to change a target's convictions. In the high-powered condition, Dutton instructed college students on how to construct persuasive arguments based upon "scientific findings" (for example, by attributing the source of the argument to a high-status person, using two-sided arguments, rational appeals, and so on). In the low-powered condition, students were informed of these principles of persuasion *but were asked to construct arguments that deliberately violated the principles.* Thus, there was one group of students who believed that they were to use arguments based upon scientific principles of persuasion and a second group of students who believed they were using arguments, perhaps equally good in content, but which directly violated these scientific principles.

Once having constructed his arguments, the student used them in attempts to convince a target person, who had initially disagreed with the student's position (government control of ecology). After hearing the student's arguments, the target person always changed his views to agree with that of the student. Thus, all students were successful in converting the target person to a new position.

The question is, did the students view the target person's conversion as being due to their own persuasiveness? The answer is mixed. When asked why the target person had changed his attitudes, students in the low-powered condition attributed the change to the target's "basic agreement on the issue once he was exposed to it." In short, the students believed that the target person made up his own mind. This belief arose, I think, because the students could not logically attribute change to the strength of their persuasive arguments. The students knew in advance that their arguments were poor and violated scientific procedures of persuasion. Yet the target person shifted his beliefs. How to account for this yielding? The answer is to assume that the persuasive arguments encouraged the target person to rethink his own position on ecology. Thus, the subsequent changes were controlled by the target person—helped, perhaps, by the student's clumsy presentation of additional facts.

Students in the "high-powered" condition attributed the changes in the target person's belief to the strength of their own arguments.

They had overwhelmed these "doubting Thomases" with precisely prepared scientific arguments.

Thus, we find that when persons believe that they have used strong and decisive arguments, then they also believe that any subsequent changes in the target's belief systems were caused by the force of their arguments, against which the target person's resistances crumbled. Contrarily, using forms of persuasion that are known to be weak, results in the belief that any subsequent changes were due to the fact that the target person made up his own mind.

Attribution and use of strong means of influence at work. At work, managers have available both strong and weak means of influence. Thus, a manager may "dangle" the promise of a promotion or pay raise in front of an employee if he improves even more than he has so far. At other times, the manager may try to influence an employee through casual conversation in which simple suggestions are offered without further mention of sanctions. Under these differing circumstances, one could expect that the manager's explanation for any subsequent compliance by his employees would differ. Changes associated with the use of sanctions would be explained in terms of the manager's own use of power. Changes associated with simple suggestions would be viewed as originating in the employee's own decision to change his behavior.

In the previously mentioned industrial-simulation study by the present writer, in which some managers were given a broad range of power to influence their workers and other managers were not given such power, evidence in support of this expectation was found.

It may be recalled that, in this study, one group of managers was delegated a range of powers to influence their employees (power to raise pay, to deduct pay or to fire, to train, and to change the employee's job). These managers had what I would call "strong" means of influence in comparison to a second group of managers who were given no delegated powers beyond telling them that they were in charge.

At the completion of the actual work, the managers were asked to evaluate their workers' performances. One set of questions asked the managers to estimate what had caused their workers to perform effectively. There were three alternatives, and each was evaluated as to its importance: "the workers' own motivations to do well";

my orders and suggestions"; and "the workers' desire for money."

More managers *without* power than *with* power attributed their workers' performances to the "workers' own motivations to do well." Thus, managers without power saw their workers as self-motivated and as determining for themselves how hard they should work. Conversely, more managers with power than without power assumed that the workers' performances were due to their desire to earn money; that is, the workers' performances were attributed to the power controlled by the managers. Thus, in terms of attribution process, managers who possessed "strong means of influence" believed that their employees were not in control of their own performances but regulated by powers controlled by the managers.

Another way of looking at the determinants of attribution is in terms of whether a relation existed between the number of actual influence attempts made by managers and their subsequent beliefs about who was in charge of the employee's performance—the employee himself or the manager.

It may be recalled that influence attempts in this study were measured by the number of times the managers talked to their employees over an intercom system. Further, it may be recalled that most of the communications made by managers with power contained explicit references to formal sanctions, whereas the communications of managers without power could only rely on persuasion or legitimacy as power bases. Within the condition in which managers controlled a range of institutional powers, a correlation of $+.65$ was found between the frequency with which managers spoke on the intercom to their employees and the manager's endorsement of the statement "my orders and influence caused the workers to perform effectively." The more managers invoked strong means of influencing their workers, the more they believed they had caused their performances. In the no-power condition, in which managers could only invoke their persuasive powers, the correlation between the frequency of speaking to employees and the endorsement of the above statement was a much lower .39. As was noted before, since the workers' performances in this study were preprogrammed, managers had no actual influence on their workers' performances. Thus, it appears that the very use of strong means induced the beliefs in managers that they controlled their employees' performances.

Similar findings have been reported by Berger (1973) in a study which used the same basic industrial-simulation design. In this study, influence attempts by the manager were dichotomized into those in which managers made explicit reference to direct and controlling means of influence through reliance upon company sanctions ("If you increase production by ten units, I'll give you a pay raise") and those influence attempts that relied on persuasion ("Try harder next time, we need more production"). The correlation between frequency of use of sanctions and the manager's belief that he was the cause of his workers' satisfactory performance was .40 (p < .01). A similar correlation, between frequency of persuasion and the manager's beliefs, was .24 (p ns) —again, much lower. What these findings suggest is that reliance on persuasion leaves lingering doubts in the manager's mind as to how influential he actually was. Relying on more controlling means such as threats of pay loss or promises of pay raises, however, produces greater certitude that the cause of behavior in the target person was the powerholder's commands.

Attribution and marriage. The distribution of power and decision-making within families is a topic of interest to both social scientists and to husbands and wives groping for ways to influence each other without anger and rancor. Here I wish to discuss the results of a study of decision-making in marriage as it pertains to the metamorphic effects of power. More particularly, the study will be discussed as it provides evidence of the relation between strong and weak means of influence and beliefs concerning "Who's in charge?"

The data of the study were gathered by myself, M. Gergen, and P. Castell through questionnaires given to married men and women. Only one partner from each family answered the questionnaire, without discussing his or her answers with the other partner. The method for obtaining respondents was simple, but probably not precise in terms of random-sampling procedures. Undergraduate students in several of my classes distributed the questionnaire to all the married persons they knew, most of whom were living in the Philadelphia area. The questionnaire explained that we were seeking information on decision-making in marriages. A stamped return envelope was also included so that each respondent could answer in privacy. Of the 180 questionnaires that were distributed, 76 usable ones were returned. These had been completed by 51 married women and 25 married men. The group covered the full range of married life from less than a year to well over fifteen years of marriage. While the low rate of returns prevents us from drawing conclusions about the distribution of decision-making in families living in the Philadelphia area, we can still use the data to examine the relationship between the respondents' beliefs concerning who was in charge of the marriage and the strength of means of influencing their spouse that they used.

One part of the questionnaire listed seventeen ways in which the respondent could change his or her spouse's mind. Each of the seventeen ways or means of influence was rated on a nine-point scale (ranging from "never" to "very often") to indicate how often that particular form of influence had been used during the last six months. The respondents were cautioned not to answer in terms of what they would like to do. Examples of the means of influence included: (1) Make my spouse realize that I know more about the matter—that I have expert knowledge; (2) argue until my spouse changes his/her mind; (3) present the facts as I see them, and let my spouse decide; (4) give up quickly since there is very little I can do to change my spouse's mind once it is made up.

The seventeen means of influence were factor-analyzed, and five factors emerged. These five factors are taken to represent the different forms of influence that husbands and wives use when attempting to convince the other party to comply. The factor names and the items defining each factor are shown in Table 9.2.

Of particular interest in terms of the present discussion were the factors labelled Authoritative Means of Influence and Accommodative Means of Influence. From what has been said so far, it could be expected that husbands or wives with high scores on the Authoritative factor or low scores on the Accommodative factor would believe that they were dominant in the marriage and controlled the spouse's behavior.

Our measure of control in the marriage was based upon the frequency with which respondents stated that they made the final decisions on a series of family matters. There were thirteen issues listed in the questionnaire: (1) handling of family finance, (2) recreation, (3) religious matters, (4) demonstration of affection, (5) friends, (6) table manners, (7) having company and parties, (8) philosophy of life, (9) ways of dealing with family, (10) wife's working, (11) intimate relations, (12) sharing household tasks, (13) politics. The instructions read as follows: "When you and your husband or wife do have a disagreement, would you say for each of these items who has the final say in a decision." The alternatives that were provided for each item were "I almost always decide," "I usually decide," "Husband-wife equal," "My spouse usually decides," "My spouse almost always decides." This measure of decision-making power in families has been used extensively in marriage research since its development by Wolfe (1959).

Table 9.2 Questionnaire Items Defining Various Dimensions of Influence Used to Change Spouse's Mind

---

Factor 1. Last Resort
1. Get angry and demand that he/she give in (.740)
2. Threaten to use physical force if my spouse does not agree (.703)

Factor 2. Accommodative Means
1. Offer to compromise, in which I give up a little if he/she gives up a little (.706)
2. Hold mutual talks in which both persons' points of view are objectively discussed without arguments (.675)

Factor 3. Authoritative Means
1. Make my spouse realize that I know more about the matter—that I have expert knowledge (.628)
2. Make my spouse realize that I have a legitimate right to demand that he/she agree with me (.600)

Factor 4. Dependency Appeals
1. Appeal to the person's love and affection for me (.717)
2. Show how much his/her stand hurts me (by crying, pouting, sulking) (.556)

Factor 5. Giving Up
1. Give up quickly since there is very little I can do to change my spouse's mind once it is made up (.463)
2. Give in on other issues so that my spouse will agree with me (.410)

NOTE: Numbers in parentheses are factor loadings.

The measure of the extent to which the respondent believed that he or she controlled the spouse's behavior consisted of the number of times the respondent answered on the thirteen items that "I almost always" or "I usually decide" when disagreements occurred. This score could range from 0 to 13. The more the respondent answered "I decide," the more he or she was considered to control the behavior of his or her spouse.

The correlation between the frequency of using Authoritative means of influence and Decision-making power was $+.27$ (p <

.05). Similarly, the correlation between the use of accommodative means of influence and decision-making power was $-.35$ (p < .01). The multiple correlation of these combined means of influence with the measure of decision-making was .45. In short the study demonstrated that, in marriage, persons who stated that they were in charge also stated that they relied upon controlling means of influence and avoided using means of influence that gave the other party the freedom to decide. Thus as in prior studies a link between the strength of influence and the powerholder's attributions of causality has been demonstrated. We hasten to add that since the findings are based upon survey data there is no way of knowing whether the use of strong means of influence caused respondents to believe that they were in charge of the marriage.

Attribution and coercion. The successful use of coercive power leaves little doubt in the mind of the powerholder that he has caused a target's behavior. It is perhaps one of the strongest means of influence available for causing compliance, although, as we shall suggest subsequently, it has great costs associated with its use. Nevertheless, there can be little doubt in the mind of the powerholder that the use of threats and force, if followed by compliance, is due to his influence. Thus, the aide employed in a psychiatric ward who says to a patient: "Stop throwing your food around or I'll tie you to this chair" is pretty sure that, if the patient complies, it was because of this threat.

A provocative prison-simulation study by Zimbardo and his associates (1974) provides evidence of how the use of coercion convinces the powerholder that he controls the target person. In this study, normal volunteers agreed to play the role of either prison guard or prisoner for an extended period of time—in fact, for almost a week. While not instructed on how to act, the guards mainly attempted to influence prisoners by commands, verbal insults, threats, and extreme disciplinary tactics. Very little use was made by the guards of simple requests. In post-interviews, the comments of these guards left little doubt that they believed they controlled the prisoners' behavior. One guard said, "I was tired of seeing the prisoners in their rags. . . . I watched them tear at each other *on orders given by us*" (italics mine), while a second guard said, "but we were always there to show them just who was the boss."

In short, the use of threats followed by compliance almost invariably convinces the powerholder that he is in command of the target person's behavior. Even a simple conversation may take on the force of a direct command, in the powerholder's view, when coercion is the only means of influence that is typically used. We have already mentioned a study by Berger (1973) in which business students served as the managers of a simulated manufacturing establishment. Findings from this study illustrate how even simple conversations can be seen by the powerholder as controlling, when coercion is his main means of influencing others. In this study, one group of managers was provided with only coercive power to influence their employees (that is, the power to deduct pay). In this condition Berger found that a reliance upon persuasion ("Try to do better next time") was just as likely to make managers believe that they had "caused" their employee's performance, as a reliance upon coercion ("If you don't work faster, I will deduct pay"). When coercion was the only formal means of influence available, the correlation between the frequency with which threats of pay deduction were used and the managers' beliefs that they had "caused" their employees to work hard was .50; while the correlation between the managers' reliance upon frequency of persuasion and the managers' beliefs was also .50. This latter correlation represents the only instance I have found in which the use of persuasion affected attributional processes to the same extent as stronger means of influence. Apparently, when powerholders can only invoke coercion, they view even informal suggestions as having the force of a formal threat.

Housewives and housemaids. The final illustration of the relation between the strength of means of influence and attributional processes is taken from a study of housewives' use of influence on their housemaids by Donna Mauch and the present writer. Our interest in this area arose from hearing many remarks about housemaids that emphasized the difficulties involved in finding satisfactory employees and in directing their work. The focus of these remarks was clearly concerned with means of influence and evaluation—both elements of the metamorphic model. The method for gathering data was to distribute questionnaires to all persons known by Mauch to employ housemaids. Of the seventy questionnaires that were distributed, twenty-five were returned. This low rate of return prevents us from making general statements concerning housewife-housemaid relations, but it does allow an examination of the correlation between influence tactics and the attributions of the housewives as to who was in charge of the maids' work behavior—housewife or housemaid.

One part of the questionnaire listed five means of influence, and respondents were asked how frequently they had used each of these means in the past few months when they found their employee's work performance needed to be improved or was unsatisfactory. Five direct means of influence were listed: (1) ask her to redo the work or to improve; (2) Admonish her; (3) Show her the correct way; (4) offer incentives for improvement; (5) discuss with her the reasons why I am dissatisfied with her work. Each of these means of influence was rated on a 4-point scale: fairly often, often, occasionally, rarely.

An analysis of the intercorrelations among these items revealed, with two exceptions, positive high correlations ranging from .36 to .61. This suggested that for all practical purposes the items were reflecting various forms of strong and directive means of influence. Therefore the responses to each of the five items were summed to form an index that was labeled "frequency of direct influence." High scores indicated that the respondents used controlling means of influence fairly often.

Our measure of attribution of causality read: "When your worker performs her work in a satisfactory manner, how important would you estimate each of these reasons is for explaining her good work? (Rate each person on a scale ranging from 1 to 7, where 1 = of no importance and 7 = very important)." Three reasons attributed the housemaid's good work to forces controlled by the housewife: "pay," "the instructions I give," and "the fact that I check up on her work." One reason attributed the good work to the free choice of the maid: "her own motivations to do well." Table 3 gives the correlations between the extent to which the housewives in this sample relied upon direct and controlling means of influence and their beliefs concerning who controlled their maids' performance—themselves or the maids.

Once again we find a relationship between the strength of the influence tactics that were selected by the powerholder and beliefs about who was in charge of the target person's behavior. Table 9.3 shows a moderately strong correlation of .56 between the housewives' use of directive means of influence and their beliefs that their "check-ups" were the cause of their maids' good work. Conversely, the absence of such use of directive means of influence was correlated at a reasonably high level (−.69), with the housewives' beliefs that the maids' good work was based upon the maids' own decisions to do such work.

Table 9.3 Relation between the use of Directive Means of Influence and Attributions of Control (N = 25)

Cause of maid's good work	Frequency of Use of Directive Influence
1. Pay offered caused maid's good work	.19
2. My instructions caused maid's good work	.14
3. My check-ups caused maid's good work	.56**
4. My maid's own motivations to do well caused her good work	−.69**

**p < .01

Of course these survey findings do not prove that the use of strong means of influence "caused" the attributions of the housewives. In fact the reverse is probably true. Simple logic would suggest that, because they felt that they could not trust their maids to work on their own, the housewives felt obligated to "check-up" on their maids. The same lack of trust also led to the use of directive and controlling means of influence. It has already been stated that cause-and-effect relations can go in both directions when power is examined. The previously cited experimental studies appear sufficient to document the point that the strength of influence tactics can guide attributions; and the reverse of this relation has probably been shown by this last study.

Evaluation of Target

The reader may question why we have dwelt for such great lengths on the development of beliefs concerning whether or not one person thinks he controls another person's behavior. The reason for taking time here is that I propose that these cognitions mediate a powerholder's subsequent relations with the target. This relation can be expressed as follows.

To the extent that powerholders believe that they have caused a target's behavior, powerholders are likely to devalue the target's worth.

If you believe you have caused someone else to do something, the suggestion made here is that you will minimize the other's worth. For example, teachers are frequently heard to "put down" the talents of a student by implying that the student did no more than carry out the detailed instructions of a teacher. And parents reserve their fondest boasts for the times when their young child spontaneously shows some early development, such as walking, without help. The child who is slow in development—a euphemism for having to be guided by others—is viewed with affectionate concern and dismay by the parents.

Sampson (1965), in his examination of power and marriage relations, discusses at length how the acceptance of power inequality in marriage during the Victorian age was buttressed by the belief of the husband (and, frequently, of the wife as well) that women were incapable of assuming the range of responsibilities of men. The accepted relation between man and wife was one of subordination, of authority and obedience. In theory, and frequently in practice, it was the husband who "caused" the wife's behavior. And these beliefs and practices were accepted not only as right and inevitable by men but also by a vast majority of women. Sampson provides a revealing statement on the pervasiveness of the belief in the inability of women to cope from a Mrs. Norton, who advocated equality under nineteenth-century British law for women but not equality in relations with men: "The wild and stupid theories advanced by a few women . . . of equal intelligence [with men] are not the opinion of the majority of their sex. I for one believe in the natural superiority of men as I do in the existence of God. The natural position of women is inferiority to man" (p. 54).

In this instance, all parties involved subscribed to the self-fulfilling belief that, if the man guides the woman's behavior, it is only because the woman is incapable of independent action.

Findings from the questionnaire survey on decision-making power in marriage that I described earlier in this chapter echoed these Victorian attitudes. It may be recalled that one set of questions measured who was in charge of decision-making when disagreements occurred. A second group of questions that was also included asked the respondents to evaluate the capabilities of their spouses. We found that if one party to the marriage believed that he or she controlled the decision-making power in the family (as indicated by a high number of "I decide" answers), this party also believed the spouse incapable of independent action. Our research found equal numbers of men and women claiming that they made most of the final decisions in their family. And, further, there were no sexist biases associated with the outcomes of controlling power; both men and women who stated that they controlled the decision-making power in the family devalued the worth of their dependent spouses.

Let me describe in more detail the data that was used to reach the above conclusions. One section of the decision-making questionnaire asked each respondent to evaluate on a five-point scale (ranging from below-average to superior) how their spouses compared with people in general on each of ten characteristics. The characteristics were (1) capable of solving problems, (2) skilled at his/her work, (3) socially adept, (4) common sense, (5) independent, (6) reliable, (7) organized, (8) intelligent, (9) physically able, and (10) persuasive. A total evaluation score for each spouse was obtained by summing the ratings over the ten characteristics. Thus, high scores meant that the respondent judged his or her spouse to be superior to people in general and low scores indicated a negative appraisal. This total was found to correlate $-.42$ with the number of times the respondent stated he or she made the final decision when disagreements arose with the spouse. The more respondents perceived that they controlled their partner's behavior, the less favorably they evaluated their spouses.

This finding is, of course, very consistent with the explanation that, if you believe you control another's behavior, then you cannot give him full credit for any actions he takes or for any products he may produce. Thus, the husband or wife who continually decides what the spouse should do is forced to conclude, ever so unwillingly perhaps, that the spouse does not measure up as a capable, skilled, and intelligent person. Every day that they conflict and that the dependent spouse agrees to do what the partner has decided, can only confirm the dominant partner's judgment that the spouse is inept.

However, because these findings are based upon survey data, alternate interpretations of them can be offered. To deal with these ambiguities, we will next turn to experimental studies within organizational settings which also examine the relation between attributional processes and evaluation of the target person.

Organizational setting and the devaluation of the target. A good part of our adult lives is spent in hierarchical organizations in which those with higher positions are given the authority to influence the behavior of those with less status. Since these hierarchical power-relations basically rely on strong means of influence, it should come as no surprise to learn that those in dominant positions at work tend to express slighting attitudes about the competence of those whose behavior they direct. Thus, for example, a study by Strickland (1958) found that when supervisors were experimentally assigned to monitor one worker but not an equally competent second worker, the very act of continually supervising the worker resulted in the supervisor distrusting the worker he had under surveillance.

A field survey by Zander, Cohen, and Stotland (1959) among staff employed in mental hospitals also showed the same tendency for those in a position of power to express slighting attitudes about the less powerful. In this survey, psychiatrists were asked to appraise the psychologists they supervised. The psychologists were also asked to evaluate themselves. The results were that the psychiatrists believed that the psychologists were only competent to test patients, not to treat them. Psychologists thought far more of their own worth and saw themselves as not only competent to test patients but to provide a variety of therapeutic, diagnostic, and research services. In this instance, then, devaluation of psychologists by psychiatrists was expressed in terms of denying that psychologists had the potential to do more demanding and responsible work.

The relation between power and evaluation of a target was also examined in a previously described industrial-simulation study of mine (Kipnis 1972) in which some managers were given a broad range of powers (rewards, coercion, ecological control, training) to influence their employees, and other managers were given no power beyond telling them that they were the bosses. At the end of this study we asked the managers to evaluate their employees' work on scales measuring quality of work, quantity of work, and willingness to promote and rehire the workers. Despite the fact that the simulated employees had turned out the same amount of work in all instances, managers *with power* evaluated their workers' performances as much poorer than did managers *without power*.

Those with power saw their employees as less competent and less deserving of promotion or rehire than managers without power. We would argue that the reason for these lower evaluations among managers with power was the managers' belief that they had "caused" their workers' performance. Hence, they discounted the worth of their workers' own contributions to the work that was achieved.

Further support for our view is found in the comments of the managers after the study was over, when they were asked what they had to do in order to be successful in their roles as managers. Managers *without power* continually stressed the importance of allowing the worker freedom to do work on his own; by being allowed this freedom, they said, the worker would be motivated to perform at high levels. For example, one manager without power said: "You must have control, but not to the point where you would dominate the worker. You must also have gentleness so you won't offend the worker." Another manager without power said: "You should have ability to show confidence in the worker, encouragement, and allow them freedom to perform their jobs in their own way."

Managers who had been given power stressed the necessity of manipulating workers as a means of raising production. One manager with power said: "You have to know how to influence the men to do more and do it better." And another manager with power said: "You have to know how to motivate the workers, even when they may not want to be motivated." Independent raters who examined these statements found that managers with power were significantly more concerned with manipulating workers than managers without power. Seventy-six percent of managers with power and 21 percent of managers without power expressed manipulatory attitudes about their workers. Thus, in this instance, the control and use of strong means of influence created what may be termed a Theory X organization, to use McGregor's term: that is, managers came to view workers as objects of control, unlikely to work unless forced to do so by the managers' orders and influence. One correlate of this unhappy state of affairs, as we have seen, was that the workers' abilities were devalued.

Similar findings were obtained by Berger (1973) using the same industrial-simulation design as mine. Berger reported a correlation of $-.31$ (p $<$ .01) between managers' evaluations of their workers and managers' attributions of causality for their workers' performances. Lower evaluations of workers were given when the managers believed that the main reason for the effort shown by the employees was the managers' orders and influence.

Of further interest in Berger's findings was that the attribution-devaluation relationship was greatest when managers were highly involved in running the simulated business. That is, in one condition Berger told the managers that their own pay was contingent on how well they ran the business, while in a second condition no such involving instructions were given. Indeed, the managers were told that they would receive a flat salary for their time. In the former condition the correlation between attribution and evaluation was $-.40$ (p $<$ .01), while in the latter the correlation was $-.21$ (p ns). A similar finding has been reported by Dutton (1973), who found that a powerholder's degree of involvement in the outcome influenced attributional processes.

We suggest, then, that the more involved an individual is in the act of influencing others, the more likely he is to assume that he is responsible for changes in the others' behavior, when strong means of influence are used. This assumption, in turn, intensifies subsequent devaluation of the target.

The final set of findings pertaining to the relationship between attribution and evaluation of the target person is taken from our survey study of housewives' use of influence among housemaids. It may be recalled that in this study twenty-five housewives described on a questionnaire the frequency with which they used controlling means of influence with their housemaids and the extent to which they believed that they controlled the behavior of the housemaids. In addition to this information, the housewives also evaluated their maids. The measure of evaluation in this instance was a summed rating of the maid's ability in five areas of housework. These were: (1) planning of work time, (2) ability to do work without supervision, (3) completeness and neatness of work, (4) inniative; and (5) the amount of work completed. The measure of attribution of control of the maid's behavior, it may be recalled, was the extent to which the housewife believed that any good work done by the maid was due either to the maid's "own motivations to do well" or to forces controlled by the housewife, such as the degree to which the housewife checked up on the maid. The correlation between the housewife's evaluations of the house-maid and the extent to which the housewife believed that her "check-ups" caused the maid's good performance was −.60. That is, the more the good work was attributed to the housewife's sur-veillance of the housemaid, the more the maid's abilities were devalued. The more the housewife attributed the maid's good work to the maid's "own motivations to do well," the more she was appreciated—the correlation in this instance between evaluations and attribution being +.80.

To summarize, then, various field and laboratory investigations have been cited in this section whose findings support the idea that a powerholder's evaluations of a target person pivots on whether or not the target person is seen to be complying freely or has been forced to comply. In the next two sections we wish to consider briefly two issues that may mediate the relationship be-tween attributions of control and evaluation.

Distinguishing between affection for a person and evaluation of his capabilities. Up to this point, it has been stated that, if a powerholder uses strong means of influence successfully, then he will feel contempt for the target of influence. Yet even a cursory reflection would suggest that we frequently like a person who is compliant and accommodating (Dutton 1973). A husband who makes all the decisions in the family may be very fond of his wife. However, devaluation of the wife may occur because at the same time the husband assumes that she is incapable of taking care of important family matters. In Henrik Ibsen's play *A Doll's House*, we find the noble person of Nora facing this dilemma in that her husband regards her as somewhat less than a child, someone to be loved and protected but never to do anything of meaning. Archie Bunker, in the popular TV series "All in the Family, continually expresses contempt for his wife's ability to cope but seemingly has a grudging admiration for her at times. Here, then, we have in-stances in which the target is liked as a person but full credit is not given for any outcomes he or she may achieve, since these outcomes are but extensions of the powerholder's ideas.

In other instances, however, we find that the individual who uses strong means of influence may express great contempt for the tar-get. During the Vietnamese War, it was commonplace to hear

American soldiers talking about "nuking the gooks," that is, using
nuclear weapons to wipe out the inferior Vietnamese. Similarly,
in the prison-simulation study conducted by Zimbardo and his
colleagues (1974) the prison guards viewed the compliant prisoners with the greatest of contempt. Zimbardo reported that, over
the five days of the experiment, guards increased significantly in
the use of deindividuating references ("Hey, you slob, come
here!") and in the use of depreciation-insults when talking to the
prisoners. In this situation, as the guards increased in their ability
to control the behavior of their prisoners, rather than the guards'
liking for the prisoners increasing, because they were so compliant,
the reverse occurred. The literature that deals with the consequence
of causing other persons to experience pain and suffering (Davis
and Jones 1960; Lerner and Simmons 1966) also indicates that
the harmdoer tends to derogate the worth of the target, presumably
as a means of protecting the harmdoer from feeling guilt.

How, then, are we to understand more precisely what determines
the scope of derogation? Why in one instance is a compliant target
seen as likable, but not talented, and in another instance seen as
generally unworthy and contemptible?

One explanation has to do with the nature of the means of
influence that are brought to bear on the target. As I mentioned
in Chapter 6, it is necessary to justify to oneself and to society
the uses of strong means of influence. This process of justification
of the use of strong means appears implicated, I believe, as a reason for devaluing the worth of a target person. For example, a
powerholder may promise food to a hungry man in exchange for
compliance, or he may threaten to take the food away in retaliation for noncompliance. In the first instance, the powerholder may
see himself as a benefactor contributing to the target's welfare. In
the second instance, the powerholder may view his threat to deprive the hungry man of food less favorably. In fact, he may be
downright depressed to find himself using threats and force in
order to get what he wants. As several writers have pointed out
(Walster, Berscheid, and Walster 1973; Lagent and Mettee 1973),
this predicament may be minimized by in some way rationalizing
one's own actions. Among these ways is the simple notion that the
target is a scoundrel and deserves this kind of harsh treatment.
Wayne Karlin and fellow writers (1973), in an introduction to
their book of stories about American soldiers in Vietnam, *Free*

Fire Zone, described how these soldiers viewed their own acts: "The agent of suffering must believe that the victim and his world are outside of humanity. *Free Fire Zone* is about men dehumanizing themselves by imagining the Indochinese as less than human, who victimized their own precious humanity by warring on the 'gooks'."

The very act of using coercion, then, may convince the powerholder that the target person is untrustworthy and a person who requires continuous surveillance (Strickland 1958). The powerholder cannot allow himself the luxury of feeling compassion for the target, for then he would have no one to blame for his acts but himself. In short, it is suggested that, when the powerholder freely chooses to use strong and harsh means of influence that are successful, he will express complete derogation of his target. On the other hand, if a powerholder uses strong but nonharsh means of influence, then it is more likely that the powerholder will derogate the target's abilities but will still retain positive feelings for him. This is because using nonharsh means still allows the powerholder to retain positive feelings about himself.

Methodological note. In studying the relation between attribution and evaluation of a target person, the researcher must be prepared for three kinds of responses. The first response—called Type A—occurs when the target person does what the powerholder wants but without the use of strong means of influence. This anticipation of a powerholder's intentions and desires has been described by several theorists (e.g., Baldwin 1971), who call attention to its role in maintaining organizational effectiveness. To the extent that a target person is willing to anticipate a leader's desires, this anticipation allows for interactions without the overt use of strong means of influence. Needless to say, when a target person does what a powerholder wants without even being asked, such acts usually are most appreciated.

The second response—called Type B—occurs when the target person does what the powerholder wants but only after strong means of influence have been brought to bear. The research described in the previous pages has mostly involved comparisons of target persons who have made Type A and Type B responses.

There is, however, a third kind of response—Type C—that the researcher must be prepared to encounter in field settings. In a Type C response the target person does not comply even after strong means of influence have been used. Thus, a child may continue to be rebellious even after the strongest threats by his parents; there seems to be simply no way in which one can make him obey the simple dictates of parents and society.

Table 9.4 shows the powerholder's reactions to each of these three types of responses to power tactics.

Table 9.4 Evaluation of Target Person as a Function of Target Compliance

	Type A	Type B	Type C
	Target Person Complies without Use of Strong Means of Influence	Target Person Complies after Strong Means of Influence Are Used	Target Person Does Not Comply Despite the Use of Strong Means of Influence
Who does the powerholder see as causing the target's behavior?	The target person's own motivations to do well	The powerholder's orders and demands	The target person's free choice, viewed by the powerholder as stubbornness
Evaluation of target person by the powerholder	High	Intermediate	Low, but perhaps grudging respect (?)

The reader may see that, if the comparison involves a comparison between Type B and Type C target persons, then we should expect to find a positive rather than negative relation between attributions of causality and evaluations of a target. This result should follow because in this instance the powerholder evaluates more favorably a person who complies with his influence attempts than one who continues to resist. However. as can also be seen, the powerholder's highest evaluations are reserved for the target person who does what the powerholder wants without any strong urgings from the powerholder, that is, does it spontaneously.

Increased Social Distance

The widespread observation (Jackson 1964; Sorokin and Lundin 1959; Zander, Cohen, and Stotland 1959) has been that those in positions of power "move away" from social contacts with the less powerful. That is, there is a preference among powerholders for social exchanges with those of equal or higher status and a tendency to avoid social "chitchat" or contact with those of lesser rank. In the previously mentioned study by Zander, Cohen, and Stotland (1959) among psychiatrists and psychologists, psychiatrists expressed much less interest in having leisure-time contacts with psychologists than psychologists did for contacts with psychiatrists. Similarly, in the industrial-simulation study by the present writer (Kipnis 1972), managers with power said they were much less willing "to have a cup of coffee or a coke with their employees now that the simulation exercise was over" than did managers without power. Finally, in our survey of decision-making power in marriage, the dominant spouse was dissatisfied with his or her marriage and with the amount of sexual satisfaction found in the marriage. The correlation between the extent to which respondents controlled the decision-making powers in the family ("I decide") and the respondent's satisfaction with his or her marriage was $-.45$. The correlation between decision-making power and enjoyment of sexual relations was $-.29$. Thus, those who controlled power in the marriage expressed the wish to "move away" from the submissive spouse, both emotionally and physically.

On the basis of these data, a fourth generalization can now be given.

Control over a target person's behavior is associated with a preference to increase social distance and psychological distance from the target person.

We do not have to look to psychological experiments to define the existence of these preferences to "move away" from the less powerful. In everyday life one finds continued instances of this drive toward segregation, ranging from executive bathrooms to the now illegal doctrine of "separate but equal facilities" espoused by Southerners as a means of maintaining separation of whites from blacks in the public school system. In general, one can expect that the more complete the control exercised by the power-holder over the target, the less the powerholder will be interested in spending time with the target.

Several explanations have been offered for this tendency of those in positions of power to move away from those without power. Zander, Cohen, and Stotland suggest that those with high power can afford to be indifferent toward those of lesser power since the less powerful are neither a threat to their security or in a position to offer any insights of interest. Mulder (1963) has argued that the movement of the more powerful away from the less powerful reflects "power gradient" motivations; that is, individuals are continually attracted to regions containing greater resources than their own and away from regions containing fewer resources. Distrust of the motives of the less powerful has also been suggested as another explanation of this movement "away" from the less powerful. Sampson (1965) has observed that some persons in positions of power are repelled by the obsequiousness of the less powerful, their lack of candor, and their penchant for flattery. There is a suspicion that whatever is said by the less powerful is designed to win favor. One can never be sure that there are not ulterior motives in any positive regard expressed by the less powerful. These suspicions may also contribute to a preference for social distance.

A final possible explanation for this preference for social distance is suggested by B. F Skinner, who points out that Western man balks at information which sets limits on his conception of himself as an agent of free will. By extension, we may also desire to avoid these persons who appear not to be in control of their own behavior but in fact are controlled by us. Fundamentally, then, it may be the target's lack of freedom of choice that provides this "movement away" from his company. To be controlled by another person robs one of those very qualities of dignity and self-worth that attract one person to another.

Power and Self-Esteem

Let us next examine how the powerholder's view of himself may vary as a function of the power he controls and uses. As Clark (1971) has pointed out, "power cannot be exercised without inducing some form of reaction." While Clark's observations were directed toward the target, it is equally true that one can expect reactions in the powerholder. While it seems reasonable to expect such variations, there has been very little published that has systematically examined this issue. Furthermore, the available literature presents contradictory findings on how the successful use of power may change the powerholder's views of himself. In some instances, favorable self-evaluations occur, and in other instances unfavorable self-evaluations occur. These latter changes appear to be particularly likely to happen if the powerholder's only means of influencing a target are coercive means.

Despite these occasional downturns in self-evaluations, as a general rule the control and use of power appears most often to increase self-esteem, if only by comparison with the self-esteem of those who possess few or no resources. Let us pursue this argument by imagining a person who has few resources that others around him give weight. He may be an unskilled, illiterate worker whose only claim on his fellow man is the fact that he is poor and helpless; or he may be an old man living alone, without relatives, in a small room in a large city. such individuals tend to act passively and believe that luck or chance controls their fate. Lacking resources, these individuals are likely to have few of their wants satisfied. Their options are limited to giving up all their wants or remaining dependent on the whims of passersby for the satisfaction of their wants.

Resources, then, enhance feelings of well-being in several ways. Most obviously, they allow the individual to live a more comfortable life. If the resources are of a material kind, then the individual can exchange his wealth for good food, good clothing, and a certain inner elegance which, in the opinion of society, marks the contented man. It should come as no surprise to learn that public opinion surveys almost always find that satisfaction with the quality of one's life is directly associated with the possession of material wealth.

Beyond the material comforts that accrue to the powerholder are the wide range of psychic comforts that also accrue. We have previously suggested that those with access to valued resources are more likely to receive flattering feedback from the less powerful. Even the most foolish of suggestions may be carried out by a target who wants to keep in the good graces of the powerholder. To the extent that one's definition of self is defined by the attitudes of others (Mead 1934), the control of valued resources heavily tips the scales in favor of a positive self-regard. The potential mental health benefits accruing to those with valued resources is suggested in a recent review by Porter and Lawler (1965) on factors influencing the satisfaction and performance of persons at work. It was found that the higher the executive level of the employee, the more likely were important psychological need systems to be satisfied. Top executives were far more fulfilled in terms of needs for esteem, autonomy, and self-actualization. Clearly, then, in comparison to the individual with few resources, those with many resources appear happier, more fulfilled, and, no doubt, more satisfied with themselves.

It is not, however, argued that the control and use of power is always associated with the development of a positive self-image. Power appears to be a necessary, but not sufficient, condition for this development to occur. Beyond the fact that the absence of resources is associated with a negative view of the self, additional information appears to be needed to predict just when the presence of power will elevate self-esteem.

Suggestions as to the kind of information that is needed can be obtained from the writings of Charles H. Cooley (1922) and George H. Mead (1934) on role-taking and the development of the self-concept. These social scientists proposed that the development of a sense of self occurs in terms of how significant others view one's own actions and behaviors. To the extent we believe that "others" disapprove of our behavior, we may come to define who we are in unfavorable terms. If we believe that others approve our behavior, then we may hold positive feelings about ourselves.

In this connection it is clear that there are shared societal expectations concerning the merit attached to using various forms of power. Society views with admiration power usage based on the distribution of rewards or the use of expert knowledge; it views with indifference and forbearance the use of legitimacy as a means of influence; but it regards with suspicion persons who use threats, force, and coercion.

It is not unreasonable to believe that those who use these various means of influence also share society's views. To use power for beneficial purposes establishes one's good name in society. In the early decades of this century, public relations advisors convinced John D. Rockefeller and others of equally great wealth to provide millions for public projects in order to overcome the negative image held of them by the general public.

On the other hand, persons who mainly use coercive power may view themselves more negatively than persons who do not have to use such power in order to influence others. Accepting society's views of one's actions leaves a person but little choice in the matter of self-appraisal. If hurting others is the main means one has of satisfying power needs, then the self will soon be seen in a negative way.

In short, it is the "price" society puts on one's use of power that may determine self-regard. In Chapter 5 I pointed out that there are instances in which society applauds the use of coercion as, for example, a means of demonstrating courage and manhood. Nevertheless, the use of coercive forms of influence is generally disapproved of by a large segment of society and, hence, may cause the powerholder to lower his sense of self-worth.

What evidence is there that the kinds of powers we use can shape our self-image? Unfortunately, there is little evidence from controlled laboratory studies that have directly examined this idea. Further, the available studies provide only contradictory results. A negative relation between the successful use of power and changes in self-regard was reported by Zimbardo and his colleagues (1974) in the previously cited prison-simulation study. It may be recalled that, in this study, volunteers served as prisoners or as prison guards for a period of five days. Twice during the progress of the simulation, each participant was asked to complete a self-description scale. The prisoners expressed increasing negative feelings as the simulation proceeded, not a particularly surprising finding since they were the targets of intensely coercive treatment. What was surprising, however, was that the wielders of coercive power, the prison guards, also increased in feelings of emotional distress, although not as much as the prisoners. Despite some of the guards' remarks that might indicate they enjoyed using power ("Acting authoritatively can be fun," "Power can be a great pleasure"), Zimbardo reported that, as a group, prison guards' self-esteem was reduced. Apparently, the experience of punishing others had severe negative consequences. Parallel findings have been reported by Milgram (1963) in his well-known studies of obedience.

Balancing these findings, however, Berger (1973) reported that the self-evaluations of powerholders became more positive when they used a broad spectrum of powers but showed no changes when only coercive power was used. In this laboratory simulation of work, one group of managers was only allowed to use coercion to influence their workers (threats of pay loss or firings); a second group was only allowed to use rewards (promise of pay raises); and a third group was allowed to use both rewards and coercion. At the end of the simulation, Berger asked his managers to evaluate their own performances on a semantic-differential scale. It was found that the more the managers used their institutional powers to influence their workers, the more favorably they evaluated their own performance. This finding, however, was mainly restricted to only one group of managers who controlled both the power to reward and to punish. Among managers who controlled only the power to reward, the results were less strong; while among managers who were given only coercive power, there was no relation between self-evaluations and the use of power.

Thus, the results appear complex. Berger's findings demonstrated in a laboratory setting that self-concepts can be influenced by the use of power. However, in this particular instance, the use of coercion did not lower self-esteem, as has been proposed here. Rather, the use of a broad spectrum of powers produced a favorable change in self-esteem.

To further cloud the issue, in two additional studies carried out by the present writer and collaborators, no relationship was found between the use of power and appraisals of the self. In the first study, involving the simulation of a business (Kipnis 1972), I found that managers who were given a broad range of institutional powers to influence their employees did not evaluate their own performance at the end of the simulation as better than that of managers who were given no institutional powers. Both groups of managers saw their own performances in equally favorable ways despite the fact that the managers with power made many more attempts to influence their workers' performances.

The second bit of negative evidence was found in the survey on decision-making powers in marriage done by the present writer, M. Gergen, and P. Castell. In this survey, each respondent evaluated himself or herself on ten characteristics (problem-solving ability, skill at work, common sense, and and so on). The ten characteristics were exactly the same as those that had previously been used to describe their spouses (p. 197). The total self-description score derived from the evaluations did not correlate with our measure of decision-making power. Respondents who stated they controlled decision-making in the marriage and respondents who said they hardly ever made the final decision described themselves in equally favorable terms. This latter finding is particularly disappointing since it was expected that persons in positions of power within the family structure would receive more favorable feedback from their spouses than those who said they did not control power.

What is most needed at this point to untangle the complex relations between power and self-evaluation are more empirical studies and a conceptualization of the problem that takes into account the basis of power, the means of power, the scope of power, and the amount of power available to the powerholder (Dahl 1957), as these contribute to the powerholder's conception of himself. At a minimum, I believe that such research will find that *the successful wielder of power will view himself in more favorable terms than he views the target of influence.* Thus, rather than stating that self-perceptions rise or fall on some absolute scale as a result of the successful use of power, I suspect these perceptions rise or fall in relation to the esteem accorded the target person. More formally, this relationship can be stated as follows:

> *Powerholders will evaluate themselves more favorably than they evaluate the target of power.*

The only evidence I am aware of to support this generalization is provided by our study of decision-making in marriage. Since each respondent evaluated himself or herself on ten characteristics and also evaluated the spouse on these same characteristics, it was possible to determine whether the respondents evaluated themselves more favorably or less favorably than their spouses. The findings showed that if respondents stated that they controlled the decision-making power in the family, they also described themselves in more flattering terms than they described their spouses. The correlation between the extent to which respondents stated that they controlled decision-making in the marriage and the degree to which they described themselves in more favorable terms than they described their spouses was $+.29$ ($p < .01$).

If further investigations confirm this finding that powerholders evaluate themselves more favorably than their targets, we may begin to understand how actual changes in self-evaluation can occur as a result of the successful use of power. That is, in addition to seeing changes that may occur through favorable feedback, flattery, and deference, we should also find that the self is viewed with increasing favor as the status of the target person rises. If the target person is respected and admired, then the act of successful influence should elevate the powerholder's self-evaluations considerably. This is because successful influence implies that the power-holder is superior to the target person.

Summary

This chapter started with the observation that the successful exercise of influence may bring about profound changes in the powerholder's views of himself and of the target person. The process through which change is believed to occur has as its central focus the attributions of the powerholder concerning "who is in charge" of the target persons behavior. To the extent that the powerholder assumes that he is in charge, then the metamorphic effects described herein are assumed to occur. Much of the chapter, then, has been devoted to examining the circumstances under which the powerholder comes to believe that he, rather than the target person, has been responsible for the eventual compliance of the target person.

The strongest available evidence centers on the likelihood of the powerholder devaluing the target person following the use of strong means of influence. It is difficult to imagine incidents in which influence tactics that allow the target person freely to choose to comply can lead to devaluation. Indeed if we fully understand how our esteem for the target person is related to the strength of the influence that we use, then we can understand seemingly paradoxical relationships, such as occur in folk myths that tell us Satan insinuates himself with soft words and persuasions rather than with outright force, which custom also says is available to him. Of what worth is a soul that was forced to choose evil as compared to one who freely chose to sin?

At this time the most equivocal evidence concerns changes in the powerholder's views of himself as a result of the successful exercise of power. The main conclusion is that powerholders who believe they control the behavior of target persons see themselves as more worthy than the target person. New techniques of studying the interactions between the powerholder and the target person that allow, for instance, for the possibility of flattering feedback from the target person over long periods of time, and that also allow for variations in the bases of power, are needed before additional statements about changes in the powerholder's self-esteem can be made.

10   Conclusion

One purpose of the social sciences is to point out new perspectives for viewing events in the world. When such a perspective is tried, it encourages a person to adjust his vantage point by a trifle, so that he may see something that had been obscured until then— although it was always there.

A goal of this book has been to sensitize psychologists to the issue of the control and use of power, and to the need of psychology to be able to account for the actions of the powerholder. The eventual usefulness of the kind of thinking presented in this book depends upon whether other social scientists accept the particular frame of reference for viewing power that has been presented here.

Chapter 9 focused attention upon the complex changes in a person's perceptions and evaluations of self and others that could result from the exercise of power. I have sketched out in the metamorphic model some of the elements that appear to be needed if one is to conceptualize these changes in any systematic fashion. Earlier chapters attempted to point out some of the environmental forces that affect the powerholder's choice of means of influence and to propose that these forces act by directly affecting the powerholder's expectations of successful influence.

What remains to be done is to tie together the reasoning on means of influence with the reasoning on the metamorphic model.

For instance it has been suggested that persons who lacked self-confidence, when placed in roles that required the exercise of influence, were rapidly attracted to the use of harsh means of influence. Since the metamorphic model proposes that persons who use harsh means of influence devalue the targets of power, does it follow necessarily that persons lacking self-confidence will typically denigrate those persons their roles require them to influence? This question can be raised, but unfortunately the empirical data needed to answer it have not been collected. Thus a future stage in the examination of the powerholder must examine the links between the powerholder's motives and expectations of successful influence, his choice of means of influence, and his perceptions of self and others following the target's compliance.

Despite the fact that there are gaps in the chain connecting power motives with the perception of the target person, and despite the lack of a broad empirical base for my ideas, I believe that the usefulness of the approach described in this book is shown by the fact that similar findings concerning the links between the powerholder's attributions, his expectations of successful influence, and his choice of strong or weak means of influence have been found in both laboratory and field settings. Similarly, the fact that one could detect the same kinds of changes among powerholders in such varied and common settings as marriage, among employers of housemaids, and in work situations suggests the usefulness of the metamorphic model. The findings are consistent with the suggestions made in Chapter 1 that the inclinations of powerholders to devalue the target of influence are not restricted to remote actors holding high office in distant lands. Rather, these inclinations may be an everyday result of the successful use of power and are due to the way humans make inferences and reach conclusions about "cause and effect" in the world around them.

In *Walden Two*, B. F. Skinner inadvertently reaches similar conclusions, I believe, but draws back from a serious consideration of them in his portrayal of Frazier, the director and founder of the novel's utopian community. The problem, of course, as critics of Skinner have often noted, is to decide who will give out the rewards. Frazier frequently discusses this problem in his conversations with Burris, a visitor from the outside world. In all of these talks Frazier denies that power has the potential to corrupt in his community. Safeguards have been developed, in the sense that managers rotate their duties and those without power continue to have the freedom to challenge. Indeed the very goal of the community is to produce autonomous persons who control their own outcomes and rewards.

Still, at the very end of the book, one is left with the strong suspicion that the exercise of power has left its mark on Frazier, who seems to consider himself superior to the rest. This is clearly revealed when he and his visitor have climbed to a high hill overlooking Walden Two.

"Then he [Frazier] flung his hand loosely in a sweeping gesture which embraced all of Walden II. 'These are my children, Burris', he said."

It would have been more convincing if Frazier had said (and believed): "These are my equals" or, better yet, "These are my superiors." Skinner, however, is too insightful a psychologist to believe that the administrator of rewards could state such humble beliefs. The transformations are there, but their consequences are minimized by Skinner.

Unopposed Power

As a final point I want to stress again that what has been said about the use of power, and particularly the metamorphic effects of power, is limited to instances in which the use of power has been relatively unchallenged for a period of time. It has long been recognized that the ultimate solution to the self-aggrandizing tendencies that potentially exist when individuals are given complete control is to institutionalize formal means of resistance. The development of formal structures that allow employees to participate in decision-making within industry, as well as the separation of powers between the executive, legislative, and judicial departments contained in the American constitution, reflect these attempts to curb the debasing effects of unresisted power. I would disagree with Professor David McClelland, who has written that checks on power in America are too often excessive and that the "American's concern about the possible misuse of power verges at times on a neurotic obsession" (1969, p. 152). He is correct in saying that such checks make the leadership role unnecessarily difficult. Yet once that is acknowledged, even a cursory examination of the modern-day world suggests that the cost of unchecked power is a world in disarray. Indeed the unchecked use of power in the second Nixon administration that eventually led to Nixon's resignation from office can be directly traced to the fact that since the early 1930s Congress has delegated to the executive department powers that had been traditionally reserved by the Constitution for the legislative branch. The argument in each of the instances in which such powers were delegated was that Congress took too long to reach decisions that required instant action. Hence such decision-making powers (e.g., the use of the army for small wars) should be given to the office of the president as a means of making leadership less difficult. The upshot of this continual delegation of powers is too well known to be discussed in this book. My only point is that per-- haps we must be willing to pay the costs of delays in management and decision-making, since to allow those in power unlimited freedom eventually leads to far greater costs.

In any case the issues raised in this book can be examined through empirical studies rather than through polemics. We can, if we so choose, examine the consequences for effective leadership of given amounts of freedom and given amounts of control. Social science technology has developed to the point where it is possible to be an "experimenting society" (Campbell 1969). I would suggest that among the questions to be studied and experimented with, in broad outline, are those that pertain to decisions concerning the use of various power tactics, how various forms of restraint modify these tactics, and how power usage under these various conditions affects the powerholder's views of himself and others.

References

Adams, J. S. Toward an understanding of inequity. *Journal of Abnormal and Social Psychology,* 1963, *67,* 422–36.

———, and Rosenbaum, W. B. The relationship of worker productivity to cognitive dissonance about wage inequities. *Journal of Applied Psychology,* 1962, *46,* 161–64.

Adler, A. *Individual psychology of Alfred Adler.* H. L. Ansbacher and R. R. Ansbacher, New York: Harper and Row, 1956.

Amory, C. *Who killed society?* New York: Harper and Row, 1960.

Atkinson, J. W. *Motives in fantasy action and society.* New York: Van Nostrand, 1958.

Bachrach, P., and Baratz, M. S. Decisions and non-decisions: An analytical framework. *American Political Science Review,* 1963, *57,* 632–42.

Baker, L. D., DiMarco, N., and Scott, W. E., Jr. Effects of supervisor's sex and level of authoritarianism on evaluation and reinforcement of blind and sighted workers. *Journal of Applied Psychology,* 1975, *60,* 28–32.

Baldwin, D. A. Internation influence revisited. *Journal of Conflict Resolution,* 1971, *15,* 471–86.

———. Economic power. In J. T. Tedeschi, ed., *Perspectives on Social Power.* Chicago: Aldine, 1974, Chap. 11.

Banks, W. C. The effects of perceived similarity and influencer's personality upon the use of rewards and punishments. Paper presented at the 1974 Eastern Psychological Association Meetings, Philadelphia, Pa.

Barnett, R. L. The game of nations. Harpers, 1971, *November,* pp. 53–59.

Bedell, J., and Sistrunk, F. Power, opportunity cost, and sex in a mixed motive game. *Journal of Personality and Social Psychology,* 1973, *2,* 270-95.

Berger, L. Use of power, Machiavellianism, and involvement in a simulated industrial setting. Ph.D. dissertation, Temple University, Philadelphia, Pa. 1973.

Berkowitz, L. The contagion of violence. In W. J. Arnold, ed., *Nebraska Symposium on Motivation, 1970.* Lincoln, Nebraska: University of Nebraska Press, 1971, pp. 95–135.

————, and Daniels, L. R. Responsibility and dependency. *Journal of Abnormal and Social Psychology,* 1963, *66,* 429–36.

Berle, A. *Power.* New York: Harcourt, Brace, and World, 1967.

Bierstedt, R. An analysis of social power. *American Sociological Review,* 1950, *15,* 730–36.

Blau, P. M. *Exchange and power in social life.* New York: Wiley, 1964.

Bowers, D. G., and Seashore, S. E. Predicting organizational effectiveness with a four factor theory of leadership. *Administrative Science Quarterly,* 1966, *September,* 238–63.

Bradley, C. Problem children: Electroencephalographic diagnosis and pharmacologic treatment. *Connecticut Medical Journal,* 1942, *6,* 773–77.

Brehm, J. W. *A theory of psychological reactance.* New York: Academic Press, 1966.

Brooks, J. *The go-go years.* New York: Ballantine, 1973.

Brown, B. R. Face-saving following experimentally induced embarrassment. *Journal of Experimental Social Psychology,* 1968, *6,* 255–71.

Buss, A. H. Aggression pays. In J. L. Singer, ed., *The control of aggression and violence.* New York: Academic Press, 1971.

Byrne, D. Interpersonal influence and attitude similarity. *Journal of Abnormal and Social Psychology,* 1961, *62,* 713–15.

Cafferty, T. P., and Streufert, S. Conflict and attitude toward the opponent. *Journal of Applied Psychology,* 1974, *59,* 48–53.

Campbell, D. T. Reforms as experiments. *American Psychologist,* 1969, *24,* 409–29.

Caplan, N., and Nelson, S. D. On being useful. *American Psychologist,* 1973, *28,* 199–211.

Cartwright, D. Influence, leadership, control. In J. G. March, ed., *Handbook of organizations.* Chicago: Rand-McNally, 1965, pp. 1–47.

————, and Zander, A. *Group dynamics.* New York: Harper and Row, 1968.

————, ed. *Studies in social power.* Ann Arbor: University of Michigan, Institute for Social Research, 1959.

Chorover, S. L. Big brother and psychotechnology. *Psychology Today,* 1973, *7,* 43–57.

Christie, R., and Geis, F. *Studies in machiavellianism.* New York: Academic Press, 1970.

Clark, K. B. The pathos of power. *American Psychologist,* 1971, *26,* 1047–57.

Cooley, C. H. *Human nature and the social order.* New York: Scribner's, 1902.

Cyert, R. M., and MacCrimmon, K. R. Organizations. In G. Lindzey and E. Aronson, eds., *The handbook of social psychology,* Reading, Mass.: Addison-Wesley, 1968.

Dahl, R. A. The concept of power. *Behavioral Science,* 1957, *2,* 201–18.

Davis, K. E., and Jones, E. E. Changes in interpersonal perception as a means of reducing cognitive dissonance. *Journal of Abnormal and Social Psychology,* 1960, *61,* 402–10.

DeCharms, R. *Personal causation.* New York: Academic Press, 1968.

Delgado, J. M. R. *Physical control of the mind.* New York: Harper and Row, 1969.

Deutsch, M. Conflicts: Productive and destructive. *Journal of Social Issues,* 1969, *25,* 7–41.

————, and Krauss, R. M. The effect of threat upon interpersonal bargaining. *Journal of Abnormal and Social Psychology,* 1960, *61,* 181–89.

Dollard, J. C.; Dobb, L.; Miller, N.; and Sears, R. *Frustration and aggression,* New Haven: Yale University Press, 1939.

Domhoff, G. W. *Who rules America?* Englewood Cliffs, New Jersey: Prentice-Hall, 1967.

Dutton, D. G. Attribution of cause for opinion change and liking for audience members. *Journal of Personality and Social Psychology,* 1973, *26,* 208–16.

Emerson, R. M. Power-defense relations. *American Sociological Review*, 1962, *27*, 31–41.

Elazar, D. *The poltics of American federalism.* Lexington, Mass.: D. C. Heath, 1969.

Erikson, E. H. Childhood and tradition in two American Indian tribes. In C. Kluckhohn & O. H. A. Murray, eds., *Personality in nature, society, and culture.* New York: Knopf, 1950.

Etzioni, A. Organizational dimensions and their interrelationship. In B. Indik and F. K. Berrien, eds., *People, groups and organizations.* New York: Teachers College Press, 1968.

Festinger, L.; Pepitone, A.; and Newcomb, T. Some consequences of de-individuation in a group. *Journal of Abnormal and Social Psychology*, 1952, *47*, 382–89.

Fleishman, E. A.; Harris, E. F.; and Burtt, H. E. *Leadership and supervision in industry.* Columbus, Ohio: Bureau of Educational Research, Ohio State University, 1955.

Foa, U. G., and Foa, E. B. *Societal structures of the mind.* Springfield, Illinois: C. C. Thomas, 1975.

Fodor, E. M. Disparagement by a subordinate as an influence on the use of power. *Journal of Applied Psychology*, 1974, *59*, 652–55.

French, J. R. P., Jr., and Snyder, R. Leadership and interpersonal power. In D. Cartwright, ed., *Studies in social power.* Ann Arbor: University of Michigan, Institute for Social Research, 1959.

French, J. R. P., Jr., and Raven, B. The bases of social power. In D. Cartwright, ed., *Studies in social power.* Ann Arbor: University of Michigan, Institute for Social Research, 1959, pp. 150–67.

Freud, S. Civilization and its discontents. London: Hogarth Press, 1957.

————. Why war? In L. Bramson & G. Goethals, eds., *War.* New York: Basic Books, 1964.

Fromm, E. Individual and social origins of neurosis. In C. Kluckhorn and H. A. Murray, eds., *Personality in nature, society, and culture.* New York: Knopf, 1959.

Fuller, J. G. *The gentlemen conspirators.* New York: Grove Press, 1962.

Galbraith, J. K. *The new industrial state.* Boston: Houghton Mifflin, 1967.

Gamson, W. A. *Power and discontent.* Homewood, Ill.: The Dorsey Press, 1968.

Godfrey, E. P.; Fiedler, F. E.; and Hall, D. M. *Boards, management and company success.* Danville, Ill.: Interstate, 1959.

Goldstein, J.; Davis, R.; and Herman, D. Escalation of aggression: Experimental studies. *Journal of Personality and Social Psychology,* 1975, *31,* 162–67.

Goodstadt, B., and Hjelle, L. A. Power to the powerless. *Journal of Personality and Social Psychology,* 1973, 27, 190–96.

————, & Kipnis, D. Situational influences on the use of power. *Journal of Applied Psychology,* 1970, *54,* 201–07.

Gottlieb, J. S.; Ashby, M. C.; and Knott, J. R. Primary behavior disorders and psychopathic personality. *Archives of Neurology and Psychiatry,* 1946, *56,* 381–400.

Grey, R. J. The influence of organizational context on supervisor's evaluative process. Ph.D. dissertation, Temple University, 1975.

Gurr, T. *Why men rebel.* Princeton, New Jersey: Princeton University Press, 1970.

Halberstam, D. *The best and the brightest.* New York: Fawcett-World, 1973.

Haroutunian, J. *Lust for power.* New York: Scribner's, 1949.

Hare, R. D. Psychopathy, autonomic functioning and the orienting response. *Journal of Abnormal Psychology,* 1968, *73,* 1–24.

Harsanyi, J. C. Measurement of social power, opportunity costs, and the theory of two-person bargaining games. *Behavioral Science,* 1962, *7,* 67–79.

Hawley, D. W., and Wirt, F. *The search for community power.* Englewood Cliffs, New Jersey: Prentice-Hall, 1968.

Hobbes, T. *Leviathan.* England: Penguin Books, 1968.

Hochbaum, G. The relation between group members' self-confidence and their reaction to group pressure to uniformity. *American Sociological Review,* 1954, *19,* 678–87.

Horney, K. *Neurosis and human growth.* New York: Norton, 1950.

Jackson, J. M. The organization and its communication problems. In H. J. Leavitt and L. R. Pondy, eds., *Readings in Managerial Psychology,* Chicago: University of Chicago Press, 1964.

Jasper, H. H.; Solomon, P.; and Bradley, C. Electroencephalographic studies of delinquent boys. *American Journal of Psychiatry,* 1938, *95,* 641–58.

Jones, E. E. *Ingratiation.* New York: Appleton-Century-Crofts, 1964.

Kahn, R. L.; Wolfe, D. M.; Quinn, R. P.; and Snoek, J. D. *Organizational Stress.* New York: Wiley, 1964.

Kaufmann, H. *Aggression and altruism.* New York: Holt, Rinehart, and Winston, 1970.

Kelley, H. H. Attribution theory in social psychology. In David Levine, ed., *Nebraska Symposium on Motivation,* Lincoln, Nebraska: The University of Nebraska Press, 1967.

Kelman, H. C., and Lawrence, L. H. Assignment of responsibility in the case of Lt. Calley. *Journal of Social Issues,* 1972, *28,* 177–212.

Kerner, O., et al. *Report of the National Advisory Commission on civil disorders.* New York: Bantam Books, 1968.

Kipnis, D. Some determinants of supervisory esteem. *Personnel Psychology,* 1960, *13,* 377–91.

Kipnis, D. Does power corrupt? *Journal of Personality and Social Psychology,* 1972, *24,* 33–41.

———. The powerholder. In J. T. Tedeschi, ed., *Perspectives on Social Power.* Chicago: Aldine, 1974, pp. 82–124.

———, and Consentino, J. Use of leadership powers in industry. *Journal of Applied Psychology,* 1969, 53, 460–66.

———, and Lane, W. P. Self-confidence and leadership. *Journal of Applied Psychology,* 1962, *46,* 291–95.

———, and Misner, P. The police officer's decision to arrest. Paper presented to Eastern Psychological Association, Philadelphia, Pa. 1974.

———, Silverman, A., and Copeland, C. The effects of emotional arousal upon the use of coercion among Negro and union employees. *Journal of Applied Psychology,* 1973, *57,* 38–43.

———, and Vanderveer, R. Ingratiation and the use of power. *Journal of Personality and Social Psychology,* 1971, *17,* 280–86.

Kite, W. R. Attribution of causality as a function of the use of reward and punishment. Ph.d. dissertation, Stanford University, 1965.

Kruglanski, A., and Cohen, M. Attributed freedom and personal causation. *Journal of Personality and Social Psychology,* 1973, *26,* 245–50.

Knott, J. R., and Gottlieb, J. S. Electroencephalographic evaluation of psychopathic personality. *Archives of Neurology and Psychiatry,* 1944, *52,* 515–19.

Lagent, P., and Mettee, D. R. Turning the other cheek versus getting even. *Journal of Personality and Social Psychology,* 1973, *2,* 243–53.

Lawler, E. E. *Pay and organizational effectiveness.* New York: McGraw-Hill, 1971.

Lerner, M. J. The justice motive: "Equity" and parity among children. *Journal of Personality and Social Psychology,* 1974, *29,* 539–45.

Lerner, M. J., and Simmons, C. H. Observer's reaction to the "innocent" victim. *Journal of Personality and Social Psychology,* 1966, *4,* 203–10.

Leventhal, G. S., and Lane, D. W. Sex, age and equity behavior. *Journal of Personality and Social Psychology,* 1970, *15,* 312–16.

Levy, H. J., and Miller, D. *Going to jail.* New York: Dell, 1970.

Lippitt, R.; Polansky, N.; Redl, F.; and Rosen, S. The dynamics of power. *Human Relations,* 1952, *5,* 37–64.

Lipset, S. Education and equality. *Society,* 1974, *11,* 56–66.

Lorenz, K. *On aggression.* New York: Harcourt, Brace, and World, 1966.

Machiavelli, N. *The prince.* New York: Mentor Books, 1952.

Macpherson, C. B. Introduction. In T. Hobbes, *Leviathan* England: Penguin, 1968.

Marwell, G., and Schmitt, D. R. Dimensions of compliance-gaining behavior. *Sociometry,* 1967, 350–64.

Maslow, A. Deficiency motivation and growth motivation. In M. R. Jones, ed., *The Nebraska symposium on motivation.* Omaha: University of Nebraska Press, 1955.

Masters, W. H., and Johnson, V. E. *Human sexual response.* Boston: Little, Brown, 1966.

May, Rollo. *Power and innocence.* New York: Norton, 1972.

McClelland, D. C. *The achieving society.* Princeton, New Jersey: Van Nostrand, 1961.

———. The two faces of power. *Journal of International Affairs,* 1969, *24,* 141–54.

Mead, G. H. *Mind, self, and society.* Chicago: University of Chicago Press, 1934.

Magargee, E. L. The role of inhibition in the assessment and understanding of violence. In J. L. Singer, ed., *The control of aggression and violence.* New York: Academic Press, 1971.

Memmi, A. *The colonizer and the colonized.* Boston: Beacon Press, 1965.

Michener, A., and Burt, M. R. Legitimacy as a base of social influence. In J. T. Tedeschi, ed., *Perspectives on social power.* Chicago: Aldine, 1974.

———; Fleishman, J.; Elliot, G.; and Skolnick, J. Influence use and target attributes. *Journal of Personality and Social Psychology,* 1976 (in press).

———, and Schwertfeger, M. Liking as a determinant of power tactic preference. *Sociometry,* 1972, *35,* 190–202.

Milgram, S. Behavioral studies of obedience. *Journal of Abnormal and Social Psychology,* 1963, *67,* 371–78.

References

Mills, C. W. *The power elite*. New York: Oxford University Press, 1956.

Minton, H. L. Power and personality. In J. T. Tedeschi, ed., *The social influence process*, Chicago: Aldine, 1972.

Mott, P. E. Power, authority and influence. In M. Aiken and P. E. Mott, eds., *The structure of community power*. New York: Random House, 1970, pp. 3–16.

Moyer, K. E. The physiology of aggression and the implications for aggression control. In J. L. Singer, ed., *The control of aggression and violence*. New York: Academic Press, 1971.

Mulder, M. *Group structure, motivation, and group performance*. The Hague: Mouton, 1963.

————, & Stemerding, A. Threat, attraction to group, and need for strong leadership. *Human Relations*, 1963, *16*, 317–34.

Nisbet, Robert A. *The social bond*. New York: Alfred A. Knopf, 1970.

Pelz, D. C. Leadership within a hierarchical organization. *Journal of Social Issues*, 1951, *7*, 49–55.

Pepitone, A. The role of justice in independent decision-making. *Journal of Experimental Social Psychology*, 1971, *7*, 144–56.

Pollard, W. E., and Mitchell, T. R. A decision theory analysis of social power. *Psychological Bulletin*, 1973, *78*, 433–46.

Porter, L., and Lawler, E. Properties of organization structure in relation to job attitude and job structure. *Psychological Bulletin*, 1965, *64*, 23–51.

Ransford, H. E. Isolation, powerlessness and violence. *Journal of Sociology*, 1968, *73*, 581–91.

Raser, J. R. Personal characteristics of political decision makers. Peace research and society. *International Papers*, 1966, *5*, 161–81.

Raven, B. H. The comparative analysis of power and influence. In J. T. Tedeschi, ed., *Perspectives on social power*. Chicago: Aldine, 1974.

————, and Kruglanski, A. W. Conflict and power. In P. Swingle, ed., *The structure of conflict*. New York: Academic Press, 1970.

Reed, W. H. Upward communication in industrial hierarchies. *Human Relations*, 1962, *15*, 3–15.

Rogow, A. A., and Lasswell, H. D. *Power, corruption, and rectitude*. Englewood Cliffs, New Jersey, Prentice-Hall, 1963.

Rothbart, M. Effects of motivation, equity, and compliance on the use of rewards and punishments. *Journal of Personality and Social Psychology*, 1968, *9*, 353–62.

Sampson, R. V. *Equality and power.* London: Heineman, 1965.

Schachter, S., and Singer, J. E. Cognitive, social, and physiological determinants of emotional states. *Psychological Review,* 1962, *69,* 377–99.

Schermerhorn, R. A. *Society and power.* New York: Random House, 1961.

Schlenker, B., and Tedeschi, J. T. Interpersonal attraction and the use of reward and coercive power. *Human Relations,* 1972, *25,* 427–40.

Schopler, J., and Bateson, N. The power of dependence. *Journal of Personality and Social Psychology,* 1965, *2,* 247–54.

Scott, J. G. *Comparative political corruption.* Englewood Cliffs, New Jersey: Prentice-Hall, 1972.

Shure, G. H.; Meeker, R. J.; and Hansford, E. A. The effectiveness of pacifist strategy. *Journal of Conflict Resolution,* 1965, *9,* 106–17.

Skinner, B. F. *Walden two.* New York: Macmillan, 1949.

———. *Beyond freedom and dignity.* New York: Bantam Books, 1971.

Sorenson, T. C. *Kennedy.* New York: Harper, 1965.

Sorokin, P. A., and Lundin, W. A. *Power and morality: Who shall guard the guardians?* Boston: Sargent, 1959.

Speer, A. *Inside the Third Reich.* New York: Avon Books, 1970.

Staub, E. The learning and unlearning of aggression. In J. L. Singer, ed., *The control of aggression and violence.* New York: Academic Press, 1971.

Stotland, E. Peer groups and reaction to power figures. In D. Cartwright, ed., *Studies in social power.* Ann Arbor: University of Michigan, Institute for Social Research, 1959.

Strickland, L. H. Surveillance and trust. *Journal of Personality,* 1958, *26,* 201–15.

Swanberg, W. A. *Citizen Hearst.* New York: Scribner's, 1961.

Swingle, P., ed., *The structure of conflict.* New York: Academic Press, 1970.

Tarbel, I. M. *The history of the Standard Oil Company.* New York: Macmillan, 1904.

Tedeschi, J. T.; Bonoma, T. V.; and Novinson, N. Behavior of a threatener: retaliation vs. fixed opportunity costs. *Journal of Conflict Resolution,* 1970, *14,* 69–76.

———; Horai, J.; Lindskold, S.; and Faley, T. The effects of opportunity costs and target compliance on the behavior of a threatening source. *Journal of Experimental Social Psychology*, 1970, *6*, 205–13.

———; Lindskold, S.; Horai, J.; and Gahagan, J. P. Social power and the credibility of promises. *Journal of Personality and Social Psychology*, 1969, *13*, 253–61.

———; Schlenker, B. R.; and Bonoma, T. V. Cognitive dissonance: Private ratiocination or private spectacle? *American Psychologist*, 1971, *26*, 685–95.

———; Schlenker, B. R.; and Bonoma, T. V., *Conflict, power, and games*. Chicago: Aldine, 1973.

———; Smith, R. B., III.; & Brown, R. C. A reconceptualization of aggression. Manuscript, State University of New York at Albany, 1972.

Terkel, S. Servant of the state, a conversation with Daniel Ellsberg. *Harpers*, 1972, *February*, 52–61.

Thibaut, J. W., and Faucheux, C. The development of contractual norms in a bargaining situation under two types of stress. *Journal of Experimental Social Psychology*, 1965, *1*, 89–102.

———, and Kelley, H. H. *The social psychology of groups*. New York: Wiley, 1959.

Toch, H. The social psychology of violence. In E. L. Megargee and J. Hokanson, eds., *The dynamics of aggression*. New York: Harper and Row, 1970, pp. 160–69.

Veroff, J. Development and validation of a projective measure of power motivation. *Journal of Abnormal and Social Psychology*, 1957, *54*, 1–8.

———, and Veroff, J. Reconsideration of a measure of power motivation. *Psychological Bulletin*, 1972, *78*, 279–91.

Walster, E.; Aronson, V.; Abrahams, D.; and Rottman, L. Importance of physical attraction and attractiveness in dating behavior. *Journal of Personality and Social Psychology*, 1966, *4*, 508–16.

———, and Berscheid, E. When does a harm-doer compensate a victim? *Journal of Personality and Social Psychology*, 1967, *6*, 435–41.

———; Berscheid, E.; and Walster, G. W. New directions in equity research. *Journal of Personality and Social Psychology*, 1973, *25*, 151–76.

Washburn, S. L., and Hamburg, D. A. Aggressive behavior in old world monkeys and apes. In P. C. Jay, ed., *Primates*. New York: Holt, Rinehart, and Winston, 1968.

Watson, D. Reinforcement theory of personality and social system. *Journal of Personality and Social Psychology*, 1972, *22*, 88–94.

Wilson, J. Q. *Varieties of police behavior*. Cambridge, Mass.: Harvard University Press, 1968.

Winter, D. G. *The power motive*. New York: The Free Press, 1973.

Wiser, W., and Wiser, C. *Behind mud walls*. Berkeley, California: University of California Press, 1967.

Wolfe, D. M. Power and authority in the family. In D. Cartwright, ed., *Studies in social power*. Ann Arbor, Michigan: Institute for Social Research, 1959, pp. 99–117.

Zander, A., Cohen, A. R., and Stotland, E. Power and the relations among the professions. In D. Cartwright, ed., *Studies in social power*. Ann Arbor: University of Michigan, Institute for Social Research, 1959.

Zimbardo, P. G. The human choice: Individuation, reason and order versus deindividuation, impulse, and chaos. In W. J. Arnold and D. Levine, eds., *Nebraska Symposium on Motivation, 1969*. Lincoln: University of Nebraska Press, 1970, pp. 237–307.

———; Haney, C.; Banks, W. C.; and Jaffe, D. Psychology of imprisonment, in Z. Rubin, ed., *Doing unto others*. Englewood Cliffs, New Jersey: Prentice-Hall, 1974.

Index